Trying to Become Atticus:
The Education of a Teacher

Tim McLean

PREFACE

I am not a researcher, and although I have taught in the state college system, at no time have I ever considered myself to be a professor of education or anything else. I was a high school social studies teacher and not markedly different from thousands of others still teaching. I worked in the Minnesota Public School system for 43 years and dearly loved most of my time in the classroom.

Much of what I describe in this book is simply a combination of memories, observations, and experiences. Though at times it may appear otherwise, little that I write should be interpreted as a negative critique of public education. I was, and will always remain, a believer in the power of the common school to shape our collective future. Of course, our current educational system has ongoing unresolved issues. There are bad teachers and underperforming schools. Too many students are functionally illiterate when they graduate. Many cannot do simple math. At times, kids are bullied and marginalized, and few parents are completely happy with their child's educational experience. Yet with all the obvious flaws, we desperately need schools and qualified motivated teachers. Covid demonstrated the damage done when the schoolhouse doors were closed. It may take years for some students to recover from lost educational and social opportunities.

This narrative is mine and may or may not represent the feelings of any other group of teachers; I hope that longevity has given me perspective and perhaps an occasional insight worth considering. I am writing now for several reasons. One of which is that in retirement I finally have the time. But more importantly, almost daily I see evidence that education, and even individual teachers are becoming the bogeymen for political movements that see even a hint of progressive idealism as a threat to the status quo and their cherished social dominance. Years ago, I never could have written that sentence, but teaching has changed me. This does not mean that I have become a liberal ideologue. I will never wear political correctness as an intellectual fashion statement. Most who know me would consider me to be conservative and I am somewhat embarrassed to admit that the first vote I cast was for Richard Nixon in 1972.

As I stated earlier, I am merely an observer, and in the past few years, I have seen firsthand that things have changed. Once staid school board meetings have sometimes become boisterous ideological scrums. Books are banned because a few parents object to the content; often without reading the supposedly offensive texts. Teachers and schools are being accused of "grooming" students to become members of any group that is currently out of favor with the political right's interpretation of history or their perception of the proper social order. In the past few years, I have seen this trend accelerate. Regrettably, the trend towards teachers quitting and taking early retirement is also accelerating. Some of the best teachers I know are walking away from the classroom at the very time that their skills are most sorely needed.

Even in retirement I occasionally look at the listings of unfilled teaching positions. When last I checked, there were 58 Social Studies positions seeking applicants. Every other discipline is similarly affected. Schools are desperate for qualified English, Math, and Science teachers. Special Ed teachers are in especially high demand. Colleges of Education are closing or cutting back on staff because, so few young people are opting for a career in teaching. There are many reasons for this. Money is of course a consideration. Teaching is not now and perhaps never will be a highly paid profession. But this has always been true, and despite the poor pay, up until the last few years we have never had a shortage of people willing and eager to teach. I think the real reason people are opting out is that the nature of the job has changed. In many schools, respect has been replaced with recrimination, and trust with suspicion. Also, in the wake of the pandemic, the workload has become crushing. This is true at every level from preschool to graduate school.

I am also writing this in support of current and prospective teachers in the hope that they will always find enough joy in the classroom to continue the good fight. If you are a teacher in training, please know that I have seldom regretted my decision to make education my life's work. With all the negatives, for me, teaching has been a tremendously fulfilling career. But know also that teaching may not be as you hope or dream. It is becoming more transactional, more like a job, and less like a calling. The cliches about the rewards of teaching are still true, but the political ground has shifted. Various groups have chosen to turn the classroom into a front line in the culture wars. You will be criticized and second-guessed often and unfairly. There may be blatant attempts at intimidation. It will be more difficult for you than it was for me but become a teacher anyway. When you stand in front of your first classroom, please, always honor the truth. You can never knowingly lie to your students to placate the ignorant or agenda-driven. Leave your classroom every day with your integrity intact. Someday that may cost you dearly, but it will cost you more if you don't.

If you are a teacher in the early years of your career and wondering honestly why you chose to do this; please be assured that it will get better. In time, you will see the good you do and the lives you affect. You will be thanked repeatedly and sincerely. A letter or two might show up on teacher appreciation day to remind you that you have had a profound effect on another human being. Please always strive to improve; that will be the key to constantly renewing your attitude and career. There are many opportunities out there for you to do so. Please take advantage of them.

If you are a veteran teacher, God bless you. You are one of the hooks upon which civil society and democracy hang. Look up the definition of Republican Citizenship and know that few other professionals deserve the description as fully as teachers. Please willingly mentor the young staff. If you are a quality teacher, don't even think about becoming an administrator!! Resolve that you will continue saving the world one child at a time and that to be called a teacher is an honor and privilege.

If you are reading this as the parent of a school-age child, please try to respect and support the efforts of your kids' teachers. I have met hundreds of educators, and none had an agenda that wasn't based on their sincerest desire to help your child become a happy well-adjusted individual. Few people will ever know and care for your students as their teachers do. For your child's sake, help them succeed. This narrative is as accurate as my memory can make it. I hope you can relate to some of it, laugh at some of it and if you're a teacher, occasionally find yourself within the text. Tim McLean

Part I

I

Of Soybeans, Corn, and Cicadas
I never really had a plan,
Just graduate, then Vietnam.
Do my year there, get my fill,
Maybe go to school on the GI Bill.
A fair deal, and even trade.
'Nam for school and I'm not afraid,
Of chasing Charlie,
The bugs, the stink,
'Nam might give me time to think.
Find who I am.
Find what I'm not.
And pray to God I don't get shot.
But what will I do If we got no war on?
Get real! Peace with Nixon, an oxymoron!
But if uncle don't need me;
And that's kind of a reach,
What the hell, I might try to teach.

As I was nearing the end of my senior year in high school, most of the future terrified me. I had no real goals and not a single viable plan for the rest of my life. I had a half-baked idea about hitchhiking to Alaska to become a salmon fisherman, but even in my own mind, that plan never had the ring of reality to it. My dad offered that maybe he could get me in at the warehouse where he worked. The pay was okay, and it was the type of grunt work he assumed I would be good at. My bench press was really pretty impressive, and my less-than-stellar academic record probably validated his opinion that anything requiring a lot of brain power was not going to be my forte. Schlepping bags of fertilizer and palletizing construction materials seemed to be right up my alley. Hell, if I applied myself, I might even master a forklift—and then the world would be my oyster!

I was one of the few people in America who kind of regretted the military drawdown which followed the signing of the Paris Peace Accords. Not the end of the Vietnam War. That debacle had cost me a friend and my country, so much more. But I regretted that the Marines were going through a reduction in force and probably weren't going to be hiring anymore. I admired the Corp, and once thought I might build a career there. The other branches of the service didn't really interest me—less *esprit*. When the time finally came to make a decision, I did the easy thing. I chose to go to college, only because I did not want to do warehouse work, and in college I could defer adulthood for a few more years. Besides, when I took the ACT my score was pretty solid. This surprised the heck out of my guidance counselor. I even got a staff member to write me a decent letter of recommendation.

Back then, the cost of most state schools was not prohibitive and finding a part time job in a college town wasn't difficult. My first quarter, I signed up for nothing but history classes. It amazed me that when I followed my interests, I did pretty well. In the next four years, I learned about distribution requirements, finished up a couple of majors, and had a heck of a good time. I learned how efficient a carbon dioxide fire extinguisher could be at cooling six packs of beer. Then, I learned that doing so will get you kicked out of your dorm. As a bonus, I had the experience of being homeless for a while as I waited for a room near campus to open up.

By the end of my senior year of college, I was writing letters of application and sending resumes to every school district within 100 miles of my hometown. Finally, I was contacted for an interview. I did well. The high school was in the town of Eagle River, and it turned out to be the home of some of the best kids in the world, and the greatest place I could ever have chosen to start a teaching career.

Eagle River was a town with very few really distinctive characteristics and a history which bore no real relationship to its name. To the best of my knowledge, few eagles had been around those parts since well before DDT, and the "river" which roughly bisected the town was little more than a muddy rivulet—less than that during dry spells. The town's name probably screamed "Hicksville" to folks with city sensibilities, but such people by and large did not live in Eagle River—and probably never would.

The townspeople were a generally contented lot, and the 800 or so souls who called Eagle River home considered themselves as being more right than wrong and more good than bad. A lot of them also carried a large chip on their shoulder regarding the moral superiority of their small-town lifestyle and could point to no fewer than five churches as evidence in support of their claim to civic piety.

It was not a rich community, and the few folks who had money seldom put their wealth on display. To do so would have been considered poor form. Oh, sometimes a guy bought a piece of farm machinery before replacement was absolutely necessary, or a tractor was pimped up with a few superfluous accessories like air conditioning or a top-end stereo. But because modesty was the norm, the poor didn't really stick out. Of course, that doesn't mean folks didn't know where they fit in the social stratum. On the farm, big blue Harvestore silos equaled money, small concrete silos or corn cribs equaled struggling. Simple, really. As is true in many small towns, the people of the community usually voted Republican, excepting of course during the FDR years. In Eagle River, conservatism was the true religion, and constancy the greatest virtue.

Even a casual observer could have seen the town was slowly dying. About one in three buildings on Main Street was now unoccupied. One of the derelict buildings had been a hardware store, another a mom-and-pop grocery—both probably unable to compete with the big box outlets just up the road in the county seat. When those stores went out of business, the locals were disappointed, but not so much that they had been willing to spend the few extra cents per item required to support these small family-owned shops. The Chevy dealership had been closed for ten years and nothing had moved into the space. What had once been a clothing store was now a second-hand shop. A couple of the most dangerously dilapidated buildings displayed rusting signage which advertised brand names and products that had not been consumer staples since the Hoover administration.

The town once had two cafes. Only one remained open now, and the waitresses who worked there usually sat around smoking endless cigarettes, drinking weak black coffee, and gossiping while waiting for the dinner rush. Invariably, the day's special was some kind of deep-fried chicken or a variation on hot beef commercial *mit* gravy *uber alles*. The people of Eagle River were especially fond of gravy.

Twice a day, the Great Northern rolled through town, and when the whistle blew, every left wrist within earshot turned in synchrony to see if it was on schedule. If one of the trains actually stopped at the grain elevator, it was newsworthy.

There were three bars in the town, each with its own set of regular patrons. Each sponsored a softball team and competed intensely for the best local talent. There were even rumors one of the bars tried to bribe a player or two into switching teams with a few bottles of Jack Daniel's—scandalous! These establishments generally spoke more of sociability than debauchery. They were places to enjoy a quiet beer and play euchre or whist with friends. By noon, the air in each was gray with cigarette smoke. All three had tables with laminated tops nearly worn down to base metal in paths aligned with the cardinal compass points. These were the trails of a million tricks being dragged and stacked by generations of calloused, well-practiced hands. All three had peeling wooden floors, slightly warped by the settling of their fieldstone foundations. If you visited each of these bars, you would have been taken with their similarities. As you walked in, there was a long wooden bar to your right and booths to the left. The vinyl backing of each booth was cracked and stained. Towards the rear were more tables. Two of the three bars had a jackalope over the door and a small collection of deer antlers. The other had what once had been a really impressive mount of the largest walleye ever caught in the area. Years ago, one of the more clever locals had put sunglasses on the fish. Imagine, a fish with sunglasses! Sadly, because even the best taxidermy has its limits, it now looked dusty, faded, and leprous. It seemed to remain on the wall in defiance of gravity, and probably mostly out of habit. Each establishment had jars of pickled eggs or turkey necks on the bar, and all the jars had labels stained by vinegar but unencumbered with expiration dates or notices of "Best used by."

The patrons of these places were mostly farmers and, because their lives were framed by a million contingencies they could not control, the people in these parts retained a rigid hold on the few things still predictable. Change wasn't really welcomed nor readily accepted. Values, of course, were collective and immutable; religion was important. The people in Eagle River went to church as families, and they were usually large families. If a couple had been blessed with only three or so kids, it was assumed that they had "problems". Families sat in the same pew, week after week. They also sat in the same order. Dad on one end, Mom on the other, the kids between, with those likely to need an occasional pinch during services seated closest to Mom. The churches annually distributed a list of who donated what during the year. As in many other cases, public shaming was an effective and time-honored means of social control. In small towns, it was often more effective than the local cop. For instance, public drunkenness was frowned upon, so even the hard-core alcoholics were discreet, and usually had enough of a work ethic to complete their chores before they quietly went home and became numb with too much blackberry brandy or peppermint schnapps.

Of course, the town knew about these folks as well as all other specimens of local sinners, and there were few really private secrets in Eagle River. If a man got drunk and was abusive to his wife and children, the town knew it. If your neighbor had a brief fling with the local trollop, the ladies' sodality would be discussing and condemning his lechery within a month. A wayward son, a spendthrift wife, an "easy" daughter, or even a mentally ill relative all became common knowledge and a source of mock indignation or consternation. However, once a secret became known it was the closely guarded property of the townsfolk alone and a thing to which outsiders and newcomers were seldom made privy. The people of the town kept their secrets well hidden from strangers.

As an old farming community, Eagle River had always been notable for two things: turning the locally grown corn and soybeans into milk and pork and converting their own sons and daughters into dissatisfied émigrés. Sadly, the town could offer little which might permanently hold children of ability and ambition. These kids graduated high school and left town searching for work; a few escaped to college. Then, they stayed away and became the entry-level workforce of more prosperous communities. Some of these ex-patriots even succumbed to radical political notions and became Democrats. May God and their parents someday forgive them.

It seemed, then, that people might grow up in the town, but often didn't retire and grow old there. Because of this, the town will probably always remain little more than a wide spot on a blue highway—a place to stop for an overpriced tank of gas and a stale candy bar, sustenance for a trip to somewhere else.

Granted, the town did have a certain timeless quality, but even that did not make it truly unique, for a thousand other small towns shared the same feeling of gray and peeling antiquity. Collectively, they were places which would never age because they were never really new. They remain forever frozen in time and memory, strangely familiar to us, but always comfortably distant. We all once had relatives who called these towns home, and most of us are no more than three generations removed from walking the streets of towns like Eagle River and wondering how in the hell we would fill up another empty Saturday night. Time often weighs heavily upon the residents of small-town America.

Even today, on the occasions when we need to drive through or visit these small places, we still might reflexively pause and consider what our own lives might have been like if our near ancestors had been a bit more conservative and a lot more satisfied with their own rural prospects. This brief speculation is usually done without regret. Except, of course, on rare and perfect spring days. Or perhaps after the first alfalfa cutting when rich country smells saturate every breath. Then we might linger, and stare, and consider; before we get back into our cars for the trip home.

There was a high school in Eagle River and, as with most small towns, that school, any school, was the vital heart of the community. People from larger cities or suburbs can never appreciate the importance a school assumes in the life of a small town. If a community had a school, it had hope—and more, for schools created occasional and necessary social diversions. A school could be the grist for endless discussions and pointed critiques. Everyone in town had an opinion about all things associated with the schools. People cared passionately about their child's elementary teacher or the local high-school athletic teams. They willingly came to open houses and concerts; they filled gyms and packed bleachers. They contributed to fundraisers. People in small towns always opposed district consolidations or anything else that might cost them their school. It was a part of their identity, and while the decision might make sense on paper, the heart wouldn't have it.

Curiously, in small-town America, these schools are usually located close together and on the same square block. That block was a large piece of the community and, if places like Eagle River had prime real estate, that block would be it. But all of it had been willingly and lovingly dedicated to the future. The schools were rays of sunshine, and most were only a right-hand turn removed from dun-colored and aging main streets. It is to the credit of small-town America that this scenario is still played out in countless communities.

It was the high school that brought me to Eagle River. I was 22 years old and newly certified by the State of Minnesota as a fully qualified Social Studies teacher. For the princely sum of $9,700 a year, I was to teach eight sections of American History and four sections of Economics, plus coach football and baseball. If the salary did not excite me, the possibilities did. I would never have considered this to be my dream job, or my last one, but it was an opportunity to teach and coach. Perhaps to take one more bite of the apple before I was forced to become an adult and find more lucrative employment. As a bonus, my parents were proud I was teaching, especially my mother. For twenty-five years, she had been a primary school teacher. She felt she had partially shaped my career decision, and maybe she was right. There was also a dozen or so of my former teachers who had played major roles in my life and my decision to teach. One or two helped carry me to a high-school diploma, and for that, I will always be grateful.

In pensive moments, I imagined teaching could also be a personal validation. On my life's resume no matter what else I did, I could list I had once been a teacher, and by extension probably a good and caring person.

But all that was in the future and a lifetime from this year. For now, I was excited, and I had cause to believe perhaps I would be a good teacher. On paper, my student teaching experience looked to have been incredibly positive. I had been placed in a large suburban school. My cooperating instructor was a history teacher and basketball coach. He believed this year, after a pretty impressive string of mediocre seasons, his team could finally be headed to the state tourney—and getting them there should be his real focus. He basically introduced me to the class, wished me luck, and then became a full-time coach. Only because his history classes were beginning a unit in which I had a deep background did I manage to muddle through. During the quarter, he observed me two or three times and at the end of my internship reported to the college that I was "a natural and would become a great teacher." In this, he really didn't have a clue, nor did I realize his glowing appraisal of my teaching was doing me no favors. He had a wealth of experience in the classroom, but never really invested the time required to help me grow professionally. He did, however, teach me one important lesson. In education and in many other fields, if you offer criticism, it becomes necessary to explain and correct. This takes time. If you offer superlatives and generalities, people are satisfied, and little explanation is required. In any case, I was flattered by his assessment. It was prominently displayed on the cover page of my applications. Perhaps that one, glowing generality had even gotten me my successful interview. Later, I wrote him a brief letter thanking him.

A lot of my friends were surprised I had chosen to teach. Most teachers are outgoing and gregarious by nature, but I was, and always will be, a shy person. Yet somehow, I found the classroom to be tremendously disinhibiting. Even as a student teacher, I often went to truly bizarre lengths to make a point or illustrate a concept. I loved laughter and walked the halls singing. When I stood in front of a class, I discovered the extrovert within. At the time I didn't know it, but I also carried and displayed a certain *smarminess*, so when I interacted with a class, my ego often trumped my ability. I thought myself to be clever. I'm sure several kids had different opinions.

Upon being hired, I decided to attack this job with a passion. On a small stage like Eagle River, I shortly expected to play a leading role. If it didn't work out that way, the worst-case scenario was I would spend two quiet years in the classroom and the next couple of summers fishing. When I got tired of the place, I anticipated a good reference, and then I could put Eagle River and teaching permanently into my rearview mirror. At 22, even the most idealistic part of me recoiled at the notion of a lifetime spent in underpaid public service, especially in a small town. So, as I contemplated reporting to my first summer football camp, it was with excitement, but also detachment. I would be a short-timer, a knight-errant with a history degree and a whistle. This would be a brief and agreeable exile to a land of soybeans, corn, and cicadas. I would stay until I had a better plan for my life, or maybe a better offer. Until then, I had a job and an identity. For as long as the titles remained agreeable, in the classroom I would be Mr. Mclean, and on the athletic field I would be Coach McLean. When I had sorted myself out, it would be time for me to move on. Regrettably, by neither training nor temperament was I prepared to fill either of these roles.

"There is very little better in life than to be young, optimistic, and ignorant."

II

Ain't in Kansas Anymore

The education of "Coach" McLean began with my first summer football camp. It was expected that with three years of college football behind me, I had enough experience to fill the role of team defensive coordinator and line coach. This was not true, for while I had played some, I had never coached. Neither had I ever taken a coaching class. My own college coaches did not consider teaching the game as their primary responsibility, and what little insight they passed on to me was always accompanied by red-faced shouting and some variation of the word "fuck." For one of them, this may have been cathartic and a partial payback for the fact he was one of the last cuts made by the Winnipeg Blue Bombers back in, '66. The rest of them had no real excuse for their vile tempers and vulgar vocabularies. They were simply angry and stupid men who chewed tobacco and didn't wipe away the disgusting brown juice which accumulated at the corners of their mouths. None of them offered much by way of being either a role model or mentor.

Even as a beginner, I realized college coaching norms would be of little use at the high-school level. The blocking and tackling were the same, but swearing was definitely out, and even a small slip into a more colorful vocabulary could quickly get me fired from my coaching and teaching position. Back then, f-bombs still had the power to shock. I also discovered that many of the techniques my college coaches had taught me were frowned upon by the Minnesota State High School League. Head slapping was out, and butt blocking was now called spearing and penalized 15 yards. Crack-backs were illegal, and unnecessary roughness was no longer an oxymoron. At the high-school level, football was still organized mayhem, but really egregious violence was discouraged.

However, some parts of the game were the same. For instance, yelling was OK; in fact, it was expected. Football is a loud game. This was the mid-seventies, and every coach at every level worshipped at the altar of Lombardi. The closer you could approximate the volume of the immortal Vince, the better. Every coaching staff had a resident screamer, and by the second day of practice the job was mine. Otherwise, I really didn't bring much to the table as far as knowing blocking techniques or running a defense. For that entire first week, I yelled myself hoarse at practice. At night, I learned a few defensive drills and schemes while sucking on cough drops or gargling with warm salt water. My ignorance may have been appalling, but no one within five blocks of the practice field could cast aspersions on my volume or intensity.

The only thing I really had going for me was my appearance. I was not cute. My girlfriend once described me as "rugged looking." Now, I had no idea what the hell this really meant, but I assumed it was female-speak for, "Thank God you've got a personality." My parents couldn't afford to give me a lot of property or cash, but they had gifted me genetically with height and bulk. I scowled magnificently and often. I had a full black beard; and a series of childhood accidents and adolescent altercations had left me a nearly perfect amount of facial scarring. I scared people. I looked like a defensive coordinator *cum ax murderer*. I also had a temper and a flair for the dramatic.

When a kid screwed up, I could confront him in a way that made it appear I was barely containing my deepest urge to do physical violence to everyone within reach. In the middle of a harangue, I would abruptly turn away from the object of my wrath and lift my eyes to call upon the heavens for the strength I needed to help me contain my berserk rage. This was wonderful acting and great theater, but horrible coaching. This was especially so when the focus of my tirade was a nice little fuzzy-cheeked kid who probably would have been more comfortable buried in the tenor section of the school choir. Most of my players were nice kids and eager as all get-out, but all the shouting in the world would not change the fact that, by and large, the youngsters who tried out for the team were small, slow, and mild-mannered. Some were truly memorable for their passivity.

My center and two guards could have been triplets. All three were wide and short. With any exertion, their faces got bright red and they sweated profusely. Their practice pants never seemed to fit correctly, so when they got into their stances, they collectively displayed an even 12 inches of butt crack. Plumbers in training, perhaps? My tackles would one day be big, strapping farmers. They had huge hands and feet; unfortunately, that day was about four years distant. For now, they were just teenagers who were kind of funny looking because they had such outsized extremities. With these stalwart blocks of granite trying to open holes in the defense, I never did get the chance to discover if my two running backs could actually have carried the ball. Either of them may have been a young Gale Sayers, but regrettably the world would never know.

My quarterback was the *pièce de résistance*. When I first met him, I was impressed. He was a slight young man but appeared to be well-made. He moved like an athlete. He could even throw the ball. Variations on the option were starting to come into vogue, and the kid looked like an honest-to-God *bona fide*, option quarterback. It took three days for me to discover he also had a number of outstanding liabilities. For one thing, nobody on the team liked him. His father owned the only grain elevator in town. In Eagle River that was the equivalent of being the scion of wealth and privilege. For this he was envied. Secondly, he stuttered when he got nervous. When I asked the head coach why this speech impediment hadn't previously disqualified him from the position, I was told he remained at quarterback because no one else wanted the job. Besides, his older brother had once been the quarterback, as had his father before him. In this boy's family, leading the mighty Screaming Eagles was a tradition. As a newcomer, I didn't feel I had a right to question such a long-standing arrangement, so I decided to work with the young man and cultivate his leadership potential. Not being a speech therapist, that was my only option. This was a wonderful example of *the inept leading the unwilling*. Quarterbacks should be team leaders, so I began to try and coach him up on the basics, things like fostering team unity and improving morale.

I noticed my quarterback hadn't yet showered with the team after practice. It may be a stupid and crude generalization, but being aloof in the locker-room has probably never enhanced anyone's role as team leader. I quietly and discreetly pulled the young man aside and suggested showering with the guys might give him the sort of common touch true leadership sometimes required. At my suggestion, the young man blushed and told me showering with the team was a bad idea. This I took as defiance, and I pressed him for the reason why he felt my idea was such a poor one. (Please remember, these were still the years of the P.E. sweat check. Getting buck naked in groups and lathering up with a really caustic orangish institutional soap was a rite of passage.) I assured the youngster I understood his desire for privacy. I explained how I had attended a Catholic school for eight years and before going to a public junior high school I had seldom even seen myself naked, much less been oogled by total strangers. (I mean, shouldn't some things be saved for marriage?) In my pristine parochial educational environment, there had been absolutely no group showering! Period! In fact, there were no showers. At Saint Stephen's, such an act was probably considered a violation of Canon Law, and as such required an immediate trip to the confessional and a hefty penance. "Bless me father for I have sinned, but I swear to God, they made me do it." The possibilities which might flow from such behavior were terrifying. What would have happened if by some freaky combination of circumstances I had been forced to get naked, take a public shower, and then later been hit by a car while crossing the street to get to a confessional? I would have been doomed to eternal perdition by a perverted P.E. teacher. The entire summer before I went into ninth grade, I woke up in cold sweats, fearing the day that I would first have to expose my chubby Catholic body to a taunting herd of depraved Protestant exhibitionists. Yes, I did understand the young man's discomfort, I really did, and his suggestion that I didn't made me all the more persistent. Then I pulled out the final, often used, and usually decisive argument in the P.E. world's war on modesty. "Unless you got something the rest of the guys don't have, you're going to shower with the team."

After eight years of waiting, I was finally able to use the argument which had gotten my corpulent juvenile backside into the showers at my old junior high school. After a further bit of evasion, he finally told me he didn't shower with the team because he thought the rest of the guys would laugh at his small "penie"… Today, I often pray God heavily discounts the sins of the young and stupid. I was

22 and had the sensitivity of a bag of hammers. I reacted badly to the young man's obvious discomfort. I started to laugh. Never in my life had I found it necessary to try and swallow so much laughter so quickly. Regrettably, I could not contain it all. My response to the young man's obvious embarrassment was a cross between a snort and a phlegmy throat clearing. Internal pressure forced snot from my nose and my eyes watered. I turned away, the issue was dropped, and from that moment on he and I had a kind of unstated pact. Neither of us would ever speak of the incident again, and where he showered was his own damn business. Neither, I suspect, was I ever forgiven. Somewhere within me, I should have found that eighth grade boy who had once spent a dozen sleepless nights terrified at the prospect of sharing a shower with thirty other people. Old fears once conquered should be buried; but never so easily forgotten. I was only five years older than this kid, nearly a peer. My reaction confirmed the basis for his discomfort. To compound my sin, I didn't keep it private. This was just too damn funny to keep to myself. That I told and retold the story to the other coaches was the equivalent of repeatedly throwing the kid under a bus. It was only in my later years that I had the maturity to be properly ashamed of myself for my conduct during the entire incident.

I made a million more mistakes with that team. More importantly, I made mistakes with kids as individuals. I was given a wonderful opportunity to teach, and at most every turn I screwed up regally. I chose to be the worst part of every bad coach I had ever had; no excuses offered. Every day of that summer camp was about anger or frustration or futility, sometimes all three. I know now that it was about me and my ego. It's very difficult for even a veteran coach to separate themselves from a team's performance. For a young one, it might be nearly impossible. We practiced diligently, but never seemed to get better. As I stood in the huddle giving instructions to this group, I often felt like the mayor of the Munchkin City. It would not have amazed me had my starting backfield broken into spontaneous song about the joys of representing the lollipop guild; in fact, this may have been appropriate, for I sure as hell wasn't in Kansas anymore.

When I first interviewed for this job, the principal told me the football team had won only a single game in the past two years. I never said it, but I was confident that with me on board, victories and athletic glory would be a simple matter of time. That interview was one of the few times in my entire life I managed to think something without then having it tumble out of my big, stupid mouth. I would later come to thank the Almighty for that one brief moment of discretion and humility, for after the first scrimmages it was pretty clear we were going to be terrible, and the athletic glory I had imagined would take a bit more time and effort than I expected.

No doubting it, during that season, bad times were going to continue for the mighty Eagle River Screaming Eagles and all the *faux* anger I could generate wasn't going to change our prospects too much. However, this realization did not stop me from trying all the usual motivational devices.

Football was, and is, the most cliché-driven sport known to man, and there was no possible football situation that could not be explained or improved upon with a good motivational poster. In a coach's world, heart and attitude would always overcome physical shortcomings. After all, everyone knows that "It's not the size of the dog in the fight that matters. It's the size of the fight in the dog." "Fatigue does make cowards of us all" and "If it's not six inches from your heart, it really won't kill you." Speaking of death, "That which does not kill you makes you stronger." "Attitude alone can determine altitude." Winning then was only an act of will, as losing was evidence of deep character flaws, and by the way, if you lose a road game you sure as hell better be quiet and reflect on your many sins on the bus ride home!!

When all else fails, coaches often appealed directly to the Almighty, for God really had nothing more important to do than to put the unfolding universe on hold and watch intently as adolescent males bludgeoned each other on a football field—really. As the season unfolded, I discovered my team must have been loaded with deep character flaws and that God loved our opponents more than she did us. We started the year with a five-touchdown loss to our biggest rivals and to my chagrin, as the season continued no matter how many inspirational posters papered our locker room walls, the Lord continued to give victory to our opponents with bigger offensive lines and faster running backs. I regret to admit it, but also to teams with better coaching. The phrase, "moral victory" began to take on new meaning, and my kids would come to develop a definite swagger in their gait if the margin of defeat was anything less than three touchdowns. Sadly, before the season was half over, I started to believe it myself.

Once again it's third and ten, .
so we probably should pass.
But every time our Q drops back,
he ends up on his ass.

Perhaps we'll run a draw play,
to get them suckered in.
Then we'll hand it to our fullback,
then we'll call his next of kin.

It's probably poor coaching,
but I have no plays to call.
No matter how I plot and scheme,
we just can't move the ball.

Our line is just offensive.
Our running backs get hurt.
Our receivers can only fetch the ball,
as a pass falls to the dirt.

We're getting good at punting though.
It's our only claim to fame.
Cuz we do a lot of punting,
about fifteen times a game.

But we just may win next Friday.
We might do a little more.
Thank God our A.D. scheduled us,
with the Sisters of the Poor.

III

Children of Ambition and Ability

The education of "Mister" McLean began on the first day school was in session. Before that day, teaching was an abstraction. But at 7:30 A.M., on August 30th 1976, teaching became real, and nothing in my background or training had really equipped me for the responsibility I now owned. All my coursework, and all my student teaching experience, had been little more than the educational equivalent of playing house. Before now, I could always have deferred to a higher authority and simply did what I was told; not so anymore.

When that first bell rang, 34 kids had an unquestioned right to expect I had something worthwhile to offer them. I was the new teacher in town. My students were curious and they were eager. I was kind of a big deal. What I didn't know then was they were also on my side. They desperately wanted me to succeed. They were the easiest house I was ever going to play for; and beginning at minute one, I screwed the pooch at every possible opportunity. What I gave them were rules. Five, to be precise, carefully mimeographed. Along with these, I delivered a lecture about what a brass-balled son of a bitch I intended to be. "Don't be tardy … no talking … assignments on time … no excuses and definitely no bathroom passes." I was Mr. McLean, and you obviously were something less. "Here is worksheet number one, open your book and get going. When you have read the chapter, perhaps I will favor you with a lecture. Any questions, raise your hand; and yes, you may have worksheet number two if you finish number one before the rest of the class." I then walked around the room, scowling. Naturally, this created the type of open, welcoming classroom I had always envisioned. The fear was palpable and I reveled in it.

For nearly five weeks, the kids cringed, and I sneered and lectured. Football practice was about wind sprints and volume; my classes were about worksheets and silence. I even imagined I was getting a few positive results in both arenas. On Friday Nights, we regularly got piss-pounded, but the scores were becoming more reasonable. Class work was getting completed on time. It was all rote memorization but correct often enough to maintain the appearance of progress.

My principal thought I was the greatest thing since the invention of multiple-choice tests, and he told me so. Once, after a very cursory classroom observation, he put his arm around my shoulder and commended me for my wonderful classroom discipline. He reminded me, "Successful teachers didn't smile at least until Christmas," and "90% of teaching is about control." This advice was consistent with the wisdom currently being dispensed in my just-completed teacher education program.

However, in college, it was referred to as behaviorism and these simple concepts were completely obfuscated with psycho-babble.

What both of us missed completely during his observation was the kids were probably learning nothing meaningful. They sat still, they suffered, and they endured, but when I remember those first few weeks, it is not with any pride in my teaching. I can say for a certainty, the kids were quiet, that's all. Were these same students locked in a room with only the text, likely they would have accomplished exactly as much.

As an undergrad I worked as a bouncer in a dive bar. My primary responsibilities were to look intimidating, check IDs and make sure no one left with a beer bottle or bar glass. What I was doing now was little different. I was a thug with a degree and so inexperienced, I saw fear and believed it to be respect. But at the time, my principal's praise flattered me. This was true even if the source of the praise didn't impress.

Despite being a 'greenhorn' I knew immediately Principal Jones was a wiener. He ventured into the halls only to get lunch or on his way outside to sneak a smoke. These trips never happened during passing time. I began to believe he was afraid of kids. I knew for sure he was afraid of the larger male ones.

One time, he asked me to step into his office to be a witness, just in case he felt the need to "get physical" with an especially incorrigible and outsized young man. What he meant was, with me in the room, the kid probably wouldn't dare to hit him back. This incident turned out to be a tempest in a teapot. There was a little screaming and nothing "physical" transpired ... unless you count a bit of spirited desk pounding! The entire episode was a truly dreadful performance by all parties involved. "Old Jonesy" was thrilled at the opportunity to pretend he was still a tough guy. I pretended I was impressed with his performance, and after a bit of ridiculous posturing, the young man pretended to be properly chastened and was sent back to class. The entire scene was made even more pathetic by the fact we all knew we were all acting. Later, this pathos was compounded by Jonesy's retelling of the tale whenever I was near enough to support his claims of macho manly firmness. The story became a running joke in the building, and Jonesy wore the tale like a bad toupee. Everyone knew it didn't fit, and the color was wrong, but no one actually told him how ridiculous he sounded. A Language Arts teacher suggested she should write an epic poem immortalizing the heroic deeds of our fearless leader. She suggested *Jonsey at the Bridge* or *The Ballad of Jonesy* might be fitting titles. A fellow Social Studies teacher wondered if Jonesy's wife was benefiting from his new rush of testosterone. A math teacher suggested we combine these two ideas and write an epic poem about his heroic rush of testosterone. The results of this collaboration were hilarious, albeit bawdy and in poor taste. Others, me included, simply felt sorry for the man and really wished the entire incident would go away.

My principal had worked in public education for 35 years. He had done important work, and at the end of this year or next he would retire. He would see no more promotions and when he finally left, all he really would take with him was a small pension, a certificate suitable for framing, a fake gold desk set, and the best wishes of the School Board. Maybe this job was once his dream, but I doubted it. When he looked in the mirror, Jonesy certainly knew his best years were behind him. Now, he desperately needed people like me to hold the lid securely in place until he could retire to a planned community in Somewhere, Arizona. It really didn't seem like he was asking for too much. For the time being, I was alright with taking the bad guy role. I honestly wanted things to work out for him; and by a happy coincidence, his infirmity played directly into my expansive ego.

At just 22, I imagined myself to be a sort of *de facto* vice-principal in the building. Teachers sometimes brought their problem children to me for reprimand, and I reveled in the perception of authority. Not even two months in the classroom and I really believed I had already mastered my profession. Teaching seemed to be so easy and formulaic. The keys to effective instruction were very simple. Silence equaled good, worksheets equaled teaching, more worksheets equaled better teaching, and screaming plus motivational posters equaled good coaching. Why the hell did anyone think this was hard?

It was about week five when David shot the first holes in my simple-minded pedagogic theories. He was a quiet boy whose family owned a mink farm on the downwind side of town. I had driven by his place a dozen times and was always amazed anyone could call such a shack home. Ramshackle was too kind a description for the property. Every wooden structure on the place was in desperate need of painting, everything metal wore a patina of rust. Nothing except a particularly hardy species of crabgrass grew in the area between the house and the outbuildings so, depending upon the weather, the "yard" was either dust or mud. There was a rusty windmill, its fan was missing about every second slat, and it was always oriented to the northeast no matter which way the wind was blowing.

David was the type of kid who never seemed to get much right. His grades were poor, and I believed he was retaking this class after failing it in the second quarter of last year. He suffered from acne wherever a greasy strand of his poorly cut hair fell across his face. His clothing was well-worn and never completely clean. Mink farming was filthy stinking work, and because it's based on death and dismemberment, David usually smelled slightly of decay. In my rural school district, most of the students had chores before school, so my classroom usually had a hint of barnyard bouquet about it. But even in this scent-rich environment, David stood out.

When I considered him at all, I concluded he was an indifferent student, and unmotivated in the extreme. Even this early in my career, I had discovered calling a kid unmotivated was a wonderful way to rationalize away any of my own shortcomings as a teacher. David's assignments were always done on time, but they were completed in pencil, often erased and rewritten. Sometimes there were small holes in the paper from his many attempts to repair his work. He never volunteered to speak in class; I'm sure he considered it the greatest good fortune when my seating chart put him in a desk at the back left corner of the room. He was so withdrawn. When he came into class, he always acknowledged any greetings with a small nod of his head and then fixed his eyes to the floor. To my knowledge, David had no close friends and few acquaintances. He didn't walk with anyone in the halls, and even the school bullies would have considered picking on David as "bringing coals to Newcastle," so he was left alone. He didn't have a nickname. This alone spoke volumes about him, for even the most marginally accepted students in the building had nicknames.

One Friday morning, an anxious looking David was tardy. It was the first period of the day, and I was more surly than usual. I expected my team was going to get the crap kicked out of it that night. We were playing the best team in the conference, and even a moral victory seemed unlikely. David became an easy and obvious scapegoat for my foul mood. Tardiness was sin number one in my hierarchy of offenses, and so I gave him particular hell. With my finest rhetorical flourishes, I suggested he was foolish and lazy. I painted for him the type of future he might look forward to if he took this slovenly attitude into the "real" world. I was so incredibly witty. As he retreated to his desk, I was actually proud of myself for the clever way I had administered such a huge dose of venom. The rest of the class laughed, David withered, and I was convinced I had accomplished at least one victory that Friday.

The following Monday, David was absent. On Tuesday, he was absent again, and I was told David's father had died in the hospital the Saturday before. I discovered that for the past two years David had been running his family's mink operation mostly by himself. He had no choice; his father was pretty much an invalid, and in the months before his death he had been bedridden with complications from diabetes. David's mother spent much of her time caring for her husband, so was of little help. The family was becoming destitute. Public assistance was available, but perhaps David and his mother saw pride as the only thing they had left which still connected them to decent society. What little income the family had was mostly David's doing. Before school, he cared for the animals. After school, he tried his best to maintain the place. Late nights were for homework and giving his mother a break from her nursing chores. On Friday afternoon, I went to a quiet and poorly attended funeral. None of David's classmates were there. I was wearing the same frayed sports coat I had already worn twice that week, but I was easily the best dressed person in the church. It was a Catholic Service; but there were no hymns, no family members read scripture or gave even the briefest of eulogies. The priest offered a well-practiced and *pro forma* homily, but when he had finished, I doubt he had convinced anyone in the church he had ever actually met the man whom he was helping to bury.

In Eagle River, as in many other places, it is traditional that after a funeral, the women of the church community provide lunch to those attending. This custom was a service and a blessing to the family of the deceased, who were often too preoccupied with grief and the details of death to offer hospitality themselves. After a brief graveside service, only about 15 of us returned to the church basement to share a bit of the sliced ham, coleslaw, rolls, coffee and cookies which were provided. I stayed because of my guilt; I hoped the other people had better motives and a genuine concern for the family. David and his mother would now need all the concern which might come their way. After lunch, and on my way out the door, a stoic, dignified looking David shook my hand and thanked me for coming. I managed a brief nod, then fixed my eyes to the floor of the church basement until I was once again safely outside. I cried for most of the drive home.

That night, I coached a football game and thanks to a collection of hometown calls and lucky bounces, we finally won. Following the contest, I went to the local Legion Club and celebrated. I think I did a pretty good job of pretending our first, and as it turned out, our only victory that year was somehow important. I left the bar two or three beers past silliness, but four or five shy of forgetfulness. In my mind, David walked me home that night, and by the time I went to bed I had formulated at least a dozen ways I could apologize to him. More than that, I was going to make his life at school better; there were things I could do. On Monday morning, David came to my room and told me he was dropping out of school. As he handed me his textbook, he thanked me again for being at the funeral. I told him how sorry I was about his father. I told him I was terribly wrong to have lectured him as I did. Rationalizations flowed, I mumbled some bullshit about nerves, and the game that night, and not knowing what he was up against, and was there anything I could do? These were words thrown into the wind and rightfully ignored as soon as they were spoken.

He said perhaps he could return to school when things got straightened out, and I desperately wanted to believe him. I told him I would help him catch up when he came back. He shook my hand again, gave me a quick nod and was gone, and on the day he walked out of Eagle River High School, he was more of a man than I was on the day I entered it.

David was a student of mine, and he had an unquestioned right to expect I had something worthwhile to offer him. I had given him only rules, worksheets, and another bitter memory. The longest conversation I had ever had with him was the few dozen words we exchanged as he was dropping out of school. A few weeks later, David and his mother were gone. Their place was abandoned and quickly became the type of rural ruin one might still find at the end of countless overgrown country driveways. It was quickly vandalized; kids went there to party and drink. Eventually, the volunteer fire department set it ablaze and then put it out: good practice, I guessed.

There were many reasons why children of ambition and ability left Eagle River. I had never seen or recognized it, but David had obviously been one of these. In all the time between then and today, I have never forgotten what I said to the poor kid when he happened to be a bit late to my first hour class and I was in a shit mood. He had a right to expect so much better, and a thousand times since I wish I had simply asked him if he was OK. Maybe that's all it would have taken. It is so damned easy to ask if there is anything you can do—after it's too late.

This entire episode was one of the lowest points of my career. I don't think that I ever hurt someone so badly or acted with more deliberate cruelty. Never was I less like a teacher. If I could undo two minutes of my life this incident might be it. I know that this sorry episode changed me. Thinking back to my first year of teaching, I believe that David was the single best teacher I ever had. What I learned from him was a gift to every other kid who ever walked into my classroom.

IV

Finally a Teacher

Winter was coming early to Eagle River that year. The leaves were changing and beginning to drop by early October. The fall bird migrations were in full swing. More than once, football practice just stopped as a flock of mallards passed overhead. When this happened, several of my kids held out their arms and pretended to draw a bead on the unsuspecting waterfowl. Some of them made fake gunshot sounds. My screaming about their lack of focus did little good, and the next flock drew the same reaction. God knows what chaos may have erupted if a buck deer had suddenly appeared on the margins of the practice field.

The ground was beginning to freeze, and a cold snap froze the small wet clods of earth that earlier in the week had been churned up by our cleats. The cold made concentration difficult, and the partially frozen ground made attempts at blocking and tackling painful and even more halfhearted and futile. My brilliant psychological riposte to my team's chicken-shit attitude was to come to practice in shorts and a tee shirt. To this day, I have no real idea what the hell I was trying to prove, or what I thought I might accomplish. Perhaps something about real men not feeling the cold, or this is what tough looks like! Then it started to rain, or rather a mixture of rain and ice pellets came down. By the middle of practice, I was slightly blue, and my nose was dripping uncontrollably. I was shivering violently and losing control of major muscle groups. Thank God, practice ended before hypothermia set in. What a wonderful example I was setting, especially the snot dripping off the end of my nose! I think the only thing I showed the team was what aggravated stupid looked like.

Next I tried threats. I was going to bench all of my starters! This was ludicrous because I had no real second string to replace them. My rants were hollow now … and the players knew it. The kids seemed to be already well satisfied with their season. My little warriors had enjoyed their few moments of gridiron glory, and they were ready to rest on their well-earned laurels until next season.

In fairness to them, my players had other concerns at this time of year. It was harvest time, and the majority of them practiced during hours that were quite literally stolen from their field work. The children of Eagle River were economic assets to their parents, and our sterling record in football made farm work seem like a more profitable use of their manpower. That they were allowed to participate in sports at all was a sacrifice for their parents. By the last two weeks of the season, football had become a thing only to be endured. Our head coach understood and accepted it. I was less willing to acknowledge the obvious. I still screamed like a maniac, but more and more I fell into predictable cadences.

Behind my back, the players laughed at me. At times I overheard when some of the braver ones did imitations of my voice and mannerisms. My quarterback had me down cold. The quality of his impersonations did great things for his status with the team. It did not however improve his execution of the offense.

Other teams with better records, fewer character flaws, and closer ties to the Almighty were sharpening up for the playoffs. Unfortunately, we were the whetstone upon which they intended to hone their games. Our last two contests were played on frost-covered fields and they were blowouts. Our last game became kind of a metaphor for the entire season. We were playing a neighboring community and sometime during the second half one of their spectators managed to get aboard our empty team bus and liberally spread deer scent all over the seats. The stink was overpowering. Sadly, my players couldn't even muster a little indignation. We had the equipment in storage by the first week in November. By then, football was just a bad memory; another subpar season in a garland of subpar seasons.

For a while, I brooded about our final losses of the year. Each time I did, it left me feeling more angry and sullen. This was especially so because, while I was in a funk, the kids had trouble hiding their jubilation. For nine long months, they were done with getting beat up every Friday night and bitched at the rest of the week. Once the corn and beans were harvested, there would be time to hunt or engage in the general goofiness which is supposed to be a part of the high school experience. This included breaking training regulations. My boys felt they had a lot of beer to catch up on before basketball or wrestling season began, and I think they gave it their best shot.

My resolution to regard Eagle River and teaching as a temporary situation was reinforced by the disappointments of that season. The entire incident with David continued to prey on my mind. It's not like I really believed I owned the blame for his decision to drop out. Circumstances had been dragging David beneath the wheel for his entire academic career. My sin was one of omission, and my cruel harangue only the final insult added to an already marginalized school life. How in the hell did I not know anything about his circumstances? All the clues were there; things a more astute teacher, or just a decent person, would have picked up on. The kid was shooting red flares at me, and I didn't even discuss his situation with his counselor. There were so many things I hadn't done. I hadn't asked him to see me after class; I hadn't sat beside him and tried to help him with his classwork. Simply saying "Hi" and wishing him a good morning would have cost me nothing. I once thought if I had one real gift to bring to the classroom, it was that I was a reflective and sensitive person. So far in my teaching and coaching career, I had seldom demonstrated either of those qualities. David never demanded my attention; he never made the smallest request of the school. He screamed silently, and I will always regret that I didn't hear him. Neither did I see him. Those first couple of months I didn't really see any of my students. I wanted to have order and completed worksheets. My students were less important than my process. I wasn't teaching kids, I was teaching economics and history, the kids be damned. Later that fall, one of the women on the faculty told me one of my female students spent a day acutely embarrassed because she was afraid to ask me to use the restroom. Seems that even with my high-powered teaching degree, I was unable to control a teenage girl's menstrual cycle. I have always detested bullies, and now I was a bully. I went home that night a smaller person, and was genuinely ashamed of myself for being such a huge prick. For the first time, I began to question if I was a good enough person to be a teacher. This is very different from wondering if I knew enough material or if I knew the mechanics of teaching. But did I have the empathy, the patience, the kindness, and sensitivity, to be trusted with a classroom full of adolescents? In the middle of my first year, the answer was—I didn't. I was becoming sullen. I knew I needed to change. In the classroom and on the athletic field, I had been living on a constant diet of cortisol and adrenaline, and it was beginning to wear on me. After only three months in the classroom, the initial flush of excitement and accomplishment was gone. Even more so than when I was a student, June now seemed so impossibly far away.

Objectively, I knew I was bored and boring. My classroom was a sterile place, and the kids came to my sections with as much enthusiasm as a miner descending into a West Virginia coal pit. Perhaps my need to change was no more than the simple and human imperative we all feel to derive joy and meaning from what we do. I thought teaching would give me huge doses of each, it hadn't—so far at least. Perhaps I was also beginning to see and understand a few simple and fundamental things about the students who had been placed in my keeping, and on almost every level I was failing them. In either case, by early winter, I had made a conscious decision to lighten up. With no football to stew about, I focused more energy on my teaching; I even generated the occasional lesson that bordered on being creative.

Once, I tried a simulation. I make no claim I created it, but it was new to Eagle River. My room was divided into eight groups. Each group was to consider itself a country. They needed to name their country, make a flag, and compose a national motto. If they could do an anthem, all the better. As they worked in their groups, for the first time there was laughter and engagement in my room. When this was done, each of these countries received a different number of paper airplanes. These represented ballistic missiles. Their objective was to prevent a war. I hoped alliances would be formed and ultimately the country with the largest number of paper airplanes, now called TAMS or terrible atomic missiles, would feel the most threatened and vulnerable. At the time, the U.S.A. and the U.S.S.R. were in the process of trying to negotiate limits on atomic weapons and I was trying to demonstrate how difficult it was to draft these arms reduction treaties. At any point during the negotiations, a "nation" was free to launch their TAMS on any unsuspecting neighbor. This was poor planning on my part and roughly equivalent to giving a kindergarten class a box full of hand grenades, or selling assault rifles to anyone without a background check. TAMS filled the air before I had completely finished giving instructions. I got pissed, end of simulation! Back to the books, never again, stomp, stomp, stomp, and scream! For the rest of the period, the kids exchanged *sub-rosa* smiles and breathed the rarefied air of co-conspiracy. I tried to fall back into severity, but I had a devil of a time keeping my eyes from smiling back at them. That night, at a few dinner tables, I wondered if the topic of conversation was the paper airplane fight that broke out in the room of the mean new Social Studies teacher. If so, a few parents probably wondered aloud what the schools were coming to. I know a couple of my colleagues did. One of our senior faculty members even gave me a few unsolicited "tips" on classroom management and shared a couple of stories from his own days as a "rookie" math teacher. Patronizing wasn't a strong enough description.

The next day, I was able to salvage a bit of a lesson from the paper blizzard of the day before. As a purpose gradually wriggled out of yesterday's chaos, more and more kids tied into my thought process. For a few seconds, every student in the room was attentive and had the wide-eyed affect of a first-grader trying to concentrate their shoelaces into a perfect bow. That precise moment was a treasure, and it was made all the better by the fact I completely and absolutely understood the minute I was living inside. That was the first time I was ever really a teacher.

Later in the day, I told a joke in class. Now, it was truly a lame joke, but after a bit of confused silence several kids actually laughed. This was due less to the quality of the joke than the unlikeliness of the source. That was the first time I remember enjoying two instructional periods in a day. It was certainly not a "Saul on the road to Damascus" sort of thing, but to this day I remember the moment, and I still smile at that dumb joke. First, I asked, "How do you sell insurance to a deaf man?" Then, I shouted loudly, "Hey, ya wanna buy some insurance?" For the few seconds it took the laughter to subside, I wasn't a horse's ass. I was a 22-year-old man telling a joke to a group of 17- and 18-year-olds. I just happened to be their teacher, and for today I was good with that. No promises for the future, no commitments to teaching as a career, but for today, I was OK with that. I think for the first time I actually considered that perhaps I might have a future in the classroom. It was about then that I stopped telling kids they couldn't use the bathroom.

The day I graduated,
I thought I knew my stuff.
Watched teachers work for all my life,
And it didn't look too tough.

Just park yourself in front of class.
Then check for who's not there.
Than pass out worksheets one and two,
Then give them all a glare.

You scowl upon occasion.
You demand they stay on task.
Then come up with the answer,
If a question they should ask.

But if you just don't know it,
Then give a dirty look.
And tell them they could find it,
If they'd only read the book!

But with time and introspection,
I soon began to see.
That if that is all I offer them\,
There's no real need for me.

I should be there to help them grow.
There's so much I could give.
To help complete the narrative
For the life they choose to live.

And that would be a victory.
Not worksheets neatly done.
But lives I helped improve upon.
Are more truly battles won.

V

The Check Stays the Same

When I talked to family or friends about becoming a teacher, the most common reaction I got was something about how difficult it would be to work with kids and, "I'd never have the patience to do it." Then, what usually followed was their honest reaction about teaching and their real reason for never considering it as a career. This almost always involved how underpaid teachers were. At the time, this was no mystery to me. My mother had been a teacher. I knew what a teacher was likely to make, and the small salary didn't scare me. I came from a family that was a bit less than well off, and I was broke while in college. When I was a student, my friends were all broke too. We lived in sketchy places, we ate chicken pot pies and a ton of mac and cheese, sometimes substituting water for milk. (This was a terrible idea.) I remember being overjoyed at finding a grocery store which sold very bad frozen pizzas for 99 cents each. I really doubt that I ate a single vegetable or fruit until some time after I graduated. Most importantly, I learned the difference between want and need. So, when I started teaching, very little changed for me. My salary was underwhelming but adequate, and I found there were ways teachers could supplement their income, especially male teachers. There was coaching, of course, but Junior High games also needed referees. Dozens of school events required chaperones, and I was willing to do homebound instruction. I even came to enjoy it.

Minnesota had just mandated that girls be given the opportunity to participate in interscholastic sports. This should have created coaching opportunities for women, however, nearly all girls' teams were coached by men. There were no female referees, and supervision of most other school events was allocated to senior (generally male) staff or coaches (almost always male) should they choose to take them. Occasionally, female teachers were considered to supervise detention, and women were always chosen to oversee the Girls Athletic Association, a quasi-competitive, intramural-style club which required supervision of the girls' locker room. The GAA typically involved girls putting on shapeless blue gym uniforms and kicking a soccer ball around or batting at a volleyball for a while. They then headed off to the Home Economics room to bake cookies. Naturally, a female teacher oversaw the cheerleading squad, and a (typically, female) language arts teacher would serve as yearbook advisor. Sadly, these positions paid less than half the amount earned by the most poorly paid male coach in the building, if the women were paid at all. Often, activities for girls were treated as "clubs" for which the adult female "advisors" were not paid.

The unfair disparities in opportunities for added compensation were compounded by the fact that it was, and is, much cheaper and easier to be a man. Appearance is a prime example. Generally, society puts far fewer expectations on men than on women. If a man, especially a single man, looks a little rumpled, even to the point of being a slob, he is a stereotype and people ignore it or maybe view it humorously. If he is married, his wife will catch hell for "letting him run around that way". As a single male teacher, if I wore the same jacket and pants for a couple days running, no one noticed, nor cared. If a woman was (is) unkempt, she was regarded as slovenly or skanky and certainly no one laughed. Women's wardrobes generally needed to be more varied and extensive. People noticed if a woman wore the same clothes twice in the same week, much less two days in a row. For some reason, women's clothing was also more expensive. Female wardrobes call for more accessories and alterations. Women wear cosmetics (worn in good taste, of course for a female teacher!) and women's hairstyles usually are more expensive to maintain. Regular trips to the salon were a necessity in those days. Men are expected to not walk around with their shoes untied, and bathe often enough they didn't stink, a rather low bar.

The school's expectations of a teacher were laid out clearly when I interviewed for my position. According to the faculty handbook, "Teachers in this district shall wear proper teaching attire. Gentlemen are required to wear jackets and ties. Female instructors will wear dresses or appropriate slacks. Part of your evaluation will be based upon your professional appearance." One thing I didn't appreciate about education at the time was that appearance was considered at least as important as substance. When a principal came to the classroom to observe a teacher's performance, they had no clue if you were actually teaching *anything*. Fair, meaningful teacher evaluations require multiple observations and a thorough understanding of pedagogy and methods. Most principals, especially in small school districts like Eagle River, lacked the time to do the former and the interest to master the nuance of the latter. The "observation" was really no more than a checklist of easily identifiable, and observable behaviors. Number one was appearance. My first year I was observed three times. Not once would I have described my appearance as anything but disheveled. My shirts were not pressed; my ties probably had food stains; my shoes likely weren't polished. In fact, on one occasion, I wasn't even wearing shoes. I had taken them off because both had those ugly white marks that appear after you've been walking in the snow. The principal thought it was funny. Not once was I given a poor evaluation for my tacky appearance. Several female teachers weren't so lucky, and at least one resented the hell out of it. Some of her bitterness she directed at me. "How do they expect me to dress more professionally, McLean? They pay me shit and expect a Gibson Girl! Not one man on this faculty has to deal with this crap, especially not you, for Christ's sake! Look at yourself!" I was offended, but she was right.

Time and the courts have changed many of the most egregious disparities, but not all. The education ranks were, and are, dominated by underpaid women, and few other professions have historically treated women so poorly. They earned less than men. They were excluded from administrative positions, and should a woman decide to start a family she was expected to resign before she began to show. "Heavens! We can't let our students see a pregnant teacher. What will they think, that our teachers actually have sex?"

In 1953, my mother lost a teaching position because of a pregnancy. I am the child who cost her that job. My mother was a bright woman, our family needed her little bit of income, but my mom got released. Had she been a man in a different occupation, she would have gotten a raise to deal with these new responsibilities, not a pink slip. This was not uncommon; it was policy in many districts.

Five years later I was in kindergarten, the largest and most ungainly child in the room, and I wasn't hitting the district's developmental markers for first grade. I became "Tiny Tim" or "Baby Huey" to my classmates. I hated those nicknames, and when I developed the smallest bit of social awareness, I died a little bit inside whenever I heard them. Those nicknames were the cause of the first fights I ever got into. I struggled with coordination. I couldn't hop on one foot. I was left-handed, so I couldn't properly use scissors; my letters were crudely formed and ugly. I was socially awkward. I was painfully shy, so I seldom spoke. I passed gas when the need arose. I doubt that I knew my right from my left. In most respects I was a hot mess. Thankfully, my kindergarten teacher, Miss Johnson, saw there was more to me than what I displayed. I think she was proof positive that at least occasionally angels do come down to earth. While the school's big decision makers were debating if I should be retained in kindergarten, she was giving me books to read while the rest of the class was learning the alphabet. To this day, I believe I owe my promotion to first grade to her advocacy. She saw in me what the "higher priced help" had not, a little potential.

Miss Johnson represented an earlier generation of teachers. When she began teaching, likely in the 1930s, all that was required was a two-year certificate from a normal school, basically a teacher college, and the genesis of the state college system of today. Because she did not have a four-year degree, she was paid little more than minimum wage, yet I believe I have never had a more important teacher. When she retired, I'm sure her pension was pathetically small. She and a million like her were the foundation of the American prosperity we have come to regard as our birthright. Miss Johnson and her peers—mostly stalwart women like her—taught America to read, write, do arithmetic, and generally function in groups. In return, they were expected to be obsequious, chaste, and dedicated heart and soul to the well-being of other people's children. But neither these women nor the men who occasionally taught have ever been offered much of a slice of the wealth they helped to generate.

The year I came to Eagle River was a negotiation year. At our first summer workshop, I was approached by the union rep, who handed me a Minnesota Federation of Teachers application. I come from a union family, so I joined eagerly. Over the course of three meetings, we agreed to a bargaining position, and formal negotiations with the board were initiated.

In Minnesota, every two years at contract time the local teacher's union and the school board get together to discuss the contract, vent about old grievances, and generate new ones. In most school districts, but in small towns especially, people take things personally, and they don't forget. Furthermore, the teachers in these small towns constituted the largest professional group in the community, and they are oftentimes better educated than the local residents who sat on the school board. The teachers' representatives did not come to negotiation meetings with hands cracked and scared by fieldwork, as those across the table from them did. Meanwhile, those farmers/board members had a definition of hard work that differed from that of the teachers', and they often believed many teachers had an attitude problem. These differences—real and imagined—brought out the worst in both parties, and the rhetoric could become heated. I say this while acknowledging that many of the board members in Eagle River were good and caring people.

I will always remember one board member in particular. He was one of the most conservative gentlemen in town, and a father of five, four of them girls. I know that he looked at being a member of the board as a civic obligation. He cared about education. So much so that in his mid-sixties he went back to school to earn his G.E.D. He felt strongly about all children. At one time it was common practice in many school districts that if a young lady became pregnant while in high school, she was placed in an alternative educational setting or on homebound instruction until she delivered. I tutored a few of these students. Once, at a board meeting called to discuss an alternative placement for a pregnant student, this gentleman asked a simple question, "What are we going to do with the boy involved?" That question, and the stunned silence which followed, changed a manifestly unjust policy. From that day pregnant students had options as to where they would attend school. Other individual board members also spoke highly about teachers and were proud of their staff. Often these feelings were reciprocated. The same gentleman who had been instrumental in changing the policy of the district on pregnant students once did a truly remarkable thing for a newly hired teacher. Shortly before the school year was to begin, she got into a terrible vehicle accident. She used up all her allotted sick leave immediately. This gentleman put forward a motion to the board that she be granted an additional twenty days of leave. She could pay this back throughout her career, a day or two a year. This was extraordinary and much appreciated. Eagle River could be an amazingly kind and caring place. But every two years money and gamesmanship polluted the relationship. This acrimony was especially hard for the teachers who lived in the community. Regrettably, such a climate of misunderstanding, untruths and exaggerations had persisted in Eagle River, and many other small towns for years.

I had never intended to make Eagle River my home, so I could deal with the feuding in a detached sort of way. My roots weren't here, my friends weren't here, and probably never would be. But the more experienced teachers in the district had given a lifetime to the community and felt these barbs more deeply than I. Some of the most senior staff had spent 25 or 30 years teaching in Eagle River. They had done much of the work that goes into community-building. They were the coaches of the local teams. They were scout leaders and Sunday school teachers. They belonged to civic organizations. They became Elks and Lions, and those who had been in the armed forces were members of the VFW or Legion or both. Through these roles, they interacted with the community on several levels, so it was tough when the community told them, "You aren't worth what you're paid, much less what you are asking for." The consensus of the board was if the teachers weren't happy with the contract, they should go somewhere else. True, that may have been possible, but for a mid-career professional this often isn't a viable option, especially not if they are supporting a family. Francis Bacon once wrote, "He that hath wife and children hath given hostages to fortune." This may be overstated, but in teaching it is not exactly wrong either. For the first several years you are in the classroom, you regularly move up the salary schedule based on added experience. Additional college credits may advance you faster, but at a point you "top out" on the schedule. Then raises, if any, become much smaller, based on whatever fraction of the rise in the cost-of-living can be wrestled from the school district in negotiations. To move to another district usually involves moving backwards in salary and seniority, probably not a good decision for people with the typical midlife responsibilities associated with raising a family. At the time in one's life when you most need the income, the paycheck stagnates and bitterness often follows.

Jim was a music teacher and had been for 35 years. In the summers he organized the local marching band, he also directed the church choir, doing both for little pay. He gave piano lessons to children for a nominal fee. When people wanted music, they called Jim. It was often expected he would provide it for little or nothing. To my knowledge, he never refused an opportunity to take on extra teaching assignments. Jim was at an age when most people could at least be contemplating retiring, but I never once heard him talk about it. I think that his savings were meager. Each of Jim's six kids qualified for free or reduced lunches. For years, he suffered the indignity of seeing his children lined up at the nurse's office every Monday morning to get their free or reduced-price meal tickets for the week. These were a different color than those issued to kids who had paid full price for their lunches.

It amazed me that the people of Eagle River, or anywhere else, accepted this practice. It was one of the most insensitive things I had ever heard of. Perhaps there was a general feeling that, "A little humiliation was good for the soul and if a few parents refused to sacrifice family pride, so their kids could get a square meal, it was their own fault and the hardworking taxpayer benefited. One less person on the dole." No one considered how the kids might feel and how many hungry afternoons were endured by students of all ages. Thank God, this practice changed over time. But not soon enough to help Jim and his family, or who knows how many other teachers or community members who found themselves in the same situation.

Carl refereed basketball games with me. He also did a little bit of everything else. Once, when we were working a game, he told me, "Stop blowing that goddamn whistle so often." He needed to get this junior high basketball game over quickly, so he could get back to school and chaperone a spectator bus to a distant wrestling match. He was 45 years old with an advanced degree in mathematics from a prestigious East Coast university. I expect he could have worked almost anywhere in or out of education. He stayed in Eagle River chiefly because he was born and raised there. He struck me as a person of high ideals. Because he stayed in teaching, his four children suffered with crooked teeth, having never gotten the braces they needed. Carl's students considered him a perpetual grump. In reality, I knew he was usually tired; and probably regretful. I previously heard the phrase, "death by altruism," after I got to know the tremendously bright person Carl was, I came to understand the concept.

The biology teacher coached three sports and walked home for lunch every day. This saved him the cost of a school meal. In the summer, he coached the Legion baseball team and maintained the field. His team held a tournament at season's end and if there was a profit, he got half. When there was a profit, he took his wife and kids out to supper.

Many of the male teachers I taught with had "side gigs." I came to know these men well. We did many of the same things because we all needed the extra money. Occasionally I was a guest in their homes for dinner. As the year wore on, and we spent more time together, they all started to give me similar advice. "You're a bright kid, Tim, get your recommendation and get out of education. Teaching is a great job for your wife to have, a nice second income, and she'll be home when the kids are. You can't eat idealism, pal, and nobody really gives a damn. Good teacher, bad teacher, or indifferent teacher, at the end of the day, the check stays the same." How incredibly cynical, but I was 22 years old, so I nodded politely and agreed. I never doubted they were telling me their personal truth, but it didn't matter. Teaching was OK for now. It wasn't my future, and no matter what happened, I would not become them. I would not let myself become them. Ten years from now, I was not going to be sitting on a frigid spectator bus hoping that we got home soon enough that I could do a little preparation for tomorrow's classes. I was not going to be screaming at kids in the detention hall, and I was not going to be driving old used cars and replacing crap tires only when my coaching checks got to the bank. If I were someday blessed to have children, they would not qualify for free or reduced lunches. They were not going without braces should they need them.

We settled that year's contract with a four percent raise over two years. Four percent nearly covered the increase in the cost of living; the contract did nothing to reduce the cost of health insurance.

In almost every line of work in America, it's presumed that if a company expects to hire *and retain* the best people, it must annually increase salaries and improve benefits. In education, it is assumed job satisfaction and the occasional apple is more important than actual financial security. For me, at this point in my career, it was. I was single with no family to take care of. But I was beginning to think that perhaps this wouldn't always be the case. At our last meeting before we were to vote on the proposed contract, an elementary teacher stood up to speak in opposition to ratification. With a very calm affect he stated, "I have been a teacher in this district for seven years. If we ratify this contract, I will make $11,800 next year. I have three kids. I cannot continue to teach for that. If we ratify this contract, you will all be moving backwards financially, and I will be a bartender. I don't want to leave the classroom, but I will have no choice." In my heart I knew he was right, but I voted "yes" and hoped with the next contract things might improve. I think many of us voted yes for the same reason. That night, Eagle River lost a pretty good teacher and perhaps someone gained a bartender. Our art teacher also resigned that spring. He opened his own shop and sold an assortment of pottery.

All I knew for certain was that despite the salary, I was actually beginning to enjoy myself. With the few additional bucks generated by my extra assignments, I could keep my creditors happy. In the classroom, my attempts at creativity and experimentation continued. On Fridays, we began to circle our desks to discuss current events. On many of these Fridays, this amounted to little more than a circular-McLean lecture, at times even resembling a napping in a circle session. But every once in a while I discovered a diamond; a child with an honest to God informed opinion. Or maybe an insight which extended beyond the railroad tracks at the edge of town. Sometimes we just talked about their plans and dreams.

I remember Andrea especially. She was a townie, which is to say her parents didn't farm. They didn't have much money, but that didn't limit her aspirations. Most high-school kids see college as a kind of terminal goal. But to Andrea, a bachelor's degree was step one. Step two was law school. Step three was to become a professional advocate for the less fortunate. I don't know how it worked out for her, but I would be surprised if over time, she did not realize at least a part of her dream. Rob wanted to join the Peace Corps and help improve the lives of farmers in less developed countries. Keith aspired to go to Annapolis and become a Marine Corps officer. At age 17 he already had a military bearing. Other kids were going to take over the family farm, but still they had thoughts about how they might improve the operation. Some just wanted to get out and see the world beyond Eagle River. I would have learned none of this had I not started to just talk to my students. God bless those kids. They will never know the joy they gave me, and how much easier it was to accept my sorry-ass financial condition after I'd had the occasional great class period. On those days, I'd look forward to my next day in class, and I'd wonder if teaching might evolve into more than the two-year commitment that I originally envisioned.

On other days when things didn't click and the kids weren't especially receptive, I'd go home asking myself, "How could anyone do this for a lifetime?" I was beginning to think that teachers probably would never be paid at a level commensurate with other professions which required an equivalent level of education but carried not a tenth of the responsibility. If I evaluated teaching only in terms of money, common sense said to get out. But I was also beginning to realize there might be other metrics to be considered. Perhaps many of the clichés about the importance of teaching and the ability to help shape the future were true.

With December came Christmas concerts by the school choir and band. There was a pretty good attempt at *A Christmas Carol* by the high-school drama club. All the events were held in the cafeteria on a makeshift stage, the audiences seated on folding chairs. We were a little lacking in ambience, but the spirit was truly spectacular and the parents in attendance beamed! The effort put forward by the directors of these productions was outstanding. There was much more going on in high school than I had ever appreciated or valued as I should. I had never considered what these teachers and advisors brought to the school, the kids, to life in Eagle River. The school had a monthly newspaper competently written, edited, and published by students. There was the yearbook which was pretty darn good! There was a math and computer club whose teacher advisors were paid almost nothing. It was really the first time I ever considered the work lovingly and willingly given by teachers in the various areas of the extracurricular AND curricular programs at the school ... MY school! As a high-school student, I never took time to appreciate kids who had gifts different from mine. Only now it occurred to me, by doing so I had been both stupid and arrogant. I began to consider the experiences I surely missed and the possible friendships I undoubtedly denied myself. But now, as I left that performance by Scrooge and Tiny Tim et al. I understood and appreciated the enthusiasm and talent of the kids and staff involved. So many kids thanked me for coming. Now, I was beginning to understand that sometimes there is much to be gained simply by showing up. That first winter living in Eagle River passed quickly and agreeably.

A prosperous and arrogant friend once asked me how much I was paid. I asked him if he wanted the number in apples, plates of cookies, thank you cards or memories. There was also the occasional certificate suitable for framing. The dollar figure wouldn't have impressed.

VI

Don't Suck Today

It was spring and the baseball season was beginning; real honest to God, that is, before aluminum bats and designated hitters baseball. Small town America has always loved the game. My students were eager to begin the season, and I was excited to be coaching again. Baseball is nearly the polar opposite of football. It's not a blood sport. I've never had to call an ambulance to collect a broken adolescent from a baseball field. Baseball coaches seldom scream; control is more important than emotion. In all the years I played, I seldom enjoyed football practice, but I always looked forward to practicing baseball. Football smelled like ammonia and sweat, baseball like leather and spring.

Well before the baseball fields were fully free of snow, my team was playing catch in the school's single, small gym or shagging fly balls in the parking lot. The bigger schools, those in the cities and suburbs, would be starting their seasons too; but theirs would begin indoors, hitting against pitching machines and throwing off artificial mounds. We didn't have those niceties. In Eagle River, spring training was a lot more basic. We did what we could, where we could, and if the temperature dipped below forty degrees, we called it a day. What we lacked in gym space and equipment, we made up for in earnestness and extra games of catch. Arms often got sore from throwing too hard too early. Hands smarted from taking pitches too close to the fists, and the locals joked the first sign winter was over was the stink of Ben Gay on every other high-school-aged boy.

I discovered spring kind of explodes in farm country. Fall and winter come by degrees, but spring arrives with a rush. Almost overnight, melting snow and spring rains convert farm driveways into open, running gashes in the gently sloped hillsides. Some springs, those driveways became so muddy, tractors were hauled out of winter storage for a quick trip to the mailbox. School buses were occasionally late because roads were barely passable. Smells which had been frozen dead in their tracks for four months were now liberated by the power of March sunshine, and it had a good earthy aroma. The farmers themselves were shaken from their mid-winter torpor. Repairs abandoned with the first snowfall were taken up again. Seed ordered two months before from the local farmers' co-op was ready for pick-up. Plans were laid and prayers were said. If everything broke just right, this could be the year when some farmers might finally turn the corner financially, but only if other farmers elsewhere in the country or the world had poor weather and small yields. It's a sad irony that one farmer's prosperity is often made possible only by another's misfortune. Bountiful harvests for all meant lower prices for crops. Also, there was an election coming up and a new farm bill due, so just maybe the support price of milk or corn would be inched upwards. At least that was the consensus of the old retirees who loitered around the feed mill. "Good way to get the farm vote." Spring in farm country was about beginnings and possibilities.

Except for my brief student teaching experience, I had never really taught in a city school, but I was a suburban kid and knew in the burbs we saw spring differently. City kids saw spring as little more than dirty icy pediments, the sorry gray remains of the huge snow piles created when they plowed the parking lot at the mall. In the city, spring was only a warmer and more convenient continuation of an indoor urban lifestyle. Little was made new, and most city kids wouldn't have been able to distinguish between the first gentle croaking of a leopard frog and a burglar alarm.

The kids in my classes could tell the difference. They knew all the spring sounds. Most of my students were farm kids, so they too were a part of the countryside. For them, spring was tonic. This made them different. Somehow, I think it also made them more aware than their urban counterparts, certainly less jaded. A country spring surrounds kids. There was energy and impatience in my classes that wasn't there a month before. Most of this was the spring season, but a big part of it may have been my newfound love of mimeograph fluid. (If you're now having a "what the hell is that?" moment, perfectly understandable. Look it up and prepare to be amazed that anything so primitive and potentially lethal, was once a necessary part of American education.) My room reeked of its penetrating stench. The fluid had methanol and isopropanol in it. Today, that stuff would be banned in all fifty states. But back then the jury was still out on most noxious chemicals and even proven carcinogens, like cigarettes. I was also going through paper by the ream. This pungent epiphany was brought about by a truly startling discovery on my part. My economics textbook sucked, and my history texts weren't far behind. One was more boring and pedantic than the next. Armed with the arrogance of the ignorant and the school's "ditto" machine, I decided I could do better!

Each morning I mined the texts for important points and concepts. I then turned these into a series of comic strips. These were not works of art. They were stick figures. The notes and thought balloons I put on them were drawn and written in a childlike scrawl. I scratched them out on "ditto" masters, ran them off, and then based my lectures on the illustrations. God, they were corny!! When space permitted, I might add a few terrible and often politically incorrect jokes. The results were amazing, especially so in economics. Now, nothing I ever did put anyone's feet on the path to being a Nobel Laureate, but lessons were taught and there was some joy and even a certain squirrelly*ness* in the room. This was all to the good. Somehow, my crude illustrations gave a few kids license to also be creative in a reciprocal sort of way. Some tests came back with cartoon characters illustrating the answers. Captain Supply, trying to catch up to the evil Doctor Demand. Production possibilities curves were illustrated with loaves of bread and cars. Some of these drawings were flat-out good; all were better than my crude etchings. One young man got so involved in answering a test's first question, he forgot he needed to answer seven others. He stayed after school the next two days to finish. Hardly best practice on my part, but that type of enthusiasm was not to be squashed.

There is no claim here that my success was universal. There were still kids, a lot of kids, who just didn't give a damn about the subject. Little that I might have done could have changed that. However, even the most disinterested students were now willing to humor me. Our relationship was less strained and adversarial, and very occasionally they joined in classroom discussions. Even the most indifferent students in the room weren't routinely giving me the thousand-yard stare as they fought to keep their heads off the desk. Basic concepts were being taught and discussed. Some of my sharper students could even make fairly accurate statements connecting these basic economic principles to public policy. One of the greatest compliments I ever received during my teaching career occurred when I overheard two students talking about my class in the hall. Neither was a particularly good student, but both agreed, "McLean's class doesn't suck so much anymore." I was so impressed with the compliment I wrote a reminder—DON'T SUCK TODAY—on a sheet of paper and taped it inside the center drawer of my desk. It was always the last thing I looked at before I began my teaching day. Funny, two students having a random conversation in the hall taught me one of the most important lessons a teacher can learn. You will often have great days when your lessons "click", and the kids are interested and engaged. You also will have some days when nothing "works;" your best efforts fail to capture and hold the students' focus. I began to think of these days as "shoveling sand." Those were days when teaching was less a passion and more like a job. But even then, smile, make eye contact, crack an occasional joke. Every day, you cannot possibly be every student's favorite teacher, but you can always manage not to suck.

I still had the occasional temper explosion. Once I was showing a filmstrip explaining the advantages of becoming an entrepreneur. The title was "*Getting Ahead in Small Business.*" The narrator on the accompanying tape began by assuring the listener, it was always possible to "get ahead by starting a small business." The giggling began immediately. By the second usage of the phrase, I suspected their reaction was based less on the stunning quality of the filmstrip than the unintended reference to *oral sex*. By the third use, the room was a bedlam. At that point, I took my pen and fired it across the room. It splattered against the wall. I halted the filmstrip and loudly threatened, "The next kid who laughs is going to be sent home in an envelope!" I continued with the most unhinged tirade I had ever employed. I derided their mental hygiene; I questioned their upbringing; I cited commandments! It was a *grand mal* tantrum. When I was finally spent, I assigned them homework, which was to include 200 reasons for keeping a clean mind. I circled the room twice, took a deep breath. Sat down and counted to ten. Then I apologized. I withdrew the punitive assignment and retreated to my desk. For the balance of the hour, the room was quiet as a tomb. At the bell, as the kids filled out, I overheard one student tell another, "That's nothing; you should hear him at half-time when we're getting our butts kicked!" Later, I wondered how many times my threat to "send them home in an envelope" was repeated around the supper tables of Eagle River. Luckily, I was never hit by any fallout from that little temper pique. Within a week it was forgotten, but the incident left me amazed by the remarkable capacity of students to forget and forgive. A person with adult sensibilities would have had a hard time walking back into my classroom again without an armed escort. I don't remember how many times that school year I made stupid threats, was needlessly cruel, deliberately tried to intimidate, or verbally berated kids. Yet, when they came back the next day, they always seemed willing to give me another chance. For some reason, despite my efforts to play the ogre at times, they were beginning to trust me. I was coming to the realization that trust is the single most important element in successful classrooms. Improving your content knowledge is essential. Staying current with best teaching practices is important. Participating in meaningful in-service experiences is vital. But none of these pursuits amounts to what my father used to call "a fart in a whirlwind" if you have not developed a basic level of trust with your kids. Be real or be quiet.

History classes offered different possibilities. In older communities like Eagle River, history surrounds you; you're just required to know what you're looking at. A walk down main street is a quick excursion through the 1920s and '30s. Many of my students lived on farms designated as *Century Farms*, having been in continuous production for at least 100 years. There were more artifacts stashed in the parlors and haylofts of these homesteads than could be found in many museums. The local church graveyards were wonderful places to connect history to lives lived and relatives dimly remembered. The reaction of my class when I said we were going to do a survey of the local graveyards was priceless. One of my dimmer bulbs mulled over my proposed course of study for a while and then asked, "Does this mean that we're going to go there?" After a few seconds of, 'what the hell kind of stupid question is that' silence, one of my more smart-assed young men chimed in, "No doofey, McLean is going to dig up all the stiffs and bring 'em here." Order was restored five minutes later.

A parent or two called the principal to suggest, "The new guy you hired is out of line with this graveyard stuff." Now, even the slightest hint of parental displeasure caused anxiety for Jonesy, and this time, his office was *flooded* with at least *two* phone calls; urgent action was required! He requested I come to his office to discuss the assignment before I did anything "rash." Of course, this was to be his clumsy attempt at intimidation. I arrived at the appointed time and there sat Jonesy firmly ensconced behind his desk. He did not immediately offer me a chair. This lack of common courtesy was fully in keeping with current management theories, which fixated on power relationships and keeping underlings such as me in their places. I was relieved to no end that we were alone. Had there been someone else present, I would have worried. Perhaps Jonesy intended to "get physical" with me. Thank God for small mercies. He assured me he understood the educational purpose behind the graveyard survey, but he was worried lest I trod too heavily upon community sensibilities or upset any of the local clergy. This was especially true for the Catholics. The two Catholic churches in Eagle River were the third rail of local politics. So much so that my kids got release time every Wednesday to attend religious instruction. How this practice jived with the establishment clause of the First Amendment is a mystery to me, but there are some questions first year teachers didn't ask.

For my part, I assured Principal Jones I was not a ghoul, and my students would behave respectfully. I told him a bald-faced lie, about a professor at Boston College using this methodology exclusively for a detailed study of the Revolutionary period. This elevated the discussion because now I was letting Jonesy in on my plans to ride the *cutting edge of historical inquiry!* That really sealed the deal. At once, he agreed my purpose was noble! Furthermore, should I get any parental flack about my cemetery excursion, I was to refer the objections to him, and he would deal with them. To his everlasting credit, Jonesy was now willing to have my back. In the *real* world of Eagle River school district politics, this may have been considered as cold comfort, but I appreciated the gesture, and thanked him repeatedly.

To begin the project, I asked my classes to bring in old family photos, and soon grainy black and whites which had not seen the light of day in at least 20 years began to appear by the box full. There were photos of grandparents and great-grandparents on their wedding day. There were baptisms, first communions, soldiers in uniform departing for, or returning from duty stations, foreign and domestic. These were the visual records of the momentous occasions and milestones in life, but not daily life. Back then you needed an occasion to haul out the camera. (I really miss those days.)

One of the pictures was very different. It was of a woman and twenty or so children standing outside a one-room schoolhouse, a teacher and her class. The students were of different ages. Some of the boys were taller than the teacher. She was a severe looking woman, but the children were all smiling, and one could get the sense that if her arms were long enough, she would be enfolding the entire group. She was what once was referred to as a "school marm." The picture was dated 1916, and some forward-thinking person with beautiful penmanship had identified all twenty students and the teacher. Her name was Miss Kimball. This became important later, because when we went to the graveyard, we discovered what I thought to be her grave. The small foot stone read, *Lavinia Kimball. 1881-1953.* I assumed she had never married. As a history teacher, there are many historical figures I wish

I somehow had the opportunity to meet and speak with, but on that day, there was no one I wanted to talk to more than Miss Lavinia Kimball. I wanted to know what opportunities she had not accepted so as to be a teacher? Maybe I could just ask, "Was it worth it, Miss Kimball? Did you deliberately choose to give up having a family of your own to become a surrogate parent to hundreds of other peoples' kids? How many memories did you carry behind those wire rimmed glasses?" I resolved that when we got back to class, I would ask my students to see if their parents or grandparents had any recollection of Miss Kimball. To this day, I regret I didn't.

Many of the surnames of Miss Kimball's pupils in 1916, still appeared on my own class rosters. This caused a real buzz in the room, as one student after another identified a grandparent or great uncle, most long deceased.

When we at last took our walks to the graveyards to record the names and dates on the stones, my students were very serious. They attacked the project with an air of conscientiousness and deliberation I hadn't seen before. Questions were asked quietly, information recorded methodically—no grab ass. Some quiet prayers were offered for the repose of the soul of a long-forgotten relative. A few monuments had a picture of the deceased embedded into the stone facing. It was as if we were being observed from beyond the grave. These small, enameled images served as a cadre of silent, stern sentinels, demanding respectful behavior. Many of my students made powerful connections to lives once lived by touching these images of the long dead. On stones worn smooth by a century of rain and ice, my kids discovered if you placed a piece of paper on the stone and rubbed it gently with a pencil, a date and name might be transferred to the paper. Sadly, sometimes it was too late to resurrect even a portion of the carving. Lichens and weather had made the soft limestone smooth and forever mute. My kids were genuinely sad when a stone was too weathered to interpret, or the only marker was a decaying wooden cross mounted on a rusted iron support. I sensed they almost felt they were being remiss in their duty to the dead.

In a short time, we collected a small mountain of raw data. We used it to draw some valid conclusions about *immigrant succession* through this part of the county. We also made some generalizations about life span and infant mortality. The students realized many of Eagle River's sons had served in America's wars; two of the earliest graves had once been of members of Minnesota regiments which fought in the Civil War. We found plagues still happened in the twentieth century. I think we also reflected a bit on our own mortality and the temporal link between all people. A little later, some of my kids were motivated to examine the records and old newspapers at the county historical society to learn a bit more. In some households, our investigations caused intergenerational dialogues about ancestors and how the town and world had changed. I even convinced one of the town's elders to come speak to my classes about the lives of some of these former neighbors. Folks who had once lived and been productive and were now "townsmen of a stiller town." Yet they would always be a permanent part of Eagle River's collective heritage. Not only did these "forefathers of Eagle River" have the same surnames as my current students, many had lived in the same houses, and a few built those very houses. Two of the class sweethearts discovered they were third cousins. I don't recall how this affected their relationship, but in a small way, it illustrates the past can at times be a minefield.

When we concluded our data gathering, we went back to the cemeteries with grass-clipping tools and rakes and trimmed around all the stones and monuments. This took a class period for each of my three history classes, but in terms of community relations, it was a priceless investment of time. The kids felt they were rendering a valuable community service. I learned that given the opportunity, many kids will exceed your wildest expectations; and when their best civic impulses are coupled with the overpowering desire to be outdoors on a glorious mid-April day, the possibilities are endless.

As we walked back to the building, I decided these would be the times I would most miss when I finally said goodbye to teaching. By now, I was nearing the end of my first year. In my mind, I was about *half done* with my "career" in education. On the day I had taken this job, I convinced myself it would be no more than a two-year commitment. Next year was a lock. I already had an offer for a second one-year contract, the only variety offered to non-tenured, probationary teachers. Besides, my baseball team had won its first seven games, and it looked like we might make a little noise in the conference, perhaps the section. I was only an assistant coach, but I still got to bask in the unaccustomed glow of victory. Life was good, and soon I would have the summer. Plus, next year, I would advance a step on the salary schedule, which meant a $450 raise. I would receive a small bump in my coaching salary as well. Things were looking up!

That spring, I made a proposal of marriage and was accepted. She and I had been going together for a couple of years now, and it seemed to be the right time for it. No date was set, sometime after I got done with my time as a teacher; when I found a real job, then we would marry. Neither of us intended to try scratching out a life on a teacher's salary. I decided to look for summer employment around Eagle River, and perhaps earn enough to buy a suitable ring. Teaching wasn't my future, but for now I had no regrets, and I was on schedule. Also, by the end of that first year, I was beginning to feel I was on the near edge of competence in the classroom. Long gone were the heady days when I thought I had a firm hold on the soul of pedagogic excellence. I still carried around a lot more ego than my teaching ability could justify, but I was figuring a few things out. The kids were cutting me a huge amount of slack in all things. That year, I discovered the real difference between teachers who succeed and those who don't, was how willing kids are to forgive the former, and how prepared they are to feast upon the mistakes of the latter. Luck is also critical. Even in my first year, it was clear the teaching profession was lousy with opportunities to commit occupational suicide. If by some chance I decided to make teaching a career, it would be another two years before I had the questionable security of tenure. Before then, I was on thin ice. A careless slip of the tongue has ended thousands of careers prematurely. The wrong bug placed in the ear of the wrong school board member could mean termination without explanation. In small towns, going to the wrong church, not going to church, drinking at the wrong bar, drinking at all, each or any of a thousand imagined sins could be the real reason contracts were discontinued. If you don't have tenure, you exist at the whim of the bureaucrats and bean counters. If tenured, you at least are guaranteed due process before dismissal.

Back then, most of the teaching contracts had a clause about "moral turpitude" or some such vacuous nonsense. This meant you had better be an exemplar of moral perfection. Either that, or be fortunate to have your personal moral failings shared by a majority of the school board. Any number of private vices could get you sacked if they became public knowledge. Perhaps I navigated this minefield successfully because at this point in my teaching "career" I really didn't give a damn. I was learning, though. Teaching was a political occupation. The real currency of education is something uncountable, so appearance and politics will always trump substance. These are things which can only be seen and understood clearly from inside the profession.

When I was in high school, I never attained enough distance from the common maelstrom to be an astute observer of the people and processes that daily surrounded me. Now I was on the other side of the faculty lounge door, and some things struck me like a thunderclap. Perhaps the most startling being the blatant sexuality of high-school students. This should not have amazed me. I was still within very few years of my own high-school experience, but I remembered it differently from what I observed at Eagle River. Like many of my male friends, I went through high school in a constant state of agitation, but I was never quite sure what I was agitated about. Most male students at Eagle River High appeared to be as naive as I had been at their age. Very few boys at the high school were what we used to call "on the make," probably a byproduct of the small size of the school and the familiarity and history the students shared. If you were a *scumbag* at Eagle River H.S., every girl in the building knew it and you were avoided. Also, and I give the boys props for this, if a male student got a little too "aggressive" with a young lady or just shot off his mouth as if he had done so, there was a good chance she had an older brother who would gladly kick his ass! And, since families in Eagle River were generally large, the older brother might be joined by an additional sibling plus a cousin or two. This borders on sexist, but this brand of chivalry was practiced in Eagle River on more than one occasion.

If the boys attending Eagle River were a bit clueless, the female students were at least a little bit less so. They seemed to know and understand agitation. Throughout the year, I got a huge kick watching high-school courtship rituals. These were intricate dances, usually led by the young lady. The male was often a willing but *unwitting* participant. However, as graduation neared, I was not entertained at all when it became obvious some senior girls considered me as a possible dance partner. This wasn't flattering; in fact, it was downright scary for a rookie male teacher. Neither was it a complete surprise. It was the logical and an unintended downside of becoming less surly in the classroom. It is easy for a kid to correctly interpret a scowl; smiles are more difficult.

As the school year was ending, a couple young women in particular seemed in constant need of individual attention. It was my practice to offer such help while kneeling beside the student's desk. More than once I looked up from the assignment to see the young lady looking at me and paying zero attention to the help being offered. This could have been benign and even cute if this was as far as it went. However, two young ladies started to come to my room between classes or during my prep period.

My counter to this was a kind of *oblique* movement. As they approached my desk, I stood and angled away from it and them. In this way, I always maintained distance without appearing to be in full retreat. Sometimes in class I would go out of my way to mention a girlfriend, later a fiancée. This was the rough equivalent of a cloud of ink being ejected by a frightened squid.

Nothing had really equipped me to deal with this. We had never discussed it in my education classes. There was no one in the building I felt comfortable talking to about the situation. God knows Jonesy would have been zero help. Addressing it with the girls in question was something I should have done but did not for fear of hurting them, embarrassing them, making them angry, or generating any of a thousand other emotions which might have a consequence I wasn't able to deal with or control. It came to a head one night after baseball practice.

As was my custom, I put the baseball gear away and then went down into an old locker room deep within the bowels of the high school. This area had been converted into a kind of crude weight room. There were a few pieces of equipment and some free weights, certainly nothing elaborate. As I was the only one there, I took off my shirt and began lifting. Shortly, I heard footsteps and assumed another coach or perhaps a baseball player was coming down to lift. It was instead a female student of mine. She was a senior, and she probably knew full well I was down there. She wore no bra under a tee shirt that was a bit tighter than it needed to be. She wore a pair of loose-fitting shorts and sandals. In my entire life, what she communicated by her presence and appearance was either the most brazen, or trusting, or clueless statement anyone has ever made to me. "Can I work out with you, Mr. McLean?" she asked. Making sure I kept most of the weights between myself and the young lady, I assured her she was certainly free to use the equipment, but I had only come down for a quick set or two of curls. My exit was less than graceful. My heart next beat when I hit the top of the steps. No matter how I spun this incident in my mind, I could see no good outcome. My career, my life, and my adult relationships were now in the hands of an eighteen-year-old girl who had already just demonstrated a huge amount of questionable judgment. Everything I did and anything I could have said was now open to the worst possible interpretation. Why in the hell did I tell her she was free to use the equipment? How did she interpret my reaction? Was she offended? Hell hath no fury ... For Christ's sake, who would believe this? I didn't even believe this! This was a bad B movie. This was not supposed to happen to homely Catholic boys. What would Mom say?

No sleep that night, nothing to eat, stomach in knots, cold sweats, back to school the next morning- then silence. The day passed, and the day after, then a blessed weekend. By Monday, I finally was able to talk to the young lady about how people might see that kind of situation. She didn't feign surprise, but she did have the decency to be embarrassed, thank God.

The next day, I went to talk to one of our senior female staff. It wasn't something I did willingly, but Sarah was as close as I had to a mentor. She was an old-school English teacher. She still taught grammar and was one of a dozen people on the planet who could explain a gerund phrase in a way that was at least marginally comprehensible. Her students became better writers, and more than one young person owed their success in freshman college English to her diligence. She had this marvelous aspect of 'been there, done that', and 'I don't give a damn anymore'. She smoked way too much, so her voice was two octaves lower than any other female on the staff. We talked a bit, she listened a lot. I finally asked her if I ever did anything to encourage the type of attention I was getting.? She told me 'no', she herself considered me to be a bit of a square, a circumspect square, but a square nonetheless. Then she told me she wasn't surprised it was happening, she had seen it coming well before I had. I asked her, "Why me?" and she said simply, "Because you're not ..." then she left me hanging for a bit. "What the hell does *that* mean, I'm not *what*?" With a smirk and more than a little matronly indulgence, she replied, "Tim, you're not too old, you're not too ugly, and you're not too likely to do anything about the flirting; you're safe, and they know that. They think that you're probably a good man. Most importantly, you're not from Eagle River. If I were a senior girl out here, I'd take a run at you myself just to see you react; you blush so beautifully. You're a good foil to practice on. It always amazes me when they put teachers as young as you in front of senior classes."

I had never been so eloquently marginalized. She had just described my best qualities in terms of negative statements, and I was thrilled and partly flattered. The offhand compliment she directed at my integrity was nice. Being referred to as "not too ugly" was almost a textbook definition of being damned by faint praise. However, on the plus side, it was nice to know I didn't look like something which lived under bridges and scared Billy goats. She also promised to talk to a few of the young ladies. This would carry some weight because Sarah was an institution and the *Grande Dame* of Eagle River High School. She could lecture the superintendent and not fear repercussions. I don't know what she said, but I do know things got better. There were still giggles, I found my name mentioned prominently in a note or two, but the year passed. Some other semi-related problems I needed to deal with myself, both professionally and personally.

Later that same spring, I received a jolt of a different kind. One morning I found a note on my desk from a young guy who was student teaching in the band program. The note suggested he wanted to get to know me better. We were only nodding acquaintances, but I'm confident I understood what he might have in mind or, at least, his sexual orientation. My first reaction was predictable, male, and poorly considered; thankfully it was also passing. Leaving the note on my desk was truly stupid, but after resisting my initial negative impulses, I began to think about why he had taken such a chance with his career. This was not an outbreak of maturity on my part by any means. Deep down, I knew he wasn't a threat to me in any way; but I was still subject to the occasional episode of testosterone poisoning. Back then, homosexuality triggered both my *fight* and *flight* impulses. Had I reported the incident to the principal, the young man would have been marched out of the building immediately. His hopes of becoming a teacher would have evaporated. A few days later, I politely told him he was barking up the wrong tree, and the issue was dropped. In the few remaining weeks of the school year, we did become a bit more than nodding acquaintances. Today, reflecting on the experience, I regret not offering him genuine friendship. At that point in my life, it wasn't possible, I wasn't capable of it. The late seventies were in the middle of a sexual revolution, but some social walls had not been breached yet. Still, during our brief acquaintance, he made me examine another of my own prejudices. Doing so made me a better teacher. In my career, I have watched kids struggle with their sexuality and sometimes become buried by confusion, guilt, and self-loathing. I have attended funerals for students who died in single vehicle "accidents" which weren't accidents. You don't run into highway bridge pillars or trees at 70 miles an hour by accident. I understand more now because I took the time to consider the loneliness of a student teacher who once tried to hit on me. I grew because of that incident. I didn't know what percentage of my students might be gay or lesbian. Previously, I had never considered sexual orientation an issue. I simply assumed that all my students were straight, and gay people existed somewhere out there on a perverted fringe. I now tried to ban potentially offensive language from my classroom and my own vocabulary. Again, I learned how very wrong you can be when you make assumptions. So many kids are carrying so much pain. Things that we only guess at after the funeral.

When you were crowned the Homecoming Queen:
It was not a coronation: but it was an affirmation ...
Of things we had all known and seen since kindergarten.

You were always a ten and a four-point-O.
All the medals you won were gold.
The Ivy's were sold. Choose: you were told

Choose you were told: and you did:
Poor kid. Locked the garage, turned the key.
You made your choice, and you chose to be free

VI

Marley's Chains

I think of the rest of that year in generalities, things I learned bit by bit from a hundred different students and staff members. This is perhaps how attitudes are best made. The occasional kid stands out, and certain kids like David will never leave me. I still wonder if he could ever possibly know, at times I still measure myself against him. I wonder if he remembers me at all. I honestly hope not, because I'm sure it would be only with a lingering bitterness. He taught me intelligence used to embarrass and humiliate is more biting than a lash. As a student, I had my share of teachers who never figured that out. Today, sadly, there are still 'educators' who can't resist being verbally *clever* at the expense of a high-school sophomore in front of a classroom of their peers. Even parents occasionally do similar things and leave scars on their own kids, which even a lifetime of accomplishment might never completely heal. David taught me common courtesy and civility cost nothing, yet can mean everything. Most importantly, he taught me never to make assumptions. I had to relearn that lesson constantly over the course of that year

During my first year of teaching, I also learned poverty is not an abstraction. I looked on my personal financial situation as temporary; but for many of my students, poverty was a permanent feature of their lives. They wore it like a tattoo. I doubt anyone sees more of the negative consequences of poverty than a teacher in a poor school district. Good teachers don't see policies and programs, they see people. I learned *real* poverty is a peanut butter sandwich in a reused and greasy brown paper bag. It's a hand-me-down, threadbare coat and oversized boots. Poverty leaves a bitter and permanent taste. In time, it becomes watery-eyed indifference, and if worn long enough it becomes the most impermeable of all shells. Teachers understand this; it explains why, in their hearts, most teachers are liberals.

I discovered some clichés are true. There really is nobility in effort. One of my students was hydrocephalic, he suffered from the buildup of fluid deep within the brain. The symptoms were numerous, unpleasant for the individual, and sometimes prevented most real learning from occurring. My student had shunts inserted in his brain to relieve the pressure. When his shunt malfunctioned, he missed a lot of school. On those occasions, I went to his home and tried to keep him current on all of his assignments. We sat at an old kitchen table made ornate by rosemaling. The boy made every effort to learn. Between my visits, his parents worked hard to help him. But we were always running in place. He could retain little. I don't know if this was related, but he was also prone to seizures. Each day was a *start over at the beginning* day. Life's deck of cards was permanently stacked against the boy, but only once did he convey his frustration to me. Before one of my visits he was told that he would never be able to get a driver's license. This would have been a blow to any teenager, but to a boy who struggled as he did every day, the thought of never being able to drive himself *someplace, some day* hurt him deeply. Later, he cried when he told me his younger brother was taking his driver's test the next morning. Aside from that single admission, he always smiled, he always tried, and always thanked me profusely for coming to help with his assignments.

His family was the soul of hospitality. As I drove in, his father always put away what he was working on and greeted me as a long-lost brother. He was a short German man but thickly constructed, and when he shook my hand it was with a grip of calloused iron. I think he was made in equal portions of power, purpose, and an obvious love for his family. His wife always had coffee brewing, good strong Scandinavian coffee. I will never forget the smell and flavor. She told me the secret was to put a bit of salt into the grounds. Several times I tried to duplicate her method, but the end result tasted and smelled like San Francisco Bay. Hell, even the German Shepherd stopped snapping at me after a while. When I left their place, I always felt like a failure.

I learned, no matter what they told me in college, bell curves only worked with middle-class white populations. I learned if I gave a kid an A when they had earned a B, I was not messing up the validity of a Harvard application. I was acknowledging great effort and making a very subjective assessment of how much actual learning had taken place. At times, I was also making it possible for a family to provide affordable auto insurance for a new driver. This may seem like I was screwing over the insurance companies, and perhaps I was, but a little reciprocity is good for the soul.

I learned a grade book isn't the only thing I should consult when making "pass or fail" decisions. Failing a student should hurt, A failing grade should be well-deserved, and should never be determined by a percentage point or two. All teenagers have a powerful sense of fairness. Being required to repeat an entire class because of a percentage point is unfair. During my first year, I had too many pointless failures. In the first two quarters of grading, I might award an F with an almost cavalier breeziness. Failing kids was a way to prove I had high standards and even high*er* expectations. This is the worst form of sophistry! By the end of the year, I was less cocky, less sure of myself, and far less ready to equate student Fs with my supposed *high* standards. I began to ask myself, was I really accomplishing anything by forcing a student to retake a class? (God, I wish more teachers would ask themselves that simple question.) If the answer was "no" I looked for a reason not to do it. We are not Heimdall guarding the Bifröst Bridge. Our subject is not the single most important thing a 16-year-old will ever learn. By the time a kid arrived in my classroom, they already knew most of what they would ever know. To paraphrase Robert Fulghum's poem, *everything I needed to know in life… " I Learned in Kindergarten."* Well, not *everything*, but should an entire future be jeopardized by an adolescent's failure to make one mindless collage, demonstrating the major exports of Argentina? There are legitimate reasons to fail a student, but most are applicable only after the student has given up on the class and you, AND themselves. Failure always has consequences, some very tangible. At a minimum, classes would have to be retaken. I learned that even a single F on a report card could be a reason for a beating at home.

I learned the faculty at Eagle River High School were usually good and well-intended people. Most were dedicated to their kids and their craft. They were not callous or indifferent. Unfortunately, some were trapped within their own history. Some were lied about by malicious former students. Like most people, some had simply made mistakes. Like Marley's chains, a negative reputation, deserved or not, can encumber a career for years.

One poor bastard I will always remember was a science teacher who had no classroom discipline. The kids ignored him completely. He was a bright man, but very slight, almost frail-looking. He had no edge; there was no firm or sharp part to his personality. His students tormented him mercilessly. They hid his things. They moved his equipment. On a couple of occasions, they locked him out of his room. In April, his wife died of breast cancer. Death came grudgingly, and only after several months of suffering—for both of them. Throughout the long ordeal, the classroom sharks knew that blood was in the water and continued to torment him. He resigned at the end of my first year. He left teaching entirely and was probably happier for it.

He wasn't unique. I was hired to replace a man who was fired for slapping a mouthy sophomore after "taking all of the shit" he could. The whole dismissal process was ugly, after which he suffered a nervous breakdown. Once he recovered, he became a furniture salesman. A twenty-year career vanished in the time it took to move his hand three feet.

One female English teacher was openly referred to as a whore by some students because she had a failed relationship with a teacher in a neighboring district. When she broke it off, the jilted asshole trashed her reputation mercilessly. Amazing how quickly a career can be shattered, even from ten miles away. Admin. did nothing, which I was discovering was sometimes the thing they did best. A few student lowlifes drew pictures of her engaged in sex acts and taped them up in the hall. The "clever" little SOBs provided labels so less-astute cretins couldn't misidentify the target of their vulgar "art. Twice I saw her sitting at her desk after school. She had been crying. I asked if there was any way I could help. She simply shook her head. I threatened some of the boys I suspected were involved, and tried reasoning with a couple more I thought were reachable. I achieved very little. She left Eagle River a year later to teach in a suburb of Saint Paul, hopefully far enough away to escape further character assassination. This happened in a time before the internet made it possible to spread lies, misogyny, and smut with the click of a mouse. Sadly, technology has made it possible for hate to metastasize and take on a life of its own. I will never understand why this bullshit is protected by the First Amendment.

James Madison would vomit. Much has been written about the cruelty of children. During my first year, I discovered a lot of it was true.

I recognized some teachers were just bitter. They were trapped in a perpetual mid-career crisis. Teaching is unique in that there is no real professional trajectory. The first day you spend in the classroom will be remarkably like your last. Unless you choose to get into administration, there is no "corporate ladder" to climb. The career moves you make will be mostly sideways. There is no path leading to greater responsibility with corresponding increases in prestige and benefits. When the school bell rings and class begins, a first-year teacher has the same duties, obligations, and responsibilities as a 30-year veteran. We all stand *in loco parentis,* in place of parent. What an amazing role is assumed. Ideally (and typically) a teacher becomes better at their craft, the longer they teach. They need to—because there's no easy way to start over.

By their mid-forties, some teachers at Eagle River were already counting the days until retirement. They formed little cliques of like-minded people. At faculty meetings, they sat in the back row, making not the smallest attempt to feign interest. I once heard them described as U-Boat commanders, ready to sink any attempt at change or innovation. To me they looked like bored freshmen in a particularly dry algebra class. When new class assignments were made for the coming school year, they lobbied to teach the same classes to avoid creating new lesson plans. The mere suggestion of taking on an additional prep was personal and professional anathema. Looking for new ways to reach a new generation of kids was the last thing they wanted to do. They had become complacent; to be frank, they were lazy. Seniority was their one perquisite, as tenure was their protection against real accountability. They played those cards whenever it suited their purpose. Eagle River had a few of these people. Three of them made a great show of waiting by the main door in their coats and leaving at exactly 3:15 every day. Except Fridays, of course, then it was OK to exit by 3:00. They thought they were making some kind of statement about the unbearable level of abuse they suffered on a daily basis. In reality, they were only compounding their problems. The kids saw their apathy and drew different conclusions.

Much of this professional ennui was probably about bitterness over money and status. *No one on the staff ever expected to get rich, and all teachers do advance on the salary schedule. However, as their own careers unfolded, most teachers saw friends and former classmates in different fields doing better financially than they were. This gap widened almost yearly, and it's hard not to have regrets about paths not taken.

That first year, I discovered most teachers still believe the clichés about the value and importance of education and teaching. These are the sentiments which drew them to the profession in the first place. However, I also came to understand the real coin of education is *respect*. Teachers need to feel valued and appreciated. From the outside, it all looks so easy. In casual conversation, people may give lip service to the idea that dealing with kids all day must be difficult and demanding. But, to themselves, they are thinking, "It must be great to have summers off," and they would willingly trade their lot for yours. Few people consider that your summer is often filled with professional development and upgrading your lessons. During my career, I filled up almost thirty-five summers with course work. At the same time, I taught summer school and coached. Most people don't see or appreciate this. I can't blame them. Memory is incredibly selective and a wonderful filter. Before I began teaching, I believed likewise. My first year in Eagle River proved how poorly my memories reflected the reality of teaching.

In all the years I went to school, I didn't appreciate many of the people who attempted to teach me, or the complexity of what many of them did. I regret that most memories I carried of my own teachers were only of the exceptional ones, or the truly poor ones. These were the frames of my educational canvas when I arrived at Eagle River. But now, I was *a teacher* and I saw dedication and caring were more the rule than the exception among my fellow teachers. However, I also discovered that over time some teachers are slowly bludgeoned into mediocrity, and some are complicit in their own undoing.

One of the things which most surprised me about our faculty was that many of them, by no means all, but many, had ceased to have a life of the mind. While trying to get others to learn, they had quit learning themselves. Part of this was due to income. College classes cost, I understood this, and in the seventies there was very little financial incentive to get an advanced degree. However, books are cheap and libraries are free. Still, a few of the folks I worked with had developed a real minimalist interpretation of their subject and their teaching. If it was in the textbook they knew it, if not, they knew it not and God help the curriculum committee who wanted to update the text! This was perhaps my greatest disappointment that first year. When I came to Eagle River, I did not join a community of scholars. We did not have discussions about our content areas. There were occasionally opinions shared about pedagogy and methods, but content wasn't talked about much. I tried to start a book club in the department once and got no takers. This amazed me, especially with regard to my fellow Social Studies teachers. This point was really driven home at the precinct caucus meetings. To my knowledge, I was the only Social Studies teacher in attendance. This ended my naïve notion that most teachers were political junkies and always ready to storm the ramparts of societal apathy and injustice. By the end of the first year, I had to accept that many of my colleagues were not unlike most people in their ability to live in one day only. This was especially odd for a profession which should be future oriented. Later I discovered by going to the Democratic caucuses I had branded myself as a 'man to be watched'. The possibility of negative repercussions may also have played a part in the lack of faculty attendance.

In my own department, I realized there was a world of difference between a history teacher and a historian who also teaches history. I resolved to at some point begin a graduate program in American History. I wanted to be a historian who also taught history. During the year, and much to my embarrassment, I learned you must always preview materials you intend to show in class. A guy I taught with was the resident projectionist. There was no topic, unit, concept, or historical event for which he could not find at least a semi-relevant film. The lights in his room were off so regularly his kids should have worn miner's hats, and his student aides were jokingly referred to as ushers. As Columbus Day approached that year, I asked this visual arts connoisseur if there was anything about Columbus in his film library; I thought a mini unit on the voyages of discovery would be a nice side trip historically speaking. He scratched his head for a bit, then he just lit up. "Tim, I got the greatest film on Columbus you ever saw. Take my word for it, it's great, the kids will love it, and it lasts the *whole* hour!" This sounded exactly like what I wanted and with such a ringing endorsement I didn't feel the need to preview the film; after all, if Jeff knew about anything it was a film. On the appointed day, I checked out a projector from the library, and carefully threaded the film through the gears, sprockets, pulleys and wheels required. Then I flipped off the light switch and looked forward to an entertaining and informative hour. For the first twenty minutes, I wasn't disappointed. The film was great! A stalwart Columbus and a scurvy-looking crew plied the endless waters of the Atlantic. However, his crew became anxious and surly. The mutinous dogs were just about to do great bodily harm to our hero when blessed land came into sight. It appeared salvation was at hand! As a longboat bearing Chris in the bow made its way through the surf, a distant group of natives came into view. No doubt they were bearing gifts and supplies for the intrepid band. I never did find out what the natives were bearing because I immediately noticed what they were wearing: almost nothing!! Dusky young maidens were rushing *and bouncing* to embrace the weary sailors. I jerked the projector cord from the wall socket so fast and hard the plug end left a bruise on the kid closest. When I expressed my feelings of horror to Jeff, he thought it was hilarious. At the time, my sense of humor deserted me. I can laugh at the episode now, but more from the realization I once believed this account of Columbus was at least partly accurate. I'm ashamed to admit, in my first few years in the classroom, the "history" I taught was sometimes low-grade fiction. Regrettably, in many classrooms, this crap still passes for history. Given the political climate, I'm afraid it may remain so, at least until teachers are willing to reclaim the truth. In this I feel we have so much more agency than we believe we have.

My first year, I learned all parents love their kids, and normally they are doing the best they can for them. Some have a simpler vision for their children, and this doesn't make them wrong or stupid. Four of my seniors would be the first members of their family to graduate from high school. To the parents of these kids, high-school graduation was the pinnacle of academic achievement. They never imagined more for their child. Colleges may as well have been on the dark side of the moon. Two of these seniors gave me handwritten invitations to their open houses. They were proud occasions and good parties.

I think I lost a lot of my certainty and arrogance that first year. A bad student does not always equal an indifferent parent. At my first parent-teacher conferences I must have reeked of condescension towards those parents of underachieving, "in my estimation," children. I wrote bad poetry about the types of people who came to discuss their child. After forty years, I still remember the verses and blush at the attitude expressed:

The Bad Conference

The parents schlep across the room,
they slouch upon a chair.
They wonder what the reason was,
the teachers asked them there.

"Our kid can read a little,
can even write a mite.
And we did fine with less than that,
less by a goddamn site.

So what if he gets only D s,
low grades don't do no harm,
Book learning it won't help a bit,
on an Eagle River farm.

So don't give me no lectures,
about future goals and such.
Don't fill his head with nonsense.
Don't make him see too much.

The best the boy can hope for,
is exactly what we got.
We see his life for what it is,
you hope for what it's not."

Then there was…

The Good Conference

The parents stride across the room,
sit upright in their chairs.
Poised eagerly to hear you speak,
the brilliance of their heirs.

You tell them what they came to hear.
They nod approvingly.
You make a joke about the fall,
of an apple from a tree.

We speak a bit of future plans,
a consensus we then reach.
You folks know how to parent,
and I know how to teach
I'll take a hundred like your child,
and want a hundred more.
Your daughter is the type of kid,
I went into teaching for.

So I hope you were prolific.
With more kids on the way,
And if you truly like the job I do,
How about a raise in pay?

I never learned more than I did that first year. More about human nature, more about human frailty, and more about the stuff which makes up our common humanity. I learned there are things a teacher should touch only indirectly because too much empathy can be crippling. Maybe teaching would ultimately be like that for me. When I first signed on, I planned to be a short-timer because of the poor pay and the minimal respect teachers received. At the end of my first year, I still intended to be a short-timer, but the reasons had changed. I discovered the workload could be staggering. I found out as a teacher, you will never run out of useful things to do. It is quite literally correct that the hours you work will be limited only by your own energy and dedication; and no one else will know if you worked them or not. Good teacher, bad teacher, indifferent teacher, the check stays the same. The days can be brutal, or they can be benign, it's your choice. There is always something that can be done better. Preparation for a class can always be more thorough. If you opt to make it so, teaching can be a well-paid, part-time job. It can also consume you. I had already met teachers at both extremes. I was coming to feel if I stayed in teaching long enough, I might eventually be sucked dry emotionally. In the same room, on the same day, there are a hundred shades of both pain and joy. By the time they reach high school, kids are seldom neutral. Eagle River kept its secrets well from outsiders, but its children were often willing to talk and just needed someone to listen. At times, they told me so much more than I really wanted to hear.

My baseball team finished with 14 wins that year. We kind of dribbled down our leg at a sub-region game, or it could have been an epic season. Most of the team would be coming back next spring, so the future was solid. One or two were even open to the possibility of playing football in the fall. For the summer, I took a job in a nearby town as a delivery man. The long drives would give me a lot of time to think. Turns out, I really didn't need Vietnam.

"All Across America we daily put teachers in charge of our collective futures.
Some are so painfully young. Twenty and thirty somethings, almost children themselves.
We pay them little, we respect them less, and now we want to arm them so they can
try to fend off psychopaths carrying assault weapons. If something terrible happens,
these same teachers will probably try to put themselves between a gunman and your child.
No doubt thoughts and prayers will be offered. Another tepid, feckless, but politically expedient re-
sponse to an American tragedy."

VIII

As Simple as This

The summer was to pass too quickly. Between my commute to work and my time in the delivery truck, I probably drove 12,000 miles in nine weeks. The company I worked for was about thirty-five miles from Eagle River and located in the only town in the county of any size. I was paid $9.65 per hour to drive a route which stretched for nearly 100 miles from end to end. At the time, I considered it to be a wonderful wage. The compensation was considerably better than I was making as a teacher and when I added that amount to my school checks, I was doing OK. I will always remember it as being a good job. After ten months surrounded by people and noise, I reveled in the solitude of driving and quiet reflection. I'm more than a little ashamed to admit my concentration on the road was not always all it should have been. I became so accustomed to traveling the two-lane county roads of my route, at times my mind would be elsewhere. More than once I came up behind a tractor or combine puttering along at a stately 15 miles per hour. The squealing brakes, or a spray of gravel as I passed on the shoulder, likely scared the *bejeezus* out of several local farmers, it did likewise to me!

At the western end of my route there was a small lake. On slow days, I had lunch at a well-shaded public access and thought about the future, especially what marriage would be like. Perhaps it was a by-product of being young and male, but in those days, my event horizon didn't really stretch much beyond quitting time. Terms like "until death do us part," or "lifetime commitment" had little real currency with me then, and the wedding was at least a year away. This was a practical eternity to a 23-year-old. So there was still time to sit in the sun and dream, and I was glad for the time. Things would happen in due course, as they always did, and I thought maybe this might become my last summer to sit by a quiet lake with no real worries and few responsibilities. Changes were coming, for sure, but not yet. Next fall I would still be Mr. McLean, and I was looking forward to it. For now, that was enough. It amazed me how much I thought about my students and players. I was also usually mentally reworking my lessons. In these quiet times, the classroom was never far from my thoughts. While marriage was still an abstraction, September was almost within reach.

The previous year, I had taught a unit on the Great Depression and had used the film *The Grapes of Wrath*, based on the novel by John Steinbeck, to personalize the plight of farmers during the Dust Bowl. In one of the concluding scenes of the film, Ma and Pa are talking about all they've been through. Ma speculates Pa has maybe become disoriented by recent events and the many sudden changes to their lives. Pa had always been attached to the land and now he was rootless. Seems Ma regarded all men as being about as adaptable as glaciers. In Ma's view, when men move at all, it is a fairly slow and spastic thing: Clueless really. Women on the other hand, "Are like rivers," Ma muses, they flow purposefully and perpetually. Throughout the story, Ma is the character who deals best with the continual disruptions to family life. Because Steinbeck depicts Ma as the stronger personality, we can conclude the female approach and psyche are superior. I don't completely accept this generalization, but it does shade towards the truth in one major respect; women will usually plan long-term, while men tend to jam their hands in their pockets, grunt some vague protest, and then go along. I was no different.

While I was kind of stuck in neutral as far as this marriage thing, my fiancée had no trouble flowing right past the acceptance phase and directly into the planning stage of a life together. When I finished my day, I would call or visit her. It was her custom to immediately present me with another portion of *my future* which *she had just planned out*. Each of these incremental "improvements" began with the phrase, "When you get done teaching next year..." Long ago, she had resolved, step one was for me to find more profitable employment, preferably in business or banking. If nothing immediately presented itself, I could always get a job with her father, a *successful* small business owner.

My increased salary would then make it possible for her to quit work entirely and get right down to having babies and setting up suburban housekeeping. In my mind, this would have been a terrible waste of a big buck, private school education on her part, but I was at the "anything you want honey" stage, so no ripples were made, no doubts expressed. In all honesty, it also wasn't a bad plan. I had a good deal of confidence I was employable in the private sector, and working with her father was not a terrible alternative. Despite the fact he was a Republican, he was a good guy and I would have judged him to have been a good employer. He liked the idea I was a teacher, and perhaps more the idea I was going to be a *former* teacher. This contradiction makes perfect sense from any father's point of view. On one hand, he wanted his daughter to marry a man who would invest himself in other people without being overly concerned about financial gain. At a certain level, being willing to teach is ennobling. At the same time, he wanted to be sure his little girl and her children—*his* grandchildren—were secure financially. A former teacher with aspirations to do a little better salary-wise was just about perfect. Integrity with income, character with coin, and someone who obviously liked kids all in the same bargain! These were things never said, but always understood; and not once objected to by me. But all that was in the future.

Everything considered, the summer passed agreeably. Drive, dream, plan, and the second verse was the same as the first. I quit work a few days before summer football camp was to begin. A little time to get away, perhaps. On my way out the door, I took some good-natured ribbing from a couple other drivers about how happy I must have been to get back to the classroom and take a vacation from the "real" world of work. In half a flash, my mind screamed, "Screw you all, you ignorant, lazy, time-wasting, seldom bathing, sons of bitches. The easiest week I've ever had in the classroom would kill the best of you before Thursday!!" It took most of the self-control I had to simply say, "It'll be nice to get back, I miss the kids." Sometime over the course of the past year, I had learned to never argue with fools.

That week, I decided to find a campsite in the Boundary Waters Canoe Area. If possible, the BWCA wilderness was even more rustic back then, or at least it was less eco-touristy. My approach in many things had always been minimalist, but when camping, primitive would have been too generous a description. I had a small tent, a canoe, and little else. So as usual, my camp site was bare bones and uncluttered by many conveniences.

It was mid-August. For me, this was the best time to be in northern Minnesota. The black flies were gone. The mosquitoes seemed to be between hatches, or perhaps they had already been sated after a long summer of gorging themselves on moose and Boy Scouts. In either case, I was left alone. The August days were already becoming agreeably cool, and the weather was unusually dry. As in most other years, summer was tiring more quickly in the North Country.

It was my third trip to this area. On each of the other two, I had intended to fish from dawn to dusk, but both times I ended up spending the majority of my time reading. This time I bowed to the inevitable and brought a good supply of books and the barest of essentials for fishing. I had five days, and I intended to spend most of my time stretched out on a low, well-shaded river bank carpeted by pine needles. In between reads, I would occasionally hike a bit to stretch my legs and make a real effort to not get lost. That year, I succeeded almost 100% of the time. For me, a personal best.

I had scouted out this particular campsite on a previous trip. It was easily accessible by canoe, and I knew from there I could cast into water deep enough to hold the occasional walleye. I baited with a dead cisco, cast out, and let it sit on the bottom. My rod was propped in the fork of a Y-shaped stick, set upright between two conveniently spaced tree roots. Then, over the course of the next couple of days I waited, read, and caught a few smallmouth bass, no walleye. My tastes in literature usually run towards biographies and histories, and my first selection was an interesting history of the First Minnesota Regiment during the Civil War. The period fascinates me. Rather, that men would willingly give their lives in support of an idea fascinated me. I think that perhaps modernity has beaten most of the altruism out of us, but it was inspirational. My second choice was a lesser-known work by Ayn Rand titled, *For the New Intellectual*, or something like that. It was a kind of history of objectivist philosophy. I had read and enjoyed a few of Rand's previous works, but objectivism now ran counter to how I was beginning to see the world. This wasn't always true. Once it was solace in a dark time for me… when life seemed intent on devouring most of what I was and anger was replacing naive trust. Then, I needed to cling to myself, if only to keep the pieces from shattering, and flying off in a hundred different directions. With time that changed, and now it was definitely a philosophy that couldn't possibly express or validate how I wanted to live my life. No matter how urgently we feel the need to be selfish, Egoism can never truly be a virtue.

My next choice was something I expected would be a bit lighter. I settled upon *To Kill a Mockingbird*. I had included the book in my pack as an afterthought. Many of my friends regarded it highly, but I was a bit leery of any book which was standard fare for high-school sophomores. Immediately, the book surprised me. It was elegantly written, and the characters were powerful and well-defined. I was especially taken with Atticus Finch, or more correctly how other characters in the book described Atticus Finch. I would never attempt to summarize this beautiful book, and trying to explain Atticus would be presumptuous. Even the small episode I describe now may be muddled by time and my frail memory. Atticus was a small-town lawyer who was called upon to defend a black man who stood charged with raping a white woman. In Depression era Maycomb, Alabama, this made him guilty. For it was his word against hers, and white womanhood against brutish black stereotypes. In such cases, trials were usually superfluous, and any man who would defend such a person was a traitor to his race as well as a fool. The judge in the case, a man of conscience, by-passed the usual public defender and asked Atticus Finch to act as counsel. It was not something Atticus wanted to do, but as a moral man in an immoral situation, he had no real choice.

Atticus' children didn't understand what motivated their father to do this; to fight battles lost well before he was born, and in doing so, risk injury and reputation. Miss Maudie, a character in the novel, tried to explain their father's motivations to his children, telling them that Atticus was acting as a kind of surrogate Christian for the entire community; "there are men in this world who were born to do the unpleasant jobs for all of us. Such unselfish acts of sacrifice and bravery elevated them and made them special." Atticus Finch, their father, was one of these men. In that one small bit of dialogue, author Harper Lee explained all anyone would ever need to know about moral philosophy. Her clarity and brevity were stunning. At any time during the next hour, the largest walleye in Minnesota could have inhaled my bait, partially digested it, and swam off with my rod to the far side of Snowbank Lake. I probably would not have known, and perhaps would not have cared.

The balance of that day and the rest of my stay in the boundary waters was remarkably quiet. I saw only two other canoes, neither within hailing distance. In the daytime, sounds were a gentle whisper, no more than the half-heard tone of a receding echo. Nighttime was the silent and persistent voice of God. Sitting by the campfire, thoughts as clear as Roman candles begged some kind of expression before they reached apogee and fell burning back to earth in a trail of sparks. The nighttime sky in Northern Minnesota has been the midwife to a thousand poems and a hundred novels. Alone in the darkness, it is impossible to look up and not feel some sliver of the infinite penetrate to the heart of your consciousness. An older way of understanding and believing crowds out any sense of modernity and cynicism. In one moment of amazing clarity, I thought somehow I now understood myself better than I ever had. Any attempt I make at description now would be a tepid thing, and I hate speaking in clichés. If you have seen and been, you understand. If you have not; I don't have the words to make you see. Some people have been intimidated by it all and dwell on human insignificance in the vastness of creation. Yet, it is impossible to be dwarfed by even this much grandeur if you will only once accept you are a rightful part of it. No one who accepts as much ever leaves canoe country feeling smaller and less human than when they entered, and any amount of time spent under an infinite explosion of stars must yield at least one fundamental, and deeply personal, new truth.

As a clueless college freshman, I once convinced myself the universe could be explained rationally; that the bricks of creation are no more than random events. "Give a tree full of monkeys typewriters, and in an eon or so out would pop the collected works of Shakespeare." "Most things happen quite by chance; a very merry circumstance." I spewed all this tripe before I spent that August night in the boundary waters. On a summer evening, after reading a book deemed appropriate for high-school sophomores, I resolved that no matter what, I might finally decide to do with my life, if I tried to become like Atticus Finch, I would be OK. Maybe it was teaching, perhaps business or banking, maybe it was carpentry, or writing poetry. Shorn of all ethical complexity, life could be as simple as trying to become Atticus. It was a good thing football was starting again, or I might have stayed at that spot long enough to cloud my own newly clarified purposes; the paralysis sometimes caused by a life too often and too deeply examined. The next day, I broke camp and headed back to Eagle River and the kids. I was just in time to begin two-a-day football practices.

"Years ago, I needed to do a summer internship to complete my licensure in Special Education. I was placed in a kindergarten classroom. Most of the students there needed a little more help before they were ready for first grade. After a while, the kids got to know me, and I was peppered with all kinds of questions. One shy little guy kind of eased himself over to me once and asked, "Mr. McLean, where do you think heaven is?" I told him that many people believed that heaven was in the sky somewhere. But I believed that, if you could handle the bugs, heaven was really just north of Ely Minnesota in a place called the Boundary Waters Canoe Area. He thought about this for a bit and then said, "I hope it's up in the sky McLean. I really don't like bugs." Sometimes I wish that I'd decided to be a kindergarten teacher.

IX

Little Things and Parents' Eyes

That year, football really began in June. The coaches encouraged the players to get together at the school twice a week in the summer to lift weights and throw the ball around. I came whenever I could. In the seventies this was an uncommon level of dedication as many programs had not bought entirely into weight training in the off season. In this regard, Eagle River was ahead of the curve, at least in our small conference. The state high-school league's rules forbade coaches from being present at these sessions. The coaches could provide a plan for the team captains, and the captains led the other boys in the workouts. This was in a more naïve time when the world was not so sue happy and seventeen-year-old boys could actually be trusted not to drop weights on their heads without an adult hovering over them. While the boys worked out, the coaches met to plan for the upcoming season. I learned a lot of football during those meetings, we drank a lot of beer, and there was real enthusiasm on the staff. This had been missing the previous year. We were going to be better this year, and this wasn't just wishful thinking. Maybe we wouldn't win the conference or make the state playoffs, but we would be respectable. As the offensive coach put it, "This year we ain't being anyone's bitch," a crude way to phrase it, but probably true.

We had reasons for optimism. The kids who took part in the summer workouts were bigger and faster than last season's crop. Many were the same kids, but each had a year of added growth and maturity. We also caught a break and had a kid transfer in from a larger, more successful program. In football speak, he looked to be kind of a shit kicker and would make the entire defensive line stronger. Several underclassmen had received a good deal of varsity playing time the previous year, and that would help us this fall. Three kids from my baseball team had decided to give football a try, and they attacked it with a will. Of course, they lacked experience, but they gave us some depth at the skill positions. They were also untainted by the failures of previous years and brought a welcome infusion of optimism.

When two-a-days finally began, there were holes to fill, but some improvements were immediately apparent. Last year's starting backfield had graduated, but in all honesty, they were replaceable, and several of the underclassmen showed some promise at running back. The outstanding thing this year was we had a junior quarterback who didn't stutter, and he actually showered with his teammates! The line would be much improved. My tackles had begun to grow bodies that complimented their already outsized feet, and they were showing signs of becoming really solid high-school linemen.

There was also a little surliness to them this year, which was great to see. Our center and both guards were back as well, each having strapped on some height and weight. They were even starting to sprout the faintest hint of facial hair. They now looked less like pudgy preschoolers and more like "husky" high-schoolers.

Another good sign: The team had developed some scruples as far as appearance went. I couldn't explain where this came from, but I appreciated it. Practice gear was washed on occasion. Players now made sure that their football pants were pulled up far enough to cover their entire asses, so the "mega-butt-crack look" was pretty much exiled from the practice field. Cleats were shined. As further evidence of their burgeoning manhood, most of the team now wore jockstraps! This may seem like a trivial observation, but the previous year not one in five of my little warriors had worn a jock. They had simply practiced in the underwear they had worn to school, then they went home "commando style." After a few days of practice, they would collect all the soiled undergarments from their lockers and start over. Once last year I thought we should address this lack of common sense and basic hygiene at a team meeting, but the head coach nixed the idea. He was probably right; at the time we had bigger problems to correct. All the same, I was thrilled this year's edition of the Eagle River Screaming Eagles would be properly attired in jocks and cups. A small victory, but a good start.

My personal goal was to be a better coach this fall. With a season's experience and a couple of clinics behind me, I knew more football. I was more self-confident, and my expectations were more realistic. Perhaps a lot of the volume I generated last year was simply over-compensation for inexperience. As long as I am rationalizing, perhaps it could have been some deeper and self-excusing psychopathy people will conveniently use to pardon their own bad behavior. Or perhaps, I was just acting like an immature horse's ass. In any case, I was going to be less volatile. Oh, there were still occasional blow ups. Once in a while, my clipboard would sail into the corn bordering our practice field. I still regularly abused my hat. But I was in better control of my temper. There was occasional laughter on our practice field. Once we even did the famous St. Johns' cloud watching drill. Several kids commented on the changes in me and saw them as an improvement. My ego was now compressed to a size that better reflected my coaching abilities. Crow is a wonderful diet food, eat enough of it and you really do shrink. Last year, it was on the menu at least once every week.

By the second year, I had pretty much disabused myself of all the cockeyed notions collected during my high school and college playing days. First, kids do have real physical limits. Will and determination do not overcome everything else on a football field. Big strong people will usually kick the hell out of smaller, weaker ones, no matter how motivated the latter may be. Second, not all injuries were to be downplayed or ignored. Once upon a time, coaches held up their charges who played with torn ligaments or broken bones as examples of macho toughness. Privately, we coaches still praised these kids because we still could not entirely escape our collective years of poor sports socialization. But we now felt compelled to lecture them on the difference between occasional pain and real injury. No one with an atom of common sense wanted a kid to do major damage to themselves to win a high-school athletic contest. Third, unnecessary suffering and discomfort were not going to be considered virtues anymore. This was a big concession for me.

When I played, water wasn't permitted on the practice field, and how more of us didn't die of heatstroke is a miracle. This was true for the entire Eagle River football staff. As players, we all thought there was a deep purpose to this and considered it part of the sport's discipline. Oddly, during games, we were allowed all the water we wanted. Of course, I now see this as a logical disconnect, but back then the bulk of the people I played with were not deep thinkers. Plus, like me, a lot of the players and coaches were Catholic, so we realized we might lessen our time in purgatory by offering up football's small inconveniences and irritants for the betterment of our souls. Kind of like the "no meat on Friday" thing but writ large. However, now as an "enlightened" coach, I realized some of our Protestant players might take umbrage at this reasoning and refuse to buy in. So, in order to accommodate their more delicate sensibilities and flabby theological structure, we became a kinder and gentler coaching staff. Now, water was always available at practice and the kids were required to drink it. We took breaks. Making kids run until they puked didn't happen anymore. If it got especially hot and humid we practiced in shorts and helmets. We started to pay attention to other small things like taping and jock itch.

A few years previous, some ingenious person invented this pink foam stuff which could be put under a tape job. It existed when I played, but it was called "sissy wrap", and "real men" simply didn't use it. During games, we "real men" had a quick spray of Nitrotan and the tape was applied directly to the skin. This gave us a kind of elevated status in the Neanderthal community of linebackers but indicated an unhealthy and abnormal relationship to needless pain. If we had time, we shaved the afflicted area first, but usually tape was just slapped on. After the game, when the tape was yanked off, there was hell to pay. However, if you managed to remain stoic throughout the removal process, your status as an insensate brute skyrocketed. This practice once cost me most of my chest hair and a small portion of my left nipple, but my newly hairless torso became an object of wonderment and awe in the locker-room. The coaches *loved* it.

You could always gauge the caliber of your performance in a game by the amount of glee displayed by the coaches at your obvious discomfort when the tape came off. I believe the jury is still out on the cosmic question of "pull fast vs. pull slow," but either way, it hurts like the devil. This year, I would expect our kids to use "sissy wrap" and there would be no backhand jabs at their manhood for doing so.

Tinea cruris, just plain-old jock itch, was the secret scourge of all football players, especially fat ones. The brownish red rash is a type of yeast infection that forms on the crotch when air flow is restricted, or cleanliness neglected. For kids with bad cases, running was agony. As a former fat kid, I could sympathize, but because it's not fatal, last year we felt free to joke about the obvious distress of those afflicted. Since then, the head coach had done a little research and found a cream which supposedly offered relief. Our chunkier kids especially were encouraged to use it. The stuff needed to be spread on by hand, so this presented us with new opportunities for coarse humor. Kids who were hurting were told, "go spread on the crotch rot stuff, and you better not come back smiling!" When our center had to use the stuff daily, the offensive coach wondered aloud if the poor kid was "worried he'd go blind." The head coach joked about needing to lock the stuff up at night. I have no idea if the cream really worked or what it cost, but if I remember it at all, it tells me it was worth it. That year there was a better feeling on the practice field and the staff's concern for little things was at least partly responsible. I knew we had arrived as a team, when one day a few mallards flew over the practice field, and no one pretended to draw a bead on them.

My relationship with my players was changing. There was no future in being a martinet. I was starting to look at my players as just kids. Inside the helmets and shoulder pads, they were simply rather large high-school students who needed almost constant reassurance. At times, this wasn't easy to give. Warm fuzzies aren't really a part of the game. In many ways, football is unlike most other sports. It's a *cruel* game. It has always involved brutally hard work and personal confrontation. Emotion is integral to the sport. It's a violent game and a serious business. It always will be. Regrettably, sometimes kids get hurt badly. After 18 players died in 1905, Teddy Roosevelt threatened to ban the sport because of the brutality and intensity of the developing rivalries. At Roosevelt's urging, many rules were changed to make the game far less life-threatening, e.g. the flying wedge was disallowed. However, despite continued efforts to make the game safer with better equipment, and more restrictive rules, the injuries didn't stop. The players today at all levels are much bigger and faster, the collisions are more violent. This has resulted in a good number of catastrophic injuries and many less functional joints. Many middle-aged men have come to regret their brief brushes with Friday night glory. All the posters and all the ringing cliché's have never once rebuilt a damaged knee or shoulder, and after a few years no one really gives a damn that your team was the lords of the Hi-way 8 Conference back in 1959. Amazingly, fathers still encourage, nay, demand, their sons play. I have often wondered how big our roster would have been if we only had kids who truly wanted to be on the team.

Aside from the obvious downside, there were still good things you could learn from the sport. Self-sacrifice and teamwork are life skills worth developing. The discipline required in football is essential for success in many fields. A lot of boys have profited from playing. But unless you intend to live in a gulag, the game is not now, and never has been, a metaphor for life. If it ever truly becomes that, God help us all. Neither will the game ever be as important to the kids as it is to the coach and many of the parents. God bless those rare kids who feel so deeply for the game they actually cry when they realize their playing days are over.

Eagle River was never a big sports town, but as in every community, there was a hard kernel of parents who lived, ate and breathed high-school athletics. Depending on the team's fortunes, these folks could be a coach's biggest boosters or a dagger in his back. Few of these "boosters" have an agenda which extends beyond their own child and personal egos. Many times, the kid gets lost somewhere within a parent's expectations.

By my second year of teaching and coaching I was beginning to understand that while parents often had *little* objectivity about their child's performance in the classroom, on the playing field they had *absolutely none*. Call it parents' eyes. It is a totally myopic view of any athletic contest or sports program. Parents' eyes can color every community's perception of the school, the team, or the coach. This disease is not unique to small-town America. In fact, some of the truly virulent outbreaks occur in the largest suburban schools. In hockey, it is pandemic. Parents will sit shivering in the stands with stopwatch in hand, and time down to the second how long their child is on the ice compared to every other kid on the team. There will be spreadsheets and flow charts. There will be "select" teams, and endless camps. Coaches will leer at each other across the ice. There have been fistfights in the stands. A parent's social status can be determined by what line their ten-year-old skates with. Fathers will ridicule preschoolers, and little boys and girls will fall asleep at their desks because they were dragged out of bed at 5:30 to get some early ice time. In football, parents' eyes could be bad, but a football field is a big place. There are really 22 potential starting spots, and coaches can usually find a place to occasionally play even the most inept kid on the team. In other sports, it isn't so easy. Take basketball for example. Parents' eyes can cripple an entire program. I never played or coached the sport, but it's been made crystal clear to me by a number of "concerned parents" of players, almost all basketball coaches "suck", and being a "dickhead" is a big part of the job description. You would receive the same assessment if you asked any parent of a player cut from a team. They are all too willing to share their feelings about the unjust treatment their child received. Many a player's parents can tell you why they believe the coach sucks, but no matter what they might say, please believe the real reason is playing time. One ball, five positions, ten players on a team, my kid sits or gets cut, and the coach sucks. Why anyone would want to coach that sport on a high-school level is beyond me. Coaching in high school is difficult, even with the best circumstances and solid parental support. As an assistant, I had the perfect job. No portion of the team's record was permanently attached to me, and a lot of the town thought I should replace the head guy anyway. On many nights someone at the local pub would buy me a beer just on the outside chance that I was the heir apparent for the head coaching job. They wanted me to remember their name, or maybe their child's name, for later reference.

High school is the first competitive level in which coaches are paid to win; nearly everything else is irrelevant. A coach can be an excellent role model, and a coach can be a paragon of virtue and fairness, but if Ls too often outnumber Ws, the coach will be down the road as soon as a more likely candidate becomes available. In most towns, a coach must also occasionally beat their community's most dearly hated rival. Doing so gives a town bragging rights along some nameless stretch of asphalt, at least until next football season. If not, coaches become expendable. In the real world, a coach is almost never dismissed for any reason other than team performance. Different reasons will be offered and some will even be believed, but the bottom line is usually wins and losses.

The head coach knew if we didn't have a pretty fair season that year, he would be asked to resign. Even in Eagle River, you couldn't lose forever without consequences. He also knew I could be a candidate to replace him. This never changed our relationship. As a young coach, I couldn't have asked for a better mentor. He ran a clean, uncompromising program. He didn't look the other way when his players broke team training or state high-school league rules. Even our "stars" were held to account. He was a role model any young man might imitate. But when the town fathers met for a few beers at the Legion Club that preceding summer, I understood that he was being trashed pretty well. The bad-mouthing probably was also going on at home, which didn't help the coach or team. It appears integrity was a wonderful thing, but only if you could couple it with enough victories. If those victories are achieved with the "right" kids getting to be the hero, all the better.

As an undergrad, I was taught that sports were designed to supplement and enrich an education program, and some marvelous teaching and learning does take place in the extracurricular areas. Relationships are established and friendships are made which will last a lifetime. Many young athletes view their coach as one of the few positive and supportive people in their lives. But by the mid-seventies, balance and perspective were gradually being lost. If many communities were asked which they would prefer, a substantial increase in high-school graduation rates or a state championship in a major sport, which would they pick? Regrettably, by my second year of teaching and coaching, I had already learned the likely answer. No one ever called me up to bitch about, or to compliment me on my teaching. The occasional parent thought me to be unfair, or perhaps a bit too liberal in my political leanings, but they never really questioned my competence. Coaching was a different matter. About ten times that second season, I was asked a variation on the question, "Coach, what can my kid do to get more time on the field?" Embedded within that question was a not-so-subtle accusation. Either you had some personal dislike of their child, or you were unfair, or you were a rock head who couldn't recognize talent if it bit you on the butt. Each time I gave them as kind and generous an assessment of their child's strengths and weaknesses as I could. Usually, what I wanted to do was to have them look at their child *objectively* and then consider having him try out for the speech team. At larger schools, a lot of talented kids got very little playing time, but if a kid wasn't good enough to play a lot in Eagle River, he was likely to be pretty bad. Thank God, as the defensive coach, I didn't get a lot of questions about plays called or not called. It was the offensive coach who had to suffer through the conversations with fathers who insisted on giving him "sure-fire, secret plays," and "can't mis'" formations bound to confuse and confound the opposition. That year, we tried one such play, which was coincidently suggested by the superintendent. Sports are not apolitical.

In a way, I saw many sports were becoming a class issue, as well. Long gone were the random associations of kids on the playground. In many schools, sports now counted the most to the people who counted the most. This group wielded a disproportionate influence in almost all school districts. This is of course wrong. The classroom can often marginalize and ignore students that desperately need advocacy, help, and support. The playing field definitely will do so; sports are indirectly designed to do so. Generally, schools do a great job of heaping rewards and recognition upon those students who need them *the least*. Extracurricular activities are often a way kids who have been programmed for success from the womb are given additional and regular infusions of confidence and self-esteem. These become the fuel for additional success. Athletics and some other extracurriculars become a meritocracy within an aristocracy. Kids of a certain class compete as equals. Kids like David who were caught in a cycle of failure would never sink the winning basket, literally or figuratively. They would never star in a play, they would never see their name in the morning announcements. No one claps them on the back and says, "Great game, guy!"

Sadly, marginal students often seemed to be in competition with the school itself, and the reward for their perseverance was being allowed to leave. In a rare moment of sunshine, they are given a diploma and a few strains of Pomp and Circumstance but, "no clapping for individual students please" mind you. Some don't even get this, and we take a perverse pleasure in their failure as a means of validating the accomplishments of their more fortunate and successful classmates. Letter jackets weren't the common outer garment of democracy in the seventies, or even today.

We were to do OK that season. We won our first game with a touchdown in the last minute. The second game, we humbled the conference champs from the year previous. We finished at a very respectable six and three. That entire season is just a warm blur now, but after forty years I still remember at least some portion of every game; and I will always remember the kids who played for us. There was Al, who once got so worked up on the sidelines that he actually left the bench to recover a fumble. The officials had to huddle for a long time to figure out that call. There was Harold who would walk up to opposing linemen and announce that, "I'm running right through you next time, you sumbitch," and then he did it. No matter where the play was called, that's where he ran. There was a defensive back named Jeff who threw himself at a 200-pound fullback and got a double compound leg fracture for his trouble, one of the truly gross things I've ever seen. I remember one half-time that season, when things were going so well, there was nothing to talk about. We spent the entire time getting our second string organized, so they could mop up.

Once, as we boarded the bus to play our greatest rival, I jumped in and banged my head on the doorway. I started to bleed like a stuck pig. We were playing the team whose fans had spread deer scent in our bus the year before, so I was really feeling jacked. The fire up speech I gave that evening was especially effective, and many of the kids thought I was throwing in the blood as a special effect. I spent the entire game with an ice pack under my cap. Needless to say, we pounded them. Later I went to the hospital E.R. to have five stitches put into my scalp. I will also always remember three of my starters on defense got caught drinking after the game and were done for the season. Partly because of this, we lost our last two games. Kids do amazingly stupid things at times. Those losses cost us a shot at the playoffs that year, and we hung up the gear with a sense of incompleteness and regret, but we were winners. For at least a year, the job of the head coach was safe. The relief we all felt was palpable. His was a job no one else really wanted, least of all me. To take it would have obligated me to another year, and I wasn't sure I wanted this to happen. Besides, we all knew the future of Eagle River football was bleak. The entire line was graduating. The quarterback was moving to a larger farm in a different state. Not one upcoming class in the next three was likely to be even mediocre, much less good. This year's record of six wins would be the high point for Eagle River football for years to come. Heaven help whoever coached the sad assemblage our team was to become in the next few years. It was wonderfully ironic that our winning season ultimately became a springboard for the head coach. His resume now boasted he was the first coach in 15 years to have a winning football team at Eagle River High School. We were acknowledged as being traditionally so bad, his boast must have carried a good deal of weight. People reading his resume probably thought, "If this guy can win at Eagle River, he must be great." A larger school with a strong program hired him to teach and coach for the next year. While I regretted his leaving, I was happy for him. People of ambition and ability seldom had long careers in Eagle River.

You really gotta go coach!
We finished in last place!
You even lost to Hooterville,
my God! you're a disgrace

I think you are a loser coach!
I know we would have won.
If you just had the common sense,
to start, and play, **My** son!

Don't you see his talent coach?
If not, you must be blind!
Or maybe you don't like the kid,
Or have you lost your mind?

I know the kids respect you coach,
and most would think you fair.
But if **my** kid sits on the bench,
his mom and I don't care!

I'm kind of a big deal coach.
I often get my way.
But I ain't a happy camper now
and someone's gonna pay!!

So do us all a favor coach.
And quit before you're fired!
The folks in town who really count,
Regret that you were hired!!!

I'm going to the board coach.
I'll state our case real clear.
They gotta find another coach
We just don't want **you** here!

Please pack your bags and go coach!
We'll get someone that's great.
My kid will be a starter,
and we'll probably go to state.

It's gonna be fantastic coach,
and all the fans will see.
My studly son will be a star.,
and he's taking after me!

I hope you learned a lesson coach!
about which kids to play.
From the right side of the railroad tracks,
It's always been that way.

X

Ice Breakers and Senior Social

My second year in the classroom was also going to be a better one. In a lot of things, experience is the best teacher; in education it may be the only one. That year, I resolved that I would learn to laugh at myself more often. I was going to sing in the halls. If I was feeling especially rebellious, occasionally I wouldn't wear a tie. That year, I would not be afraid of the kids. Much of my rigidity from the year previous was probably a result of fear. New situations, new responsibilities, and a million chances to screw-up. By my second year, I was not so afraid of failure, and everything wasn't so blasted serious. If I once failed to deliver the consummate lesson, my students would not be scarred forever, and the gates of Princeton would not be barred to them if I occasionally missed the mark with a poorly aimed pedagogic broadside. This year, tangents and side trips would be O.K.

On the first day of faculty workshops, as per usual, a motivational speaker came in to fire up the troops. The Eagle River school district employed about 65 teachers, and we were all seated on folding chairs in the high-school gym. She began by singing *"You Needed Me"* with all the tear-jerking false emotion she could generate. The woman was terrible! By the second chorus I was giggling and by the third I had to leave the gym before I embarrassed us all. It was in the hall outside the gym where I had my first real conversation with the new principal of Eagle River High School; and he wasn't thrilled at my reaction to the speaker. I had seen the guy in passing a few times during the summer and been introduced, but we had never really spoken. It was one of those situations where any explanation I offered would have sounded contrived and silly because we both knew what I was doing out there.

"Shouldn't you be in the gym, Mr. McLean?"

"You needed me, you needed meeeeeee!"

"Yes, I just stepped out for a minute."

"And I can't believe it's truuuu, I can't believe it's truuuu."

"Well, when she finishes, you probably should go back in."

"I needed you, and you were thererere!!!!!!"

"Sure thing, see you at the staff meeting."

"And I'll never leave, why should I leave, I'd be a fooooool."

"She really is bad, isn't she?"

"God awful."

"Well, maybe she motivates better than she sings."

"I'm thinking 'hat's a pretty good bet, for sure it won't be worse."

"Have a good day, Mr. McLean."

"You too."

"Because you needed MEEEE!!!!!!!"

It didn't occur to me to ask him what he was doing in the hall, but as an administrator, he had options I didn't. As I remember, she wasn't much better at motivating than she was as a songstress. But the year was officially inaugurated all the same.

In the seventies, this B.S. was what generally passed for staff development. The pattern was simple: Motivational speech, then breakout sessions. Invariably, each breakout session would begin with an *icebreaker*. Most icebreakers involved you doing something that was both uncharacteristic and inane. If you have ever been subjected to *Two Truths and a Lie*, you know exactly what I mean. In this particular session, we broke into small groups and each of us took a turn reading from what I believe was one of the lesser-known works of Dr. Seuss. When we concluded, we were each to share with the group a little bit about someone in our lives we considered to be a "Who Buddy." Now, according to Seuss, a "Who Buddy" is someone who is important to you and has been a powerful shaping force in your life. Many of the folks in my small group described former teachers, which, I believe, was the intent of the exercise and would thus allow all of us to walk away validated in our decision to become educators and professional "Who Buddies"! When my turn to speak came, I managed to choke out something about Coach Bud Grant of the Minnesota Vikings as my "Who Buddy." This really per-turbed the second-grade teacher who was leading our little group. She was convinced I was not giving this exercise the proper *gravitas*. I assured her it was never my intent to marginalize Dr. Seuss, and Mr. Grant was in fact a powerful role model and shaping force in my life. She didn't buy it, and her condescending reminder, "We are here for a reason" became a personal challenge. Being young and stupid, I decided this was a wonderful opportunity to push a few buttons. By the time it was my turn to describe another "Who Buddy," I had composed a short *Suessical* verse

> *I hope all you teachers don't think me a fool,*
> *but I really believe that Bud Grant is so cool.*
> *You may think this silly, but try not to show it,*
> *for he's my Who Buddy and you may as well know it.*
> *Oh, I could have picked Halas, or I could have picked Bear,*
> *or Landry in Dallas, and why should you care?*
> *Well gone are the days when the Vikes were so cruddy,*
> *Bud Grant is the reason: so he's my Who Buddy.*

That day I discovered, in certain situations, the world of education broke rather cleanly between elementary and secondary teachers. I honestly believe the lady in charge of our group ranked my little take-off on *McElligot's Pool* as akin to admitting that in my spare time I enjoyed strangling puppies or urinating on sacred objects. If there had been someone there who gave a tinker's damn, I believe she would have run right up and "telled" on me. My high-school cronies loved it, but our elementary colleagues sat silently. I hoped they would feel free to laugh once they were out of earshot of the second grade Seuss Nazi, but elementary teachers might have a different sense of humor, so maybe not.

These days of "workshops" were a farce and normally, every teacher in the room felt slightly demeaned for having participated. Even giddy first year teachers probably walked out of their initial workshop session feeling compromised and less idealistic than when they entered. That day I resolved that should I ever stay in teaching long enough to get tenure, I was going to take a pass on anything which required me to wear a name tag or discuss Whos, Sneetches, Grinches, or variously colored fish. However, Cats in Hats and Lorax would still be in play.

Over the summer there had been some changes at Eagle River. As I mentioned, we got a new principal, and he brought with him a guy who was assigned to be vice-principal and teach a couple of sections of speech. I could now lose all pretensions of being the building badass. By this point, the shoe no longer fit anyway. This gentleman was one of the biggest nuts ever to grace an administrative office; I liked him right off. By October, we were doing duets of tunes from West Side Story in the halls, these were complete with finger snaps and shoulder shrugs. Not much dignity in that; but the kids liked it. There was very little the man could take seriously.

I seldom resorted to the office to enforce my classroom discipline, but once I thought I would take advantage of the additional administrator by bringing one of my little miscreants to him for reprimand. In a very obvious state of agitation, I escorted the young man into the Vice Principal's office and began to relay a litany of the boy's countless sins. Halfway through my diatribe, the V.P. looked me squarely in the face and told me that "under no circumstances would he have sex with me that night." However, he was "open to the possibility of getting a Dairy Queen after school." Stunned would be too mild a description of my reaction. Then the laughter began. *All* three of us became nearly immobilized with gales of it. Situation defused, he prescribed an appropriate penance, gave a brief absolution, and all involved giggled the rest of the day. In Eagle River, you could get away with the occasional amazingly stupid statement.

One of our Social Studies teachers left for another district over the summer, so his classes were to be absorbed by the rest of us in the department. I was assigned the Senior Social classes. This was more or less in addition to my economics and history sections. It would mean prepping for another subject, but for each class I received an additional $300. With my step on the salary schedule, this raised my basic compensation for teaching and coaching to over eleven thousand dollars a year. In the mid-seventies, this was a decent salary for a single guy. I never had so much income. Regrettably, my fiancé was unimpressed with my new-found affluence because I was also working longer hours and had little time to contribute to the endless minutia required if a couple was to stage a socially acceptable wedding celebration. This made for a long, cold winter.

Senior Social proved to be a challenge. It was a general class and required for graduation. The idea of the class was valid and worthwhile: Have the kids examine a menu of social problems and explore possible policy solutions. Done correctly, the class would raise social awareness and help the kids understand there was a larger world outside of Eagle River. Done incorrectly, and the class was a crashing bore that related not one iota to the lives and futures of my students. Regrettably, my first go at the class was somewhat less correct than it should have been. In my own defense, the post-Vietnam, post-Watergate period was not the best time to teach a class on public policy. Cynicism was as common as air. Even the least ingenious student knew the social revolutions and revolutionaries of the sixties had changed nothing. The U.S. government and its leaders had failed on many fronts. Vietnam was a colossal and divisive mistake; political corruption continued; poverty persisted; racism remained virulent; the communists appeared to be winning; and the planet remained overpopulated and under-cared for. It seemed the best technologies we could develop were usually bent towards the development of newer and more deadly bombs or a really effective antiperspirant. It was one of the few times in American history when ignorance truly was bliss. For if the kids in my class knew and really understood the news of the day, they could have been immobilized with pessimism. It was a good time to be a nihilist and a shallow thinker. This perhaps explains disco, and the Reagan majority in 1980.

However, there was a silliness in those Senior Social classes which was lacking in many of my other sections. There were reasons for this. These kids were only a few months separated from the 'real' world, and many weren't really comfortable with that. Senior year is scary when a kid doesn't know what comes next. Many of them would be leaving town for college or work opportunities. A few had no clue as to what the next year might bring. I understood this, they were little different than I was as a senior.

About the second week of class, I walked into the room to find one of my seniors lying on the floor under his desk. When I asked him if he was OK, he assured me he was, and said he was only giving his desk its yearly check-up. He also decided as long as he had it up on the hoist, he figured he'd change the oil. I laughed, and it creeped me out some when he didn't laugh back. In the same class, I had two young men confide to me that the night before they had a contest to see which of them would swallow the greatest number of .22 caliber rifle shells, and did I think this would cause them any real harm. It seemed the "winner" of the contest had three or four live rounds somewhere in his digestive tract. The loser knew for a certainty he had only consumed two. I told them to go directly to the nurse and, as they headed out the door, suggested they be careful not to bend over and shoot any of their classmates! The nurse found less humor in the situation and had them on their way to the nearest emergency room within the hour. Both were unharmed, but shortly the young men were celebrities of a sort, and it was unfortunately the type of celebrity which could follow you negatively your entire life. For the balance of the year, that singularly stupid act became the comparative whenever any member of the class did something really bone-headed. Sort of like "Ya, that was really stupid, but not nearly as dumb as….." Both youngsters involved got new and unrepeatable nicknames and whenever they were jostled in the hall someone would flee in mock terror lest they might blow up.

That year, two of my senior boys played the ultimate country practical joke on me and convinced me "cow tipping" was an entertaining way to spend an evening. These guys were my football captains. Later, they were the ushers at my wedding! Why would I not believe them? Of course, they never showed up at the designated field at the appointed time. After half an hour or so, I figured this out, and felt like a dumb shit for at least a month. Thank God, I didn't accept any invitations to go snipe hunting. In spite of it all, these kids had a wonderful way of ingratiating themselves to me. They were becoming special. I began to think of them as **My** kids. The majority worked hard and appreciated small things. They were often naïve, which I came to think of as a virtue. Because I was a teacher and coach, they trusted me implicitly. In return, I tried to be entirely worthy of their trust. Sometimes I failed, and those failings are the only real regret I still carry from my Eagle River years. The entire time I taught there, I never completely mastered my temper. But much of it was because I wanted so much for my students. I wanted them to be as good as I thought they could become. Looking back, I realize my students were not perfect. They lied to me at times, they cheated, and they often carried the same negative social baggage which weighed down their urban counterparts. They threw spitballs, they farted in class, they smoked dope, and they were often cruel to each other. But they were usually also in the process of becoming good, solid, level-headed people. On balance, Eagle River grew decent, stable kids.

During my second year, grading student work began to consume most of my spare time. To take on the extra classes, I had to give up my prep time for the year. Even with the energy of youth on my side, it was sometimes difficult to keep up with the volume of correcting required to give the kids meaningful, and timely feedback. The money from the extra classes was nice, but the price exacted was higher than I anticipated. I doubt that I would have taken on the additional load had I known how difficult it would be to keep up. A lot of this was of my own doing.

Even as a high-school student, I had been disdainful of teachers who kept files full of old assignments and relied on multiple choice or scantron testing. Now I was able to see the other side of it.

Such testing was quick and easy; why spend endless hours at night correcting poorly written essays or short answer tests? Teachers who rely on a pedagogy of routine and automation have decided what they gain in leisure time is more important than what they lose in efficacy. Based on my experience as a student and a teacher, they also lose the respect of their students and become bad clichés and poor caricatures of their profession. In Eagle River, I knew teachers who bragged about never taking anything home with them. Some even pretended by doing so they were making a principled stand against the exploitative policies of the local school board and administration. I learned there is even a phrase for this questionable noblesse oblige; it's called "work-to-rule," a job action also known as an Italian strike, which offers a clue to its roots. These faculty lounge minimalists gave some credibility to the old saying, "Those who can't do, teach." The expression made me wretch, but by my second year I knew where it came from and why it was believed.

The truth was, I discovered that teaching could be a very well-paid part-time job if you chose to make it that. Eight hours a day, nine months a year, holidays off. On every faculty there are several people who will do the minimum required under the contract and no more. If they are given ten sick days, they will call in sick ten times. If they have a couple of personal days, they will use them. They will not willingly take on extra assignments. These people never seem to improve or change. They learn nothing new about their craft; because they have had the *same year of experience over and over again*. Neither are they happy in their work. Kids don't remember these people as bad teachers, they simply don't remember them at all, and the worst thing a student can ever say about a teacher is to say nothing at all.

I discovered in teaching getting lazy is such an easy pit to fall into. Every textbook sold comes with enough support material and packaged lessons to vaccinate entire departments for years against possible outbreaks of creativity. Even the dimmest bulb with a teaching degree knows worksheets are often busy work, and that any kind of authentic assessment requires the student to do a considerable amount of writing. This is true in Social Studies, even more so in English. Correcting this student writing demands that the teachers do a lot of homework. Regrettably, the faculty minimalists are all too correct in one regard: good teacher, bad teacher, or indifferent teacher, the check always stays the same and creativity is often a time-consuming option. It is so damned easy to be boring. Of course, this is not always the case, and many teachers work an amazing number of hours trying to keep their presentations fresh and relevant. I was privileged to work with some truly outstanding teachers. Their kids profited from their association with them, and they were true exemplars of what was once called Republican Citizenship.

In graduate school, I was told there are perhaps three general types of teachers, but you can opt to be only two of these types. The other type you cannot choose. It is almost as if there are unique individuals who don't choose to be teachers—instead teaching chooses them. I believe some people truly are born instructors. Their skill set matches the professional and affective characteristics needed to deliver comprehensive and meaningful lessons. They seldom have discipline issues. Kids like them. Parents try to get their kids placed in these instructors' classes. Such teachers are rare, and if a student has two of these instructors during their academic career, they are lucky. These teachers love their craft, they love their kids, and they love the entire classroom dynamic.

Throughout this narrative, I have not used any real names or place names. The two individuals I now mention are very real. Sister Perpetua was a Presentation nun that taught at Saint Stephen's Catholic School in Anoka, Minnesota. Her patience, kindness, and gentleness made school a joy for me. She understood middle schoolers more completely than any other teacher I have ever been associated with. The lady also had some steel. There was a construction project going on in our schoolyard once, and the noise the workmen were causing made instruction and learning difficult. Once, Sister stopped a math lesson right in the middle and stormed out the door to confront the workers. I'm sure there was no cussing, but the finger wagging and body language was impressive. From that moment on, we were all pretty much in awe of her. She was the first teacher I had who actually convinced me that I was a competent student. It is a very powerful thing when a teacher tells you that you are smart and makes you believe it. She hugged me once after a playground scuffle, I almost cried. It was she who made me first see teaching as a possible career.

The other teacher I will cite is Lyle Bradley, one of my biology teachers. A former fighter pilot in the Korean War, Mr. Bradley could control a class with a raised eyebrow. I remember his room as always reeking of dead things, and you could begin to smell Mr. Bradley's class about three doors down. The man kept a colony of flesh-eating beetles! He also kept a fair number of critters in cages throughout the room. His walls were covered with curiosities, and there was at least one potential lesson on every table.

It was fall and one of our assignments was to assemble an insect collection. I had been really diligent and had put together a pretty impressive one. On the night before it was to be graded, one of his critters escaped from its cage. I don't remember what it was, but it spent the night feasting on my collection. All that was left was a scattering of unidentifiable insect parts pinned to a Styrofoam board. The next day, Mr. Bradley gave me the bad news and told me that he hadn't seen my collection and evaluation would be impossible. He asked me how good I thought it was. I told him honestly that it was really complete, and I was proud of it. I even had a giant water beetle! He suggested I should probably give myself an A then. This kind of floored me! I never imagined any teacher would trust me so far as to grade myself. He went on to explain that I was a good student and had never to his knowledge lied to him. Besides, the critter must have thought my collection outstanding because it was the only one that got eaten! That day, Mr. Bradley taught me a great lesson, one which I subsequently carried with me into my own classroom. As a teacher, your default setting should always be to believe and trust students. At times, dogs do actually eat homework. Parents get sick and need your student to watch younger siblings. Family tragedies do happen. Brothers overdose and relatives die. Any one of a million things can become more important than a five-paragraph essay about what I did on my summer vacation. Your students have lives apart from school, and many are dealing with more than you will ever know: Honor that. In my career, I have been lied to. I probably had more of my students' grandparents die than most teachers. But I never questioned if believing kids was the right thing to do. Some students may laugh at you behind your back for your naïveté. Some of those will later apologize to you, or at least regret their dishonesty and learn from the episode. Mr. Bradley taught me that.

I think few have ever loved teaching and their academic discipline as much as he. He took his students on dinosaur digs in the Dakotas and lost few opportunities to explore the natural world around the high school. We visited museums. We went digging in bogs to try and locate bison bones. His curiosity was endless, his intellect unquestioned, his dedication unfailing. If I had a role model as a teacher, it was Mr. Bradley. I really wish that I had expressed my appreciation to these two remarkable teachers. I regret that in both cases it's too late.

Unfortunately, these types of teachers are becoming increasingly rare. In my experience the majority of them are women, and as more and more professional opportunities present themselves, these remarkable ladies are opting out of education. I think their absence is the single biggest reason schools are becoming less effective. I do not pretend this is my own assessment, but it is what I've come to believe.

A second type of teacher is truly a professional educator, and if their name appears on your child's schedule, you as a parent should be thrilled. They are mentors and role models. To them, teaching is a verb. They stay absolutely current with best practices, they give timely feedback, create authentic assessments, and constantly try to improve their personal scholarship. They read extensively to better master their academic discipline. They take classes. Their standards are high, but they create ways for kids to meet them. These teachers are the backbone of every successful school. You can choose to be this teacher; you can also choose not to be. During your career you will be presented with a thousand opportunities to be mediocre and the choices you make in this regard will ultimately define you. Regrettably, if you strive to become the best teacher you are capable of being, you will not be paid one cent more than your position on the salary schedule dictates. The administration will reward your diligence by giving you the most challenging students, and you will serve on every make-work committee that comes down the pike. You will write hundreds of letters of recommendation, sometimes because you're the only teacher who will. But, you will also sign a thousand yearbooks and receive more invitations to graduation open houses than you can possibly attend. Your kids will come back to visit you years after they have graduated. Many will thank you. None will forget you. You will never regret your vocation. You will be totally deserving of your title. Truly, you will be a teacher.

The third type of "teacher" deserves little notice and requires less explanation. We have all had dozens of them. They spend their entire careers trying to minimize their workload. They bitch a lot. Occasionally, they manage to generate a creative lesson plan, but it is clearly the exception, not the rule. Any break in their routine is anathema. Their text is their bible, and working overtime is the bane of their existence. They prefer order to spontaneity, and usually their desks are immaculate. They will retire at the first opportunity, and in doing so they will perform the greatest service they have ever rendered to public education. These people will not be remembered, nor missed.

It was during my second year that I found out how it feels when one of your favorite kids dies. Jack was an amazing student. Even in middle school, his potential was always on display. I considered it one of the highlights of my career that he once asked me to write a letter of recommendation for him to a well-regarded Minnesota private college. Any member of the faculty would have happily done so, and I was flattered he asked me. Often, our schools and teachers are criticized for the poor performance of our students relative to their peers globally. There's a lot of truth in this. We do not do well on the PISA test. "Programme for International Student Assessment" and many countries' students outperform America's on this standardized achievement test. But in all aspects, Jack was a world-class student. He was a National Merit Scholar before rich parents would routinely pay for enough tutoring and test prep to make the honor nearly meaningless. A class leader, a talented musician, and an accomplished athlete. I deeply regret that I never got to send the letter. On a snowy day, Jack got his coat entangled in a tractor's power take-off. He was working alone. The results were too ghastly to describe. It was an incredibly sad funeral.

A powerful lesson that the community of Eagle River taught me is this; Farming has always been a dangerous occupation, and a good number of farmers carry lifelong scars from run-ins with machinery or gravity. At times during my stay in Eagle River, I shook hands with men who had fingers chopped off or pulled out by corn pickers. Farmers were sometimes crushed when a tractor rolled over. Farmers occasionally suffocate in grain bins or are overcome by silo gas. Cheap food often comes at a very high cost. Eagle River taught me to respect farmers deeply. I also came to respect their kids for the work ethic many learned at home. I will always be thankful some people are willing to bear a disproportionate share of the cost of affordable food for the rest of us.

That year I learned some teachers can be the pettiest people to inhabit the planet. In March, the students in National Honor Society selected me to speak at their annual induction ceremony. I was happy to do so, but it seemed that this was an affront to every more experienced teacher in the building.

Once it was known I would be the speaker, whenever I came into the lounge, conversation pretty much stopped for a bit as gears shifted and throats cleared. It seemed the faculty had established a sort of *de facto* rotation as far as who would speak at induction. The N.H.S. advisor was informally charged with maintaining the integrity of the "selection process" by making sure the faculty member selected was well-placed on the seniority list. I came in under the radar. I was the beneficiary of a write-in campaign, and much to the chagrin of the N.H.S. advisor, I was selected. In a system where much of the salary money and perks are doled out based upon longevity, this was an outrage! As a second-year teacher, it simply wasn't my turn yet. Several senior staff felt they had been unjustly passed over. To them, being asked to speak at *anything* was an honor long in coming. Of course, nothing was said to me directly. Later, I learned one of the faculty "mavens of correctitude" had approached the principal and suggested he might wish to speak to me about my egregious lack of deference. To his credit, he gave the matter all the consideration it was due. At the time, I didn't understand that giving such a speech may have been the only recognition which would ever accrue to some teachers during their entire career; and my speaking may have been viewed as a net subtraction from someone's allotted fifteen minutes of fame.

Were teachers so starved for any form of recognition, this was actually an issue? Was mine such a demoralized profession, teachers were willing to squabble over the most minor patch of sunlight? If I stayed in the classroom, would I become them? For the hundredth time the question consumed me, and for the first time I needed to confront it directly. There were so many negatives to staying in education. On top of the poor salary, all of us were expected to do so much that was demeaning and seemingly designed to be so. Once during my second year, I was assigned to bathroom duty. We had a few kids smoking in the john, so the obvious solution was to station a teacher in there during passing time. For an entire quarter, I stood there and watched kids pee. I have seldom felt more ridiculous, and at least a little like a pervert!

I had come to terms finally with the reality that there was no real hope the money issue would ever be resolved. If I continued in the classroom, I would always live with the public's expectation that job satisfaction was an adequate replacement for financial security. My two years were nearly up. The promises and commitments I had made to myself the first day I arrived in Eagle River all came with an expiration date. The promise I made to my fiancé was likewise dated. If I intended to resign, it needed to be done quickly. I owed my employer that much. I was also sure any decision to continue in education would end my engagement. My fiancé had no intention of living in a small town on a smaller income. For this, she really could not be faulted. Many teachers come from a blue-collar background. Becoming a teacher is the first rung on the professional ladder. To be a teacher was really rather a lofty goal. If you came from more favored circumstances, aspiring to teach was really rather *déclassé*. Without explaining the economic gulf between us, I can simply say my fiancé considered teaching to be definitely *déclassé*. For a year and a half, I had agreed with her, but during my second year I gradually came to the realization that teaching had become a huge part of my life, of me. I also came to believe I was good at it, maybe better than anything else I had done in my life. For years, I had wondered what I might do to make both a living and a difference. I was not a religious person, but it seemed this was the thing which God had given me. I would not cure cancer, nor would I write the great American epic poem, but I could teach. I had always thought any decision I came to would be more difficult, more wrenching, more like the stuff of bad movies. By spring, I was totally at peace with my decision. Everything considered, I think I gave a hell of a speech at the N.H.S. ceremony.

Later that night, I told my fiancée I was going to teach in the upcoming year. I told her there was really no other choice I could make. I apologized to her for not being honest with her before this, but it was only tonight I had finally resolved the last doubt. I lied; I told her it would only be for one more year. I said I didn't want to lose her. I said we would really be OK and I could work summers and coach another sport. There were a couple of things that I really wanted to try in the classroom yet, and a phys-ed teacher I liked and respected had agreed to be a co-head football coach with me that fall, should I choose to take the job. She railed at me some, she told me that I was being stupid and selfish. I will always remember the sneer she had on her face when she suggested that perhaps if I stayed in education, we could afford to have our reception in the dance hall just down the road. She said that I was not aiming high enough and I would come to regret opportunities lost. Finally, there was silence and resignation. She said that my pronouncement really didn't surprise her, then she pretty much said goodbye. There were no tears, there was no ugly scene complete with a ring being ripped off and slammed on the table.

She was right, of course. There was no argument I could have offered that would have changed anything. I was to see her occasionally over the summer. She called me whenever memories became too oppressive and she needed to be held. Once, she asked me to be her escort at a girlfriend's wedding. I really wish I had begged off. It was a totally over the top affair. Six bridesmaids, champagne, prime rib dinner. The obvious opulence was maybe a poorly concealed backhand slap, perhaps not. We left the reception early; I haven't seen her since. In the fall, I began the course work for an advanced degree in education. I found out later she ultimately married some guy who was hooked up with a major retailer. Executive type, well-paid. I'm told she has three kids and a nice home. I hope so, there is no happiness she doesn't deserve, truly one of the outstanding people who I've ever met.

My smaller dreams

I never really lied to you.
The things you still want,
I once wanted too.

Now we have our degrees,
and the world should unfold.
Suburban streets, all paved in gold.

But, could we maybe wait another year?
Just one more time, September to June?
You see, I think I'm really needed here.

But if not, if never, I'll understand.
Living inside my smaller dreams,
wasn't really what you'd planned.

XI

More than a Diploma

I was to spend two more years teaching in Eagle River. During that time, I coached two really awful football teams, got tenure, and became a girl's track coach. I buried myself in my work and resolved that I would probably be single forever. It was a bad time for me. I had never really accepted that depression was anything but a lack of discipline and focus. But looking back, I now understand that I was probably depressed. I was dwelling too often on what might have been and paths I could have taken. It seemed that I was truly alive only when I was at school. Teaching could still completely engage my feeble mind, and during my hours in class I was OK. Thank God, I had my job, because during these years, I was privileged to teach and coach some of the neatest kids in the world. As planned, I began and completed a graduate degree in education. For several reasons my memories of those two years are less precise than those of my first two. It's almost as if once I decided teaching would shape the arc of my life, the individual years became less important and discreet. The amount of scotch I was drinking also probably played a role. Thankfully, that's in the past now. What remains are memories of children who in my mind will forever be yearbook young.

I remember Ann, who I first met as a slender eighth grader who ran track. She was the best and most endearing parts of all adolescence. At every track meet, she asked me to station myself at an appropriate point on the track's infield. When she reached that point, I was to yell, "Kick it down and run fast." Ann then sprinted with all her might, passing as many runners as possible, occasionally winning the race. On the occasions she didn't win, it was probably because of my incorrect positioning. When she became a freshman, I had her as a student in American History. Such a bright child! She never stopped smiling and seldom stopped talking. Once, I became exasperated with her chattering to the point I asked her, "Can't you please shut-up?" The look that came to her eyes was much akin to a puppy which has just been whacked too hard on the nose for simply doing the things puppies naturally do. She was quiet the rest of the period, and I hated the silence.

I remember Thomas. By the age of sixteen, he had become the personification of many of the characteristics, both good and bad, which made the students of Eagle River unique. He was a big strong kid. He never participated in sports, but I tried to talk him into football on more than one occasion. I think he belonged to the Future Farmers of America, but that was about the extent of his extracurricular involvement. Tom would give anyone the shirt off his back and have the good grace never to remind you of the debt owed. He was an indifferent student. I attribute this to the fact he couldn't read. All of his teachers knew it, many wanted to help, but none knew how.

In the era before Special Education and intensive remediation programs, kids like Tom were largely ignored. If a student was severely disabled there was usually some programming available, but it was usually offered in small cramped rooms well away from the rest of the student body. These rooms were little more than glorified janitors' closets. The children packed into these spaces were spoken of in hushed tones, and the people who taught them existed apart from the rest of the faculty. The students thus assigned were really only the visible tip of a very large and ugly educational iceberg and, as is the case with all icebergs, 90% of the problem existed below the waterline and hidden from view. Tom was one of these invisible students.

With a month left in his senior year, Tom stayed after class and asked if there was something he could do to accumulate enough points to pass. He told me flat out anything requiring additional reading or writing wasn't possible. There was no "please pity me" in his voice, he didn't whine about the workload, and he didn't want me to slap him on the back and let him slide through. Tom was simply asking me if there was something he could do with his hands; something he could make, which would earn him a passing grade. I told him I had decided months ago if the only thing which kept him from getting a diploma was passing my class, I wasn't going to be the one who wrecked his mother's plans for a graduation open house. He tried hard the rest of the year. As I remember, he did well enough to pass anyway. His open house was outstanding.

Tom's class was my last one on the last day of school that year. In the final seconds of class, a student with whom I occasionally had a few discipline issues decided to try and get the class to count down the final seconds until they were free of "this goddamn prison." He began his countdown at 20 seconds. At 18 seconds, Tom stood up, pointed a thick finger at the young man and said, "Will you shut the hell up?!! Maybe you think McLean can't do nothing to you now, but you know I can. You count anymore, and *I'm* gonna get down on you!" The young man just about crapped! We finished the year laughing. Later I found out Tom settled down to live in Eagle River and was raising a large family there. He became a skilled electrician and member of several civic organizations. He was a volunteer fireman and wanted to become a paramedic. One winter day, he was involved in a car accident. He insisted medical attention be given first to an injured woman in the other vehicle. By the time the medics got to him, it was too late. He died of internal injuries on his way to the hospital. Tom couldn't read, but his short life carried as much meaning as any student I have ever taught. I learned so much from him. His life was a lesson in sacrifice, dignity, and integrity. The world has missed deeply the gifts his generous spirit may have given us.

Kevin was a problem child. Rumor had it that as an elementary student, he had the habit of running out of the building and hiding in the corn field which bordered the school. More than once, the principal spent a good part of his day and most of his patience chasing Kevin between rows of seven-foot corn stalks. When he cornered him, the real battle began. Against a malevolent elementary school kid, any adult handicapped by an appropriate level of mental hygiene has few defenses, and human bites are filthy things. The elusive little gremlin once managed to avoid capture for two hours and was finally corralled only with the help of the local police. By Kevin's fourth year in the building, the principal in question had resigned his position and bought a turkey farm in Central Minnesota.

When Kevin reached high school, little had changed, but now he hid in book closets and jumped out at people. After startling the daylights out of someone, he would treat us all to gales of nearly hebephrenic laughter. I was Kevin's history teacher. At this point in my career, coffee was a huge part of my day, and by our fifth period I had usually swilled a gallon of the stuff. Between caffeine and fatigue, I was Kevin's ready-made victim. On the third day of class, he nailed me with the jump-out-of-the-closet shtick. My reaction was volcanic! Stuff flew, kids howled, and Kevin carried on like a demented hyena for five minutes. From that day on, whenever Kevin wasn't in his assigned seat, I automatically placed a chair in front of the book closet door in such a way it was effectively locked. I trapped him once, and to his credit, he laughed equally hard when the joke was on him. I left him there for the class period. Shortly after that Kevin was arrested for breaking into a car wash. It was his third offense, and he was tried as an adult. Many times I have wondered if while in prison he got the help he so desperately needed; probably not.

Linda owned four cotton print dresses. These dresses were simply and modestly styled and sewn by hand. They all went from collar bone to mid-calf. Even today, I can clearly remember the color and pattern of each. When she was in my class, I could have told you what day of the week it was by which of these she chose to wear. This wasn't unique in Eagle River, as many children make fashion choices solely based upon their mother's laundry schedule. In all but the worst weather, Linda wore simple pink cloth shoes and white anklets. Nothing in her manner of dress was superfluous, and I very much doubt she owned even a single piece of jewelry. I know she never used make-up. Linda wore her brown hair long and usually in a ponytail drawn tightly. Her black framed glasses were not quite the cat's eye models common in the fifties, but they were years out of style. When she was reading, which was usually, she held the book a scant few inches from her nose, so I came to believe her prescription and lenses were similarly dated. Linda's middle name was Constance and if ever a person wore their name well it was Linda, for she was constantly cheerful, constantly curious, and constantly studying. The fact she was also constantly ignored by her more fashion-conscious classmates was also painfully obvious, so she was constantly alone. I think her apartness endeared her to many of her teachers, it made her special and singular. We all regarded her as a pearl of great price. In all respects, she was peerless, and easily the brightest child in her class.

Her family was one of the few in town which belonged to the Evangelical Church, and along with other members of the congregation, they formed their own subculture within the community's larger Catholic mainstream. Few in this group were her age. Linda's religious beliefs precluded things like dancing and card playing, so two of the town's main social outlets were forbidden to her. When she had time, she read a great deal of good and classic literature. I know that she sewed and did needlepoint. She also baked. At Christmas time she gave each of her teachers a box of the most amazing cookies wrapped with a bit of newspaper and a red ribbon made into a perfect bow.

I don't have any idea what her parents considered Linda's best future to be. I was her teacher for three separate classes in high school, and not once did they come to a conference. This wasn't at all unusual. Parents of many high achieving kids are content as long as the As keep coming, and with Linda, the As were another constant. Several times during her senior year, I asked her about plans for the upcoming fall, and never did I get an answer which was direct enough to convince me any plans existed. By April of that year, I stopped asking because the question made her uncomfortable and application deadlines had passed months before.

It was nearly prom time in Eagle River, and the level of excitement in the building was ratcheted up almost exponentially. In a small town, prom can be a huge deal, and one of the few occasions when excess is tolerated. The school would be decorated with miles of paper streamers in the school colors and hundreds of flowers, both real and artificial. There would be a Grand March attended by much of the town, and the couples would enter the gym through an arch made ornate by the best efforts of the Junior class. Kids without escorts went anyway and paired up long enough to be announced and make their entrance. Many a grandmother drew incorrect conclusions about these random couplings and smiled all the way home.

It was rumored some of the more debonair gentlemen in the senior class were even considering the unheard-of extravagance of renting a limo and escorting their *ladies fair* to a distant metropolis for a meal at a truly pricey restaurant. I can't remember if anything ever came of it, but in Eagle River, a guy could elevate his social standing by merely discussing such extravagance as a real possibility.

Perhaps a week before the dance, I was working late in my room. Track practice was long over, but as it was now early May, the light from my single outside window was still sufficient for my purposes and my classroom lights were off. My room was at the end of the hall on the second floor of the building. At the opposite end of the same hall, there were two large windows. Against these, a padded bench had been built. It was a perfect spot to gossip or sit in the sun and study. This little lounge was quickly appropriated by the seniors, and being allowed to sit there was an honor that came to you only when you reached that elevated status.

When I finished for the evening and was leaving my room, I noticed a solitary figure sitting on the senior bench. I knew immediately it was Linda. She was staring into the gathering dusk, and my footfalls on the linoleum tile floor did not alert her to my presence until I had covered half the length of the hall. She turned and smiled at me, but her eyes carried neither joy nor greeting. She was embarrassed I had come upon her and she quickly gathered her books to leave. Only my request that she stay kept her from being two flights of stairs away by the time I reached her. I asked how things were and if there was something I could help her with. That she started to talk to me at all was a surprise, because Linda usually spent few words on topics unrelated to school. Neither was I a person a kid would seek out for serious conversation or advice. I was glib, and I was funny, but there was little depth to me, and I was years away from any pretensions of wisdom. She talked to me only because I was there and willing to listen. She said she really didn't want to graduate. For her, next year was pretty empty. Her parents had tried to find tuition so she could attend a small Midwestern Bible college, but that wasn't going to happen this fall. Such colleges were Linda's only real option. State schools were never considered due to her family's religious orientation; and besides, those schools had "questionable" reputations. So next year she would help around home. Perhaps she might find a job doing sewing or cleaning, and in one of the years following she could go on to school. She understood the reasons for this, there was no bitterness in her. She also expressed to me, she knew ultimately she would go to college, a way would be found; she was determined to go on to school.

Linda said the reason she came to school tonight was not to consider her future, but to maybe try and absorb as much of the high school as she could. That bench and her classes were the only parts of being a senior she had ever really experienced. When she graduated, she would carry with her none of the normal trappings of high school. She had no letter jacket, no class ring, no senior picture, and few friends she would cry with on commencement night. I think that she had signed a few yearbooks, but I'm guessing, did not own one herself. She said that in her four years with us, she had never been to a high-school athletic event or dance. I doubt that she would even know how to dress for a football game, much less a dance. She belonged to no clubs. She told me now there would never be another opportunity for her to do any of the usual high-school activities. She would never go to a prom, and while understanding why she couldn't go, it didn't lessen the pain. "If someone had only just asked me, Mr. McLean, I couldn't have ever gone, but even considering it for a week would have been nice; it would have been a memory." Her tone was so incredibly mature, winsome almost. It was as if she was discussing a long-ago heartache now mostly healed and largely forgotten.

For the first time in three years of teaching I hugged a student, and then for the only time in my life, I asked a fantastic young woman if she would do me the honor of being my escort at prom. She completely understood the nature of the invitation, but understanding did not stop her from blushing beautifully as she gracefully declined. She was smiling as she turned to go. That was the last real conversation I had with Linda. Two years later, she was able to go away to college. I would be amazed if today she were not a success in every sense of the word.

Every kid should be able to walk away from high school with something more than a diploma. There should be friends, memories, and enough joy to soften the pain. Because there will be pain. Should Linda ever read this, I would like her to know that on a May evening a long time ago, her Senior Social teacher was trying to tell her exactly how special she was. I wanted her to know, every guy who did not ask her to prom lost a wonderful opportunity to spend some time with an extraordinary person, and in forty-plus years of teaching I have never had a student as kind or possessing a more dignified spirit.

When I think of Linda now, it is almost as a modern version of Hester Prynne. She personified dignity through adversity, and few kids in any high school could wear their personal scarlet letters as well as Linda did. In time I learned that every student carried their own individual marks of distinction. Some were good and positive, some not. For the lucky ones it was intelligence or athleticism or perhaps an offbeat sense of humor. Others were quiet or beautiful. A few of the less lucky kids were pariahs who wore their uniqueness like an open wound; or perhaps the stain of a leper. Because high school is a dynamic period in a kid's life, they are always in the process of becoming something more or something different. High school is a time when kids need to individuate, but still crave the acceptance of the group. Because of this, the halls are always full of joy, pain, and doubt. Smiles and tears are both transitory and always very close to the surface. There are children who laugh too loud and sad, sad children who seem to lurch from crisis to crisis. There is not a high-school kid in America who is exempt from sometimes hurting. At the end of the day, the homecoming queen and the captain of the football team were still just insecure children.

It amazes me, but most kids will grow in spite of it all. They are accepted as they eventually find their clique and their level. These kids usually remember their school days with fondness and a nostalgic glow. Some others are not so lucky, and for some students even the best high schools are unspeakably cruel places. Many students will suffer through four years of purgatory or anomie. Some kids at Eagle River were never wanted at lunch tables. They were jostled in the halls, but not in the good-natured way of adolescents. They were the butt of jokes, or worse yet, they were ignored completely. If group work was assigned in class, no one clambered to include them. When these kids were finally *assigned* to a group, they sat on the margin and wrote notes to mythical friends. They would sometimes doodle or draw; they would fix their eyes on their desk. More than anything else, they would hope to God the other kids persisted in their feeble and half-hearted attempts to include them in the task at hand. By senior high, rules of the game require marginal kids to resist social interaction, especially with their "betters," that they be dragged against their will to the place they really want to be. With their silence, they will then express their gratitude for temporary and grudging acceptance. If one of these children refuses to be obsequious, they are usually labeled as behavior problems. When I was in high school, I was customarily an asshole to these kids. I was also an asshole to kids who were mature enough to be decent to these kids. Sometimes watching the students in your classroom can be a very ugly and painful reflection of your own past. It can also be a second chance.

There's a word for people like us.
Our betters, call us pit dwellers.
You know, the kids without cell phones.
Not to our faces ... we're tough.
But in other places,
like bathroom stalls, or in the halls;
scratched on the front of our lockers.

Dumb asses! Going to all that trouble,
just to tell us what we already know,
and see, every time we look down
at our old generic tennis shoes.
We're the kids who take the bus.
No cars for us, no starter jackets.
Just worn-out jeans, before they became cool.

XII

Shattered Covenant

As I mentioned, in my third year at Eagle River, I began a graduate program in education. I did it for reasons both practical and professional. If, as it now appeared, teaching was to be my career, common sense dictated I try to advance on the salary schedule as fast and as far as possible. Secondly, I truly wanted to improve as a teacher, and almost daily it was made obvious to me, in the classroom Mr. McLean was still pretty inept. Even a partial listing of mistakes I made and repeated could keep a faculty lounge in stitches for a week's worth of lunch periods. Perhaps and more importantly, by the middle of my third year, I didn't feel I was making a difference for a lot of my students. It's true that an unexamined life is not worth living. However, it's also true that a life too often examined can be a cause for melancholy and kind of a pain in the ass. Oftentimes, at the end of a day, I found myself alone in my small sparsely furnished apartment reflecting upon what I had accomplished. At times there was satisfaction. Occasionally, I thought the day was well spent. However, so many days I had nothing but question marks. I was doing an insane amount of work, but outcomes were never equal to inputs. I stopped celebrating what I hoped were my successes and dwelled on what I was sure were my failures. There were always the kids I didn't seem to reach. To them, my classes and I were a cipher, something to endure and move on. I've always felt any student placed in my keeping had an unquestioned right to expect I had something worthwhile to offer them; and lately, if I were being honest with myself, I had to admit that often I didn't.

Regrettably, my first two quarters of graduate work did very little to improve my teaching or my outlook. Nor did they lighten the crushing load of ignorance I carried. The classes I took were largely taught by professors who were old enough to have attended seminars led by a mature John Dewey. They wore Liberalism as a badge of academic honor, and had probably voted for F.D.R., all *four* times he ran. To their credit, these gentlemen, "yes they were all men," were steeped in classical learning theory and cared deeply about what they did. Unfortunately, the purity of their intentions and lessons could seldom be translated neatly into my everyday life as a teacher. I have heard students decry the fact that much of what they learn in grad school was ivory tower stuff. In my case, it could have been better described as ruminations from Narnia. It was totally unfair of me, but sometimes I tried to imagine my professors leading a Senior Social class at Eagle River. They would have survived for about fifteen minutes in an honest-to-God high-school situation. They were no doubt very well intended, but unless they were fortunate enough to teach in a Catholic girl's preparatory high school in Iowa, nice old guys with good intentions such as they, would shortly become the preferred prey of the senior class. Consequently, I came to take much of what they gave me with a large grain of salt.

In one instance, this was especially true. One of the instructors in my program was a failed junior-high principal and a living validation of the Peter Principle. If the rumors were true, as a school administrator, he had already risen to his level of incompetence and was shunted out of his district. However, flying in the face of logic, he was rewarded for his ineptitude with a college teaching position. He now held a job which allowed him to instruct uncounted others in the most efficacious and state-of-the-art ways to fuck up an entire generation of prospective teachers. Think of the possibilities. This man could now have acolytes!! He would perhaps become the peak of an educational Ponzi pyramid of incompetence. The only remotely analogous situation I can think of is the nomination and election of Warren G. Harding to the presidency. Typhoid Mary might also offer a useful comparison, but the historical record is less clear in her case. I have no idea how this person was still employed in education. Thankfully his class was as devoid of real content as it was of academic rigor, so it could be easily ignored. Overall, my initial experience with post-graduate education reminded me of Winston Churchill's assessment of Clement Attlee: "There was much less there than meets the eye."

Thankfully, things improved as I progressed through the program, and what I did ultimately take from these graduate classes was a degree of respect for the entire K-12 educational process. I began to view education in a more holistic way. In my daily teaching, I tended to view my students through a very narrow lens. In this I was wrong. I have heard elementary teachers complain about their colleagues at the high-school level being entirely too subject oriented. Amid the graphs and equations, we lose the child. Through my graduate work, I began to discover some truth in that accusation. Every kid is a collection of inputs, attitudes, and expectations. All of these are protean and shifting. Both research and intuition tell us that even the most sophisticated appearing seventeen-year-old is little more than an emotional lava lamp. They all have needs which they daily carry with them to school, and these needs will be addressed in order of personal importance. The academic agenda I present will be a secondary consideration. It is a rare high-school kid who can successfully stow all emotional baggage and immediately concentrate on the task at hand. As I was to learn later, college students are often only a little better. Maslow and his hierarchy hardly needed to be validated by the observations of a shuffle-butted newbie Social Studies teacher, but for me his work was a rare intersection of theory and practical understanding.

The best elementary-school teachers understand this intuitively and they begin their days by establishing a positive climate in the classroom. They move towards the academic only when the affective stuff has been dealt with. First, they build bridges, and then they march their class across them. No bridge: no progress, make camp, fix s'mores. High-school people can learn a lot from this approach.

Regrettably, in high school even if we don't have a bridge, we attempt to ford the stream anyway. In doing so, a few of the poorer swimmers drown. In high school especially, all failures are not owned by the teacher, but it is a rare failure in which the teacher is not at least partly complicit.

Please do not interpret the previous statement as an indication that my graduate studies were helping me to appreciate the value of Who Buddy workshops and other such warm and fuzzy tripe. I remained convinced one needn't become childish to be child centered, but in any classroom a bit of empathy goes a long way and bridges do need to be built. Teaching is a human activity, and to learn is a human imperative. Trust is essential to learning, and it does not spring from indifference or antagonism. Trust grows from positive interactions, fairness, and consistency. Plus, every once in a while, no matter how good things are going, you still need to occasionally stop, build a fire, and make s'mores. Eagle River taught me nothing is more important than respect and trust, but empathy is essential to building both. I have never met a good teacher who did not display it on a nearly daily basis.

I once had a student get so mad at me, he kind of shouted the only difference between me and a five-gallon pail of cow shit was the pail. I knew the boy's parents and if I called them about the incident, the consequences might have been brutal. He immediately recoiled in horror from what he had just said, and an apology followed almost before an exclamation point was placed on the curse. He looked terrified by what had just fallen out of his mouth. I told him his apology was accepted, but as a gentle reminder, perhaps he should come up with 25 good reasons a young man would be well advised to not describe his teacher as five gallons of cow shit. He agreed, and the matter was dropped. I read his reasons out loud in class the next day. It was freaking hilarious!! He had trusted me not to escalate, involve the office, or call home. I trusted the episode would not be repeated and he was sincere in his apology. Neither of us was compromised by the incident. Nor did the rest of the class begin acting on the assumption that calling me five gallons of cow manure would meet with only minor consequences. That whole incident was a small victory for each of us.

There were other parts of grad school I really appreciated. One blessing was you were no longer expected to do mythical lesson plans *ad nauseam*. Your instructors assumed in this regard you had already earned your spurs. This was accurate, for as an undergrad I had written dozens of them. As with a lot of teachers of my age and experience, it seemed the bulk of my education classes were directed towards the sole end purpose of constructing the consummate lesson plan. It appeared this was truly the holy grail of teacher training and the *sine qua non* of my undergraduate existence. There were reasons for this fixation. In a college classroom it would have been difficult to actually measure how well a potential teacher could *deliver* a coherent lesson, but by thunder and Horace Mann, professors could endlessly critique *the writing* of lesson plans! In reality, for me and a whole generation of prospective teachers, these plans were the educational equivalent of an appendix. Everyone knows they probably have some important purpose, but no one knows exactly what the hell they do. Also, people who have them cut out immediately feel better.

Neither did the pain end when I got a teaching position. Every teacher at Eagle River High School had to file a weekly lesson plan. By my third year, I was coming to view these as the bane of my existence and a canker upon the *corpus* of education. To anyone who has never written a comprehensive lesson plan, nor even cast eyes upon a planning book, let me assure you, your life is better for the omission. In no way am I minimizing *planning*. Every decent teacher plans extensively, but the dynamic of a good classroom is such that detailed plans faithfully executed will become rigid and meaningless. During an average week, I taught four discrete subjects at least five different times each. There were literally hundreds of daily interruptions. Much of the time, schools simply aren't very conducive to learning, and certainly not amenable to the execution of detailed plans. In my first year, I diligently tried to record all of my goals and the objectives for each of my classes. The pages I submitted to the office were masterful and breathtaking in all respects. If education had epic poetry, my lesson plans would have become the stuff of pedagogic legend. In reality, before the ink was fully dry, they were also on their way to becoming complete works of fiction and low-grade compost. The progression typically went something like this: By 9:05 on Tuesdays, these plans had become wish lists; by 10:10 on Wednesday, they were mere guidelines; by Friday, they were the teaching analogue to a child's optimistic requests to Santa. In the early stages of my career, I worried that one day an administrator was going to drop by my room and compare the day's observed activities to my proposed course of action as expressed in my lesson plan. As it turned out, my fears were groundless. Each of these plans, lovingly written, was checked off, held for a year, and then summarily disposed of. My plans were unexamined, unread, and "un-given a damn" about. My elegant plans were reduced to a series of check marks next to my name, and as long as the little boxes were properly inked, the world kept spinning. In no other pursuit have I ever wasted so much time for so little purpose. Several of the people I worked with illustrated this point by filling in their planning sheets with ridiculous, vulgar, or physically impossible proposed classroom activities. We had a P.E. teacher who simply wrote "Ball Skills" across the top of the page with arrows going across each day of the week, and another arrow going down through the hours of the day. There was never a consequence for this flippant disregard of sacred teaching writ. I never had the chutzpah to do likewise, but in time I did become indifferent to the content of my weekly plan, and toward the end of my fourth year, I stopped filing these plans all together. At about that time, I had decided to resign from Eagle River. There were a dozen reasons, but the real precipitating event was my striking a student. This was something I had never believed to be possible, and even today I have trouble accepting I did it. When I mentally replay the incident, it is as if I am watching myself from inside our coaches' office. There is no apparent rage on my face, the entire time I maintain flat affect, almost like a poisonous snake deciding if the prey was worth the venom.

I was helping out with the wrestling team and heard a commotion in the shower room. One of the team's heavyweights was holding our honorary manager under a shower. Normally I would have contained myself, but the poor little guy had Down's syndrome and was screaming at the top of his lungs. It was perhaps the most pathetic and cruel thing I had ever witnessed in a school setting. The wrestler laughed at him. I was livid, but I can offer no real justification for slapping him. In my almost four years of teaching, I had been nearly as mad several times and had controlled myself. But that day, at that moment, I made a conscious decision to punish the larger boy. I had to move several steps to initiate the confrontation. It was in no way spontaneous. I planned to do it, and in doing so I have never been more wrong or ashamed of myself. Reflecting on the whole episode, I am surprised I used an open hand instead of a fist. I still remember the crack of my hand against his cheek. I still remember holding his head under a shower until he blubbered out an apology. Sadly, I remember enjoying it. We got dressed and I hauled the kid to the Athletic Director's office and told the A.D. exactly what had happened. Then I went back to the coaching office and wrote the incident up. I had one of the wrestling coaches sign the confession and attest to the truth of my account. The kid went home with my hand-print across his face so I assumed shortly I would face consequences, perhaps dismissal. Amazingly, I could not make myself care. The next morning, when I came to school, the news was all over the building. Several kids stopped me to ask if it were true. Most were absolutely giddy. Seems the young man I slapped was not really in the running for Mister Congeniality. After a week went by, I went to see the principal to ask if he had read my account and had any parental contact regarding the incident. He said he had read the report, but no, he had not spoken to the parents and he really didn't expect to. Then he asked me a question. "If your 300-pound son had just been slapped for tormenting a student with Down's syndrome, would you want to make a big deal of it?" He knew the parents in question; he felt that they were good people and were dealing with the situation, perhaps more harshly than I had. He did suggest that I really needed to examine my anger issues. I deserved any consequence which might come my way, but now it seemed that I was being given a ticket to walk away clean. After a lot of soul-searching, I resigned my teaching position. I had no other choice.

Seven or eight years ago I was going through some of my old stuff and I found a yearbook from my Eagle River days. In it, there were a hundred expressions of good will and assurances I would be missed and remembered. There was also a copy of a poorly written draft of my letter informing the superintendent I would not be back to teach and coach next year. I clearly remember writing it, but time has softened the pain and cynicism expressed between the lines. I remember in the weeks before I submitted it, I was torn and depressed. I loved the classroom, I had come to love the town, but I wasn't moving the needle. I wanted to do something which could change lives. I know now I was being totally unrealistic, and at times I still wonder what type of life and career I might have built had I stayed in Eagle River. But I had struck a kid and nothing could be the same, a covenant had been shattered.

Superintendent Nelson,

Please consider this letter as representing my intent to resign my teaching position effective at the end of the current school year. The reasons for this are many, but please be assured I have no specific grievance against the administration of this district nor Eagle River High School. I have always been dealt with in a fair and consistent manner. I have come to deeply appreciate my students and this community. Neither do I have immediate plans to accept another teaching position. However, more and more I now justify myself and my salary only in terms of the hours I work, and not the amount of teaching I really do. What have I accomplished, Mr. Nelson? It seems much of the past four years I have been running in place. You also know about the recent incident in the locker room. I apologize again for my lack of self-control and personal discipline. Two years ago, I was given the Teacher of the Year Award, and at the time I treasured it. Now, I'm not sure it really was anything more than a prize in a popularity contest. After all, that's what a lot of my colleagues called it.

By resigning, I will now have the time to go back to school and become a reading teacher. I think I will get a lot of meaning from being able to teach a kid something which will make a real difference in their lives, something that will last. In my four years here, I have seen so many kids who read poorly or not at all. Thank you for the opportunity you've given me to teach here, I resign with more than a little regret.

Sincerely,

McLean, Social Studies, Eagle River High School.

When the superintendent read my resignation, he made a very good show of expressing his sorrow at my departure. He even gave me a week in which I could reconsider and rescind it. On a personal level, he was being sincere. I had been his own child's teacher and coach; perhaps he had come to like and respect me. But as an officer of the district, he knew that my letter presented him with new possibilities. Here was a chance to hire someone for a smaller salary. Perhaps some enthusiastic young teacher, newly certified by the state of Minnesota as a qualified Social Studies instructor. A knight errant with a history degree and a whistle.

By this point, I had four years' experience and a master's degree. I was no longer a bargain-basement teacher. He could now try and find a coach who would restore the glory days of Eagle River football. For the past two years, I had pretty much screwed the pooch as far as winning went. Even in Eagle River, you could not lose forever without consequences, and I understood a few of the boys at the Legion Club were beginning to trash me and my co-head coach pretty good. This was kind of in the nature of things. One of the last lessons that Eagle River taught me was that education is a business. In all things, the books need to be balanced. Good teacher, bad teacher, indifferent teacher, the check stays the same and the smaller a district can keep the check, the better. Even in the early eighties, teaching and learning were slowly being turned over to accountants and executive types. School administrators were being taught management skills instead of learning theory. Over my career this trend was to accelerate and it continues unabated today. This is a mistake. Schools cannot be run like businesses. As sentient beings, teachers and students cannot really be managed, only lead. You cannot teach someone to think by issuing a steady stream of orders and directives. More so than in almost any other endeavor, quality education requires the full participation of all parties involved. As we discovered in Vietnam, occupying territory is fairly easy. Winning hearts and minds is the true victory, and only possible in non-coercive relationships built on trust and honesty. When kids and teachers are made to feel like cyphers, the school has failed. The same is true when we define the relative quality of schools by comparing standardized test scores.

One of my last official duties at Eagle River was to coach my team at the section track meet. By this time, Ann was an accomplished middle-distance runner who no longer needed me to tell her when to run fast. By chance, that day I was introduced to her older sister. She was a nurse and a brilliant, beautiful and accomplished woman; but that was in the future. That summer, I went back to my hometown and stayed with my parents for a couple of months. I was going to be a broke college kid again, and the rent there was agreeable. I began another graduate program. This time I would study the nature of learning disabilities and basic remediation in reading. That was a great summer. I went to school and occasionally got to fish. I was even able to carve out a couple of days in the Boundary Waters. The weather was rancid, but I had one night of stars and reaffirmation. My possibilities were again endless, and that summer I was truly happy and hopeful. I took a job as a park director. On Fridays, we had almost two hundred kids from ages five to nine chasing around the park, swinging bats, and running bases. Few balls were fielded, and no scores were kept. At the end of the games, everyone got a popsicle. Players, siblings, and parents, we always made sure there were enough popsicles to go around. "It's OK to have another, just be sure the wrappers and sticks go into the trash barrels, you bet, you're very welcome."

I'm sorry that I need to leave.
I much regret this day.
But I did something really stupid,
and there's a penalty to pay

I'll always treasure these four years,
and the time I spent with you.
I never will forget this place,
whatever else I choose to do.

You've taught me how to teach, you know,
and no matter what comes next
you were my favorite teachers,
my classroom, and my text.

Forgive me for the many times,
I screamed for no real reason.
The times I took it out on you,
when we had a losing season

There is so much more I'm sorry for,
like the kids I didn't reach.
I know there were times you failed to learn.
But there were times I failed to teach.

And I'm certain that in future years,
When my thoughts turn back to this day
I will wonder how different life may have been.
If only ... I had opted to stay.

Part II

The Kingdom of Spec. Ed.

The Promise

Come along now child
Walk with me
trust me deeply
and I promise I'll be
Your booster rocket

I'm going to carry you
At least for part of your way
And set you down the very day
Your own motor igniters
Then I'll fall away

So you come along
You promise to learn
And I promise to teach
And perhaps place your hands
Where my own never quite reached

You go be my ripples
If I was your stone
But in the stream of forever
What we started together
We each must now finish alone

Then, go and exceed me child
You will honor all I give
If someday
I'm only a footnote
In the fantastic life you live

And that's really OK.
Because on that day
I'll point to you
And be proud to say
I was your booster rocket

Crossing the Rubicon

By my fourth year of teaching, the evidence of my own eyes had convinced me many schools were failing in their core mission. Every day in the classroom, it became increasingly plain to me that a lot of my students were locked in a cycle of failure and poor performance. The problem seemed to be fundamental. Nothing was going to change for these kids until they improved their basic skills in reading and math. As a secondary consideration, these non-readers were forcing all of their teachers to modify and simplify their entire curriculum. This was creating a system which served no one very well and would continue to spiral downward. This was a mystery to no one associated with the schools. I believe it remains true today.

When I first began teaching, I considered the problem to be entirely socio-economic. Rich public schools with a great tax base and prosperous students did well. Private schools performed even a little better because their students were usually better off financially, and they could be more selective in choosing their clientele. Private schools were not mandated to offer any Special Ed. services, nor anything else really. Poor rural schools and inner-city schools were at the bottom of the economic food chain and often had the most challenging students. The research seemed to support these same simple conclusions.

Poverty as the root cause of most social and educational ills was a mantra of the Johnson administration, and as early as 1965, these discrepancies were recognized and attempts were made to correct some of the inequalities. Title I was enacted to try to remedy some of these educational disparities. This program funneled money into schools in low-income areas and provided a boost to economically disadvantaged students. Head Start was initiated at about the same time with essentially the same goals and had some success meeting the educational, social, and emotional needs of economically disadvantaged preschoolers and elementary students. It was especially effective in rural areas. What wasn't being addressed was the unique challenge posed to the schools by kids who had a limited capacity to learn or a disability which hindered their progress in regular classrooms. For these kids, a more prescriptive way to teach was required.

In the late sixties and early seventies, what became Special education was still in its infancy. There was no national mandate that specific services be provided. Some of the more enlightened and prosperous school districts made an effort to provide for students suffering from obvious and severe handicapping conditions, but only the profoundly handicapped, such as children with Down syndrome or cerebral palsy were occasionally seen walking, or being wheeled, through the hallways of public schools. I have come to believe though that when it did happen, it was probably an accident or poor planning on the part of the teacher assigned to care for those students. Most schools didn't willingly display their handicapped populations, and great pains were taken to shelter the "normal" kids from seeing what was then considered to be an unpleasant reality. During my own high-school years, there were perhaps a dozen severely handicapped kids in my building. In a student body of three thousand, these few were deliberately made invisible to the eye and memory. To my knowledge, at no time during the day were they allowed to interact freely with the rest of their classmates. They were always excluded from the pages of yearbooks; they didn't go to pep fests or assemblies. Were it not for the randomness once created by a bomb threat, I probably never would have known they existed in the building at all. During that evacuation, one of the handicapped students smiled at me while being escorted from the building, and when I returned the smile and asked him, "How's it going?" he was delighted. He tried to respond to me, but his best attempt at speech was little more than a guttural, "Hi." To this day I don't think I've ever given another human being greater joy, and all it took was three words. My friends gave me a lot of crap for that incident. "Hey McLean, talk to any tards lately?" A couple of my teammates even managed a pretty accurate impression of the poor kid's response. It became an inside joke, and I laughed along with my group. On more than one occasion, I mimicked the kid myself. In doing so, we were being cocky little pricks with well-decorated letter jackets. We were so young and arrogant that it never occurred to us to be humbled by the blessing we had received when we were born strong and whole.

By segregating these kids, most of the people associated with schools were not being deliberately mean-spirited. They had convinced themselves that exclusion was mercy, and it spared the handicapped students having to deal with the endless leers, taunts, and thoughtless cruelty so common in high school. This was of course ridiculous. But it did rationalize exclusion and justify making handicapped students invisible.

Regrettably, neither were these students really being educated. While in school, they were given a few years of cursory instruction in life skills before being shunted into group homes or state institutions. In the fifties, sixties, and early seventies, many of these institutions were little better than human warehouses. Places which reeked of neglect and urine. While there, the few skills so tediously acquired at school often withered and died from lack of stimulation and social interaction. Kids with names and feelings became patients and numbers. Their minds then turned in upon themselves and often they died young... social ciphers buried under institutional headstones; and there but for the grace of God, and a lucky roll of the genetic dice go I.

As time passed, there were also some positive things happening for the handicapped. Some school buildings had been modified to provide wheelchair access, and more were in the process of being modified. But these accommodations were hardly the norm, and they were spendy. Many school districts fought the mandates eventually passed to provide accommodations and access for the handicapped. Transportation to school was sometimes provided, but in different buses. Predictably, these "short buses" became another source of crude humor, and you could always get a cheap laugh by accusing someone of taking the "short bus." In some districts there was a curriculum in place, and a little cognitive progress was made. There were some work programs that provided for a little rudimentary training. Upon aging out of the school system, many of the handicapped lived out their lives with their parents. They usually found love and acceptance, but seldom became adults in any meaningful way. They were never encouraged or allowed to live anything resembling an independent life. Parents spent endless hours worrying about what would happen to their kids when they became too old or infirm to be their caretakers. This is still true today.

In this model, both parent and student were supplicants to the schools, and as such were grateful for any help offered. Parents were also usually thrilled with any successes their child achieved and made few legal demands for a larger piece of the educational pie. Very little service was required by law, and little was really expected. Some large districts built centers where the bulk of the handicapped student population was instructed. If a district had a shrewd eye for the bottom line, these facilities were opened to the children of neighboring districts and services were provided for a fee. Kind of like commodifying the handicapped.

The kids with less obvious educational infirmities were largely ignored. They were simply expected to attend the appropriate local school. The key to survival was to look and act relatively normal. If you could do so, you were allowed to join the herd. It was just kind of assumed these kids would muddle through school somehow, or perhaps they would eventually drop out and become the foundation and pillars of the burgeoning fast-food industry, sometimes for no more than a "training wage" which, in my opinion, was crass exploitation. This was only to be expected. After all, school wasn't for everyone and then there was the "horse and water" thing. By the time these students got to high school they were labeled as lazy, or indifferent, or simply stupid. While at Eagle River, I had already dealt with dozens of kids who wore such a label. In my ignorance, I believed them.

Most of my high-school colleagues thought the real root of the problem for these students was always "down there" somewhere, as in the lower grades. By the time these "slow learners" got to high school, there were few expectations held for them. Maybe they were placed in a work program, and for their electives were given a long list of shop or Home Ec. classes. Their academic records contained little evidence of achievement, and their attendance was often spotty at best.

When in high school, I had little contact with that segment of the student population. I was fortunate to be placed in what were labeled "advanced" classes. Sometimes called the "college track." It was almost a school within a school. The students in my track took physics and chemistry. Most of us had a few years of foreign languages, in my case now long forgotten and never really excelled at. Many of us were also in the band, choir, or orchestra, so even the general elective classes were scheduled to accommodate the "advanced." It's amazing the number of ways a school can be segregated.

When I became a teacher, and because high school was the last stop on the educational express for most kids, I was now free to hurl verbal thunderbolts of unwarranted criticism at all the elementary and junior-high teachers who had obviously screwed these kids up before I ever saw them. "What in the hell do they do *down there*?" "Did those people *down there* teach these kids anything?" "Jesus Christ! Why did those people *down there* pass these kids?" At the high-school level, failing kids *before* they got to us was now offered as a kind of universal solution. "If they just failed a few of these kids down there, the rest might figure it out and shape up." If you were an elementary or junior-high teacher, it was still possible to push the blame downward, but now the excuses and reasons were shifted to things like poor parenting, a deficient environment, or moldy sperm cells.

These students became the source of a nearly infinite amount of hand wringing and mock administrative concern. They were "unmotivated" and that became the single most overused and self-excusing descriptor ever invented. With that single word, the focus of the problem was shifted, and the student owned both the problem and the solution. Teachers could self-righteously proclaim that, "They had presented the material, what more was to be expected?"

School districts bought into the validity of this description and responded to the problem by trying to teach the staff to be motivational powerhouses and educational snake oil salesmen. Almost overnight, an entire industry grew up around the need to create in-service training for teachers in motivational techniques. If these programs were good, the staff was entertained for a morning and then went about their business exactly as before. If the program was bad, the staff suffered through it, cursed the administration for requiring their attendance, and then went about their business exactly as before. Few teachers had either the attitude or the aptitude to implement the suggested motivational paradigm shifts. The results were predictably bad. Sappy songs and Who Buddy workshops were common. They were cheap and fast but solved absolutely nothing and motivated absolutely no one. Neither did they address the real issues.

A good number of individual teachers saw the problem differently. They recognized that a large number of "unmotivated" students simply couldn't read at a level that made success likely. The reasons for this were not fully understood and it really didn't matter. These individual instructors responded to the problem in concrete and practical ways. They modified their curricula. They read the material to students. They let the less capable kids work with the stronger students.

When I was in elementary school, a boy in my class had some real disabilities. His speech was halting and disjointed. He walked with difficulty and his vision was poor. He wore thick glasses that made his eyes appear huge. Each day, our teachers assigned a different one of us to be Richard's helper for the day. As I remember, our class responded to his obvious infirmities in a way that I can only describe as heroic. Kids competed for the honor of being Richard's helper. It was a Catholic school, so staff referred to the service as an act of grace. It was, for both Richard and the kids who helped him. This acceptance was most obvious on the playground. Without being told to, kids modified their games to allow Richard to be a participant. Once at lunch, after Richard had been a bit sloppy, I saw a young lady wiping his face with a paper napkin. Her affect was almost angelic, her tenderness almost sacred, Richard beamed. Once, Richard messed himself. To my knowledge, not one kid in that class made fun of him. Think of that, there was not one student in an upper-elementary classroom who was willing to cheap shot an obviously handicapped classmate. Would a room full of adults be so kind? This moral heroism happened at every grade level until we all left and went to different high schools. Richard was in my eighth-grade class picture. I doubt he moved on to high school with the rest of us, but I don't think that any of us in the picture will forget him or the kind and loving teachers who made it possible for Richard to be in that picture with the rest of his classmates. At times, I have found kids to be unspeakably cruel to each other. But, if you can make them see each other as individuals, they will almost always respond positively to a cry for help.

Other teachers found different ways to accommodate poor students. Alternate testing strategies were used. They offered extra help, worked mountains of overtime, and reworked all their lessons, in some cases, going so far as to write an entirely separate curriculum to accommodate only a few students. To them, teaching was a verb, and it existed only if learning actually took place. In a thousand ways, these special teachers expressed the care and concern *each child* should have a right to expect from *every teacher.* As a wonderful by-product, these few and special teachers also seemed to have few unmotivated kids, and they enjoyed coming to school. They did some wonderful work, and millions of students owed their diplomas and futures to the efforts of these kind and caring professionals. This was especially true in elementary school. Their students were the lucky ones. Many kids just drifted. Much later in my teaching career a vice principal, who I had known for years asked me if I was related to a former teacher of hers. I was, and she asked me to thank that teacher for all she had done for her in the second grade. Seems she was a poor reader and the intervention of that one outstanding woman had made all the difference in her life. My principal was fortunate. Many students weren't. The educational system had not crafted a unified response to the problem of poor fundamental skills. Neither was it known what the root causes of the deficiencies were, or how to make corrections.

The first major step towards changing this model was the passage of P.L. 94-142 in 1975. This federal law was titled the Education For All Handicapped Children Act. States were now charged with the development and implementation of educational policies and plans which were consistent with the new federal law. All students were to receive a free and appropriate public education, and the definition of a handicapping condition was expanded to include children suffering from specific learning disabilities and emotional or behavioral problems. School districts responded by building nearly parallel educational systems which attempted to provide for the unique needs of these kids. In retrospect, the development of this parallel system was perhaps a mistake, as it fostered separation instead of inclusion and integration. It also required a good deal of new staffing and teaching methodologies, which at the time didn't exist. Expenses multiplied. To its credit, Congress realized doing this would be an expensive proposition and pledged to provide 40% of the funds required to offer the mandated services. States and school districts would pay the balance. Even in the initial phases of implementation, much of this promised federal largess never materialized. So when dollars were needed to support special education staffing and to purchase materials, states and individual school districts bore the lion's share of the expense without adequate reimbursement. Only once, in 2009, did the federal government fund even half of their promised contribution. This was done as a one-time payment and part of a plan to give districts a cash infusion at the start of the Great Recession.

The predictable happened, Special Education programs came to be viewed by the mainstream as a bottomless money pit and a direct subtraction from a district's efforts to provide for the balance of the student body. Partly because of Congress and the courts, groups of kids were now forced to compete with each other for limited dollars. Please do not interpret this as a partisan political rant against tight-fisted conservatives. It is not, in this case both Democrats and Republicans have lied to the schools with equal facility, and neither party has ever had any intention of fully funding the programs created and mandated. The Democrats will occasionally offer bills to fully fund Special Education, but with the possible exception of former Senator Paul Wellstone's efforts, these were really nothing more than cynical attempts to embarrass the then current administration. This is a very easy point to prove. When, on a couple of occasions, Democrats controlled the two chambers of Congress and the White House, Special Education was still never given the promised funds. "Sorry guys, we really want to help, but that darn filibuster just makes it impossible."

It is important to understand a little about the history, funding, and the politics of Special Education because it explains a good deal about the developing relationship between these classes and the mainstream. Both handicapped and non-handicapped students are entitled to a free and appropriate public education. However, one group now had the legal right to demand it. Advocacy groups grew and became much more assertive. Lawsuits followed, and due process made its way into state legislation. Special Ed. was beginning to get the first call on a district's resources. The balance of the student population got what was left. It was assumed the "normal kids" would be OK. If you are an administrator, you might rail at that oversimplification, but at the end of the day you know it to be true.

I was still in Eagle River when that district was making its initial attempts to implement 94-142. On one of our interminable workshop days, we were being given an in-service on what the new law might mean to a classroom teacher. The district had already hired three special education teachers and someone who for part of their day acted as the coordinator of Special Services. She was leading this particular in-service. As was my custom, I had my workshop face firmly in place and had already reflexively shut down most of my brain. Our icebreaker was based on a game of musical chairs. Eight teachers were marched around a row of seven chairs. When the music stopped, they all tried to find a way to sit down. At first, this required a bit of squeezing, but was easily accomplished. One of the chairs was now removed, and the exercise was repeated. This continued until there were four chairs holding eight people. Now, each male member of the group had a female sitting on his lap. (Today, even the notion of this happening is truly cringe-worthy.) At this point I kind of woke up and was really quite interested in how the next accommodation was to be made. Since a few of the teachers involved were a bit rotund, the possibilities for low humor or serious injury seemed imminent. But at this point our new coordinator of Special Services stopped the game and stated, "You see, there will always be a way found to accommodate everyone, and it's fun!" She then proceeded to make a fifteen-minute speech on the joys and benefits of including the handicapped kids. She got a brief round of applause, but as she was walking away Carl, our craggy math teacher, asked her if she would mind a question. She nodded her head and said she would be happy to answer any questions. Carl was a very direct man, bright and insightful. Experience had made him cynical, and then often events validated his cynicism. He wanted to know what would happen in this little game if a chair was reserved for one person and everyone else in the game had to fight over what was left. She muttered something about fairness and that such would never be the case. She obviously didn't understand the point Carl was making—and he didn't elaborate.

It took years for me to completely appreciate the implications of his question. At the time of that little demonstration, I had only the vaguest notion of becoming a Special Ed teacher, but I was glad there would finally be some help offered to handicapped kids. The need was urgent, and I believed the work could be tremendously rewarding. Certainly, a special education for these kids must be of direct benefit to every classroom teacher and of indirect benefit to all students.

I never appreciated how difficult it would all be. Neither did I realize, when I finally made the decision to become a Special Ed teacher, I was crossing an educational Rubicon. I was forfeiting my citizenship in one teaching community and moving to a completely new residence in the Kingdom of Special Ed. This was indeed to be a foreign land. As I was to discover; within the kingdom, the blind routinely led the blind and the people all spoke a separate language based almost entirely upon acronyms. The citizens of the kingdom had strange and unique rituals which had to be followed with the precision of a Japanese tea ceremony. Within the kingdom, school rules no longer applied, and the national motto was, "Cover your ass."

"I've never met a Special Ed teacher who wasn't an optimist and idealist: At least when they started."

XIV

What You Wish For

Even with the passage of the EHA, special education spent a good deal of time trying to invent itself. Back then it was usually about little rooms and kindly, soft-spoken female teachers who kept jars of hard red candy or Werthers butterscotch on their desks. They often tried to teach reading using variations on the same strategies which had been failing kids such as these since the days of Daniel Webster. They were almost universally kind and willing to help. No uniform level of service was provided to students, nor was there a common method of determining who should receive those services. Nevertheless, these teachers did some amazing work. Perhaps most importantly, they gave their students someone to talk to. There was no blaming and shaming. But at this point, most of their skills were *affective*. Research had given us only a few real clues on how to be *effective* when teaching these students. Many were graduating, but barely literate. The reasons for this were unimportant to me at the time. Invariably, the true *causes* of academic failure are complex and societal, while the *effects* are obvious and individual. This has always been the case, but now we would be entering a new era in education based upon more prescriptive instruction. Students with learning disabilities would be given the opportunity to work with a well-trained and caring group of professionals. I finally resolved that I would be one of them.

I don't think I have ever felt as altruistic as I did the summer of 1980, when I began taking the coursework necessary to become a teacher of the learning-disabled. I was 26, and on a mission again. The possibilities and rewards seemed limitless. I wanted to become a Special Ed. teacher because I thought by doing so, I could help kids in a very important and fundamental way. I thought I would become one of those amazing teachers I so admired. Finally, I would be conforming to my own idealized notion of what a teacher was, and could be. I first went into teaching because I didn't have a better plan. It was to be a pleasant way-station on my road to something else. I decided to stay in teaching because I discovered the classroom gave me both purpose and identity. In my four years, I had come to see teaching as a truly Christian activity. Now I would be a Special Education teacher and have the opportunity to both teach and, in a sense, heal. Maybe it was the *most important* thing I was capable of doing.

As I said, I never felt more altruistic than I did on the day I registered for the classes which would lead eventually to certification as a teacher of the learning-disabled. That fall I moved back to a boarding house near the college from which I had already twice graduated and became a full-time student again. Seven years later, I never felt as relieved as when I directed the state to drop the Special Ed. endorsement from my teaching license, and I left the Kingdom of Special Ed. for good. Along the way, I found the answer to Carl's question.

XV

Ear Wax

That fall, I took a job as a bartender. My living accommodations were shit, but I really didn't need much. I was happy to be in school again. The coursework required to be a Special Ed. teacher wasn't proving to be overly rigorous. Most of us in the program could carry outsized credit loads, work nearly full-time, and still manage a social life. This was important to me personally because I had begun to date a wonderful woman. She was Ann's older sister and a nurse at a major metropolitan hospital. I had first met her at a track meet the previous spring, and towards the end of summer she called and asked if I would like to attend a Gordon Lightfoot concert with her. Immediately, she became important to me. By the end of the fall, I began to hope that perhaps I might someday share a life with her. The time I could spend with her made the rest of my week tolerable. But at the end of the day, I was still basically a broke college student who lived in a dump. She was the reason I started to apply for Special Ed. positions the second I had enough credits to get a temporary license. These interim licenses, called variances, allowed you to teach for two years while completing the class work required for full certification.

In the early eighties, finding a teaching position was difficult. For any opening, there might be at least a dozen applicants. It was mid-February, and this late in the school year, about the best which might be hoped for was a little substitute teaching. If I were really lucky, the sub job might be long term, but the competition for these positions was also intense. Back then, I thought there would always be more people willing to teach than there were teaching jobs; this has changed, especially in Special Ed.

I filled out applications and sent resumes with no real expectation it would do any good. Each one I mailed was sort of like a "message in a bottle" cast adrift by a shipwrecked sailor. Only by dumb luck and a favorable tide might it drift into the hands of a person with a position to fill and a job to offer. I was fortunate, that a vice-principal at a large urban middle school fit both of these stipulations and called me to ask if I could interview for a position working with at-risk students. The job would mainly involve teaching Social Studies to kids with behavior issues. Most of the students in the program were classified as emotionally disturbed, but I wouldn't have a real Special Ed, caseload. Many were simply deemed to be uncontrollable in a regular classroom setting. It would be challenging, but if I did a good job, there was the possibility I could be rehired or catch on somewhere else in the district. It was a mega-district and there were usually openings. This job could be a Godsend. If I got it, I would leave the dump where I was staying. Maybe I could start to plan a future. I *needed* this job.

For the interview, I decided to purchase a second suit. The one I owned was black, and I still occasionally wear it to funerals. It doesn't fit anymore but at a funeral no one is really trying to make a fashion statement. This one was pricey and gray. In no way could I afford it, but sometimes desperation trumps prudence and I needed this job. Before I walked into the principal's office, I was intent on eliminating every physical characteristic which anyone might find objectionable. I got my hair cut, shaved my beard, and trimmed all that could be trimmed. I used tweezers to pluck anything the scissors or razor couldn't reach. I ironed, polished, and buffed. Quite normally it would be fair to describe me as a bit rough-hewn, but on the day of the interview, I glistened! For a solid hour, I looked as if I had stepped out of the pages of GQ! While waiting in the office reception area, I began to worry that perhaps I looked too good. Maybe the expensive suit would lead the gentleman to believe I really didn't need the work. Perhaps he might see my polished wingtips and conclude that I was a member of the Young Republicans League, or maybe my round wire-rimmed glasses branded me a Democrat; either assumption could be fatal to my prospects. Thankfully, I was called into the principal's office before I could worry myself into full-fledged apoplexy.

As expected, the interview began with introductions and pleasantries. These dragged on for so long, the dialogue became rather inane. Next, we talked about football. For ten minutes, he rambled on about his own glory days at some small school in Montana. Seems once upon a time he was a stud of the first order in seven-man football. Due to his lack of stature, this seemed unlikely. Then he offered his completely clueless insights on the Viking's prospects for the upcoming season. Throughout his monologue, I tried to convey interest and attention, but I couldn't stop myself from staring at the man's ears. They were huge! He looked like a two-handled coffee mug! He was holding a pencil and kept sticking the eraser into them. Not just a little bit, but way down there. The man's ear drums must have been located almost directly behind his eyeballs. Then, when he had finished excavating, he withdrew the pencil from his ear and put it in his mouth. When he decided that an eraser infused with ear wax didn't taste good, he reversed the process and stuck it back in his ear. He did this three times during the course of the interview. All the while I was trying to be attentive and hoping like hell he wouldn't repeat the trick, but this time use his nose as the mine shaft. I would have laughed, no matter how desperately I wanted this job, I *just know* I would have laughed. Even the imagery of him doing it nearly had me giggling. Several times I was close to excusing myself to make a self-composure run to the bathroom.

In the half hour we met, he asked me exactly one question I thought relevant to the position being offered, and he made just one mention of my coursework and experience with at-risk kids. I asked no questions and had the job in hand before I got out of the chair, and "By the way, could you start on Monday?" Later, I learned I had been the only candidate interviewed for the position. I was either truly spectacular, or the man was so incredibly lazy, he probably more or less drew my name from the applicant pile at random. Then he gave my references a quick glance, and it was likely he decided to hire me as soon as he saw I was a normal looking human being and could articulate a reasonably coherent sentence. The fact I was male and large didn't hurt either. I probably could have shown up in a dirty, sweaty, tee shirt and it would have made little difference. I was a warm body and I was qualified. Most importantly, he would need to waste no more of his valuable time trying to select a teacher to provide instruction to some of the most challenging students in his building. I wonder if he went home that night congratulating himself on his decisiveness. The entire process had taken about sixty-five minutes and left me with a good deal of foreboding, but I had a job. Later I was to discover the reason the position was open was the woman initially assigned to it had suffered a nervous breakdown two weeks previous.

I was once teaching a Social Studies methods class to a group of prospective elementary teachers. After class, a young man came up to me and asked what the minimum amount was he could do to get a B. I told him that the class wasn't overly demanding and that with a little effort an A was a really good possibility. He shrugged his shoulders and told me that he was going to be an administrator and only needed this class to get his elementary certification before beginning his admin. coursework. He only really needed a B. Many times I've wondered what happened to this minimalist, and said a small prayer for any school that was so clueless as to hire him to be their instructional leader. I wish I could have found a way to give him a C.

XVI

The Wisdom of the Dog

I now had four days to move my entire life fifty miles to the south. This was one of those occasions when being propertyless was a blessing. It took no more than two hours to pack up my few belongings. Most of the furniture I had accumulated went into a dumpster. A table and chairs were left at the curb with a sign proclaiming them to be free for the taking. What I decided was worth keeping, fit easily into the back seat and trunk of a 1973 Plymouth Duster. In another hour, I had squared things with my slumlord, and got my name off the utility bills. I left him a note with an address that he could use to send me back my damage deposit; still waiting on that one. With the remaining couple of days, I found a small apartment near Minneapolis and spent some quiet time with Mary. For the first time, we talked about a future together. She had accepted my decision to be a career teacher, and she understood what that could mean. The next day, I withdrew every dime I had accumulated in my teacher's retirement account and bought an engagement ring. This was really a dumb move, but when you're young and in love, the future happens in one-month increments, and it was a beautiful solitaire.

On the appointed Monday, I reported to the office to get my class rosters and any final instructions. On the way to class, I stopped by the principal's office to thank him for the opportunity, and to assure him I intended to do a good job for the school and kids. The man barely looked up from his desk; he acknowledged my sincere gratitude with some really brief and totally non-sequitur muttering. At the time, I thought that perhaps he was deep in thought. With familiarity I came to appreciate it wasn't possible for him to concentrate deeply on much of anything. The reality was he didn't seem very bright, and there was a distinct possibility he never remembered hiring me in the first place. He did have a doctorate in education. The rumor was, his wife, a journalism teacher, had written most of his dissertation. Funny how rumors spread.

The program I was now a part of was housed in four portable classrooms behind the main building. Portables tend to be singularly ugly affairs, and these were no different. They were quite old and age had not improved their appearance. Originally a light green color, but time, sun, and rain had modified the shade considerably, plus now a few rust streaks were thrown in for contrast. Most pole barns had more style, and at the back of the main building was a logical place for them.

I assumed there would be some in-service associated with taking the position, but in this I was mistaken. I should have asked about it during the interview, but I didn't want to look like a wimp; remember, I needed this job. The guy who taught the math component of the program soon came in, gave me a quick fifteen minutes on the lay of the land and wished me luck. Ten minutes later, I was surrounded by sixteen kids who now had an unquestioned right to expect I had something meaningful to offer them; and I had nothing. I made it through hour one by sharing a bit about myself and flying by the seat of my pants. The next hour I had a different group, so the second verse worked as well as the first. The third hour was to be a sorely needed prep period, but right before the end of class period two, an office aide came into the portable and informed me I had been assigned to supervise the "modified learning center" during that day's third period. Any preparation I needed to do would be on the fly.

I had no real clue what a modified learning center was. Neither did I know doing occasional supervision there was to be a part of my job. Everything I knew about the "MLC" I learned by consulting the faculty handbook while I walked to my new duty station. It seemed the school had just gone to a policy of never suspending kids *no matter what* their behavior. At the time, this seemed to make sense, as many students had come to regard a suspension as no more than a brief vacation from class. A few got themselves suspended whenever the pressures and demands of seventh grade became intolerable. Offenses which could land a student in the MLC ranged from continually forgetting to bring a pencil to class to assaultive behavior, and students assigned there ran the gamut from slightly squirrelly to sociopathic.

The idea behind the MLC was to create an environment within the school which was so strict and regimented that no kid wanted to be there. There was to be absolute silence and endless homework. Kids assigned there ate lunch at their desks and had few breaks. Modified Learning Centers were usually located in drab rooms without clocks or windows. Lacking a proper dungeon, this particular middle school had located their MLC in a cramped old phys-ed storage area. This room had no iron maiden and only a few thumb screws, but it smelled funky enough to qualify as subterranean and nasty. Nine student desks were crammed in and when I arrived seven of the desks were occupied. The teacher I relieved shot past me while the door was still only partially opened. To my cheerful "Good morning" he only grunted something about the class list being on the desk, and he was gone. Thus began the longest hour of my life.

For five entire minutes, things went well. The kids were quiet and homework was being attempted. By about minute six, a few of the kids were over their initial shock at seeing a new face and resumed their screwing around. The talking and giggling was intermittent at first, but despite my best efforts, by the thirty-minute mark the conversations flowed freely. These were mostly hushed, but twice the room echoed to a staccato yelp from someone who had just been the recipient of a titty twister. (I think the more modern term is Purple Nurple.) My admonitions to be quiet meant nothing. Moving around the room and standing next to the little miscreants did no good. Separating them only meant that they had to talk louder. This should not have surprised me. After all, they had no real reason to listen to me. There was simply no coercive force I could wield. They couldn't be suspended, they already were. They generally had no fears that their grades would suffer, most were already failing; besides, junior-high grade point averages meant nothing. This particular district had bought into a policy of no retention—none, period—and these kids were completely happy with the idea of a social promotion. The office wanted nothing to do with them and stated as much in the policies and procedures they had established for the Modified Learning Center. The only viable threat I could level at them was that they would get additional days in MLC, and why would a kid want to leave? For the first time in my brief teaching career, I was being totally and completely ignored by students. To them, I was no more than a petty annoyance. Of the seven students present, only three were truly obnoxious, but those three kept the rest of the room spinning. As I was trying to keep some kind of order, I grew panicked that a principal might walk by and see my complete impotence. I would be fired and disgraced before my first lunch. Thank God the bell rang before I resorted to hurling any meaningless threats or actually doing anything physical. As I was to learn later, the possibility that a principal might walk by was remote at best, but I was told another young teacher's career had once been short-circuited when they got fed up and grabbed one of the little detainees. This was duly reported by an outraged parent, and the teacher was terminated.

By the end of the week, I had talked to enough people to know that my experience that day was more or less typical. Every teacher in the building hated supervising the MLC and if it could be avoided or pushed on to someone else, it was. On my first day, someone had pushed this duty off onto me by scheduling a Special Ed staffing during their supervision period. As a rookie I couldn't really complain to anyone, neither could I refuse. During the rest of that winter and spring, I supervised the MLC three times because it was my "normal" turn to do so. I supervised it three additional times because other teachers found ways to avoid the duty by whatever means possible. One long-time staff member routinely called in sick on the days he was scheduled to supervise in-school suspension. This was widely known and always winked at; one of the perks of longevity. I rediscovered that being at the bottom of the seniority list sucks. I began to dread the appearance of office aides at the door of my portable. In addition to MLC duty, I was called upon to chaperone dances, supervise lunch, and monitor after-school detention. None of these "opportunities" was worded as a request. Most carried a little extra compensation, but a few were *gratis*. The lunchroom was an especially interesting duty station. You were to monitor the behavior of 400 students and also make sure their dirty lunch trays were properly stacked on a table near the kitchen door. If you failed in this, a largish lunch lady dropped whatever she was doing and sought you out for reprimand, usually loudly. She reveled in her authority. These scenes did wonders for your status in the building.

In the classroom, things weren't going much better. After a very brief honeymoon period, it became painfully obvious why my students had been assigned to me. All of them were in their early teens and several were already well-acquainted with the workings of the family court system. My kids had few social skills and fewer inhibitions. They were deeply jealous of kids who succeeded, but they laughed about their own failures and labeled everyone who did well a "sporto." Status among this group was achieved and measured by the severity of their aberrant behavior. The boy who stood atop this perverse pyramid earned the position by pushing a female faculty member. Because he was considered to be conduct-disordered, his consequences were minimal, and he was now regarded by his peers as the epitome of rebel cool. All my students would willingly declare they were in this program because they were considered to be losers. Few could sit still for more than a few minutes, and their attention spans ranged from five minutes to three nanoseconds. Between the thirty of them assigned to my classes, I doubt there were thirty courses they legitimately passed that entire school year. Most were angry at the school, or their parents, and some had excellent reasons. A few carried more negative personal baggage than any 13-year-old should ever need to bear. The extra weight of it sometimes made them wobble when they tried to walk a straight line.

Talking to these kids was scary. One extremely immature seventh-grade girl once asked me if I "got my rocks off" telling kids what to do. Shocking question coming from the mouth of a little girl who had yet to establish a bra size. Greg, the one who had pushed a female staff member, was positive the only reason I was hired was because they needed some "Big, sporto, motherfucker, to control him." As spring wore on, I came to believe he was at least partly right. Now in eighth grade, Greg was already well on his way to serious involvement with the legal system. Regrettably, he was bound to take a few other marginal kids with him. The boy was both corrosive and a leader—a bad combination. With Greg egging him on, another of the boys once took a swing at me. His lack of pugilistic technique was laughable, and I don't believe that his heart truly was in it, but this one inept whiff was a bridge definitely crossed and burned. It put him on the other side of a lot of things. For this he got three days in MLC and a rep as a badass. A little later on, the same boy verbally threatened a female vice principal. This time he was expelled. There are after all some things which simply cannot be ignored or tolerated.

Jason was sure he was going to be a professional BMX rider. He was certain he had life by the short hairs. He was going to turn 16, drop out, and win races; many, many, races Then would come magazine interviews, sponsorships, and groupies. He was going to drive a sports car that would cost more than those, "sporto dickhead classmates of his could make in five years." Two other boys in class were going to be his crew, gonna ride his coattails to the big time and easy street. He wasn't unusual, many of the 30 kids in the program had big dreams, but only the smallest kernels of real hope. They boasted about future plans; their braggadocio convinced no one, least of all themselves.

I didn't plan it that way, but that spring I was taking a graduate class with a title something like, *Educating the Emotionally Disabled Student.* That moniker isn't correct, but it's close. The instructor was a new guy. A freshly minted Ph.D. who by his own admission had never taught in a classroom setting. He was a veritable font of information and opinions regarding the proper way to integrate conduct-disordered students into the classroom. As I have rediscovered many times since, opinions without experience are worthless. I tried a few of his ideas, none worked. I wrote as much on my final class evaluation. I recall also telling him I would never again take a class from someone who had never been told to "fuck-off" or side-stepped a punch. He had very little to tell me, and less that was worth listening to.

Throughout that spring, it appeared that I was to be pretty much on my own in terms of both managing student behavior and the content of the class. In the time I worked there, I never located anything resembling a curriculum.

The physical separation my kids had from the building helped to create a kind of "out of sight, out of mind" attitude in the office. To the administration, the portables at the back of the building were a holding tank and quarantine zone. There is often a fine line between being empowered and being ignored. If a program such as this was to work, it was crucial that the teachers be given the freedom to experiment and be creative. It is also imperative they be given direction and support. We received neither. The office had a rationale for this, maybe even a pseudo-philosophy and justification, but at the end of the day what really mattered was my students were literally out of the building and out of their hair.

Because my students generally lacked basic academic tools, I decided my classroom approach should be hands-on and project based. The early eighties was one of those rare periods of heightened environmental awareness, so I decided perhaps we could look at some pollution-related issues. We opened a collection center for aluminum cans. If we made a profit recycling the cans, we were going to use the proceeds to buy a stereo for the portable. The kids were enthused. The rest of the student body basically considered my kids as pariahs, but a few of them did bring in their aluminum cans from home. Soon, we were spending the occasional class periods wandering the school grounds and the adjacent parks looking for throwaways. There was a lot of grab-ass going on during these excursions, but we always came back with bags of stuff. I was even able to devote a bit of classroom time to the issue of recycling and solid waste pollution. Several of my kids decided we weren't accumulating aluminum fast enough and asked if it would be OK to bring in other aluminum objects. I told them to go ahead and expressed appreciation for their initiative. The next day, when I took the morning roll, three of my class were absent. At the end of that day, I was informed all three were in juvenile detention. It seems they were apprehended attempting to steal aluminum screen doors from a construction site. For good measure, they had also vandalized one of the nearly complete houses. They took two by fours and destroyed much of the drywall. It was a terrible reflection on my class and school. It was made worse by the fact the kids involved were really three of my favorites. I will always believe they were fundamentally good kids who got caught up in a bad situation which was at least partly of my making.

When I was a sophomore in a high-school biology class, it was required that we dissect a frog. Usually the poor beast wasn't killed beforehand, it was pithed. A wire was inserted into the spinal column. This destroyed most of the central nervous system, but the heart continues to beat. This seems unspeakably cruel, but it served the purpose of allowing the student to observe a heart actually pumping blood. When I heard about the arrest of those kids, I was suddenly able to relate to the frog I had once so eagerly disemboweled. For about a half hour, I was effectively immobilized. I went home that night, questioning my vocation and wondering why I had ever left Eagle River.

The next day, my principal found out about the incident and gave me particular hell. During his tirade, he must have repeated twenty times he never authorized me to get into this recycling stuff. Gutless cur that I was, I took his dressing down and apologized for my lack of foresight. I really needed this job. The week previous, I had asked Mary to be my wife. She had accepted. A late summer wedding was being planned, and even back then weddings were ridiculously expensive. Aside from that, a personal blow-up now could put a blot on my record that no explanation or amount of righteous indignation could erase. In a very competitive job market, I no longer had the luxury of slamming doors shut, literally or figuratively. Not once did I point out to the bastard that only two days previously, he had commended me for the hands-on approach I was taking with my kids. At the end of his "blowification" he made sure I knew he would be watching me, and he wanted an exact accounting of every penny we raised when we cashed in the aluminum already collected. That the man challenged my competency, I had to accept. I had just given him ample reason to do so. The fact he was now questioning my honesty was almost more than I could bear. In a better time and culture, I would have demanded satisfaction and challenged him to a duel, but I *needed* this job, and I took his abuse without complaint.

If there were repercussions from the screen door incident, my principal wanted to be sure he was staking out a position which was well removed from any culpability. He was affixing blame and criticism before it even existed. No doubt this was a well-honed survival skill and had served him often over the years. Give the man credit; he had completely mastered the art of the dog. He knew where to lick and where to scratch. I believe had my project really succeeded, and a stereo was purchased, he would have been somewhere near the head of the line to accept any notice or praise from the district higher-ups. He probably had career plans which were bigger than a principal's desk in a suburban middle school school. Maybe he had a vision for public education which could only be implemented from a loftier pulpit. Or perhaps, he was only a craven little man with a questionable Ph.D. and a knack for survival. In any case, I was a completely blamable, non-tenured teacher.

The rest of my time there, I concentrated on keeping my nose clean. In class, we did nothing creative or different; I resorted to using the same materials and methods which had failed with these kids all through their academic careers, and they usually reacted terribly. I did discover that they enjoyed being read to. None of my kids would willingly read anything independently, but they all loved a good story. They especially enjoyed dark fiction or gruesome non-fiction. I read portions of *Night* by Elie Wiesel aloud to them, and the days melted. This was too advanced for the students in this class, and I needed to modify a lot of the vocabulary, but for a solid week they were normal kids reacting in predictable ways to a mind-numbing evil. Some of the questions they asked about the Holocaust bordered on the philosophical. Those days were golden.

Near the end of the school year, the principal again called me into his office. When I arrived, he and his three assistant principals were sitting at a table, all obviously nervous. He barely looked up from his desk as he informed me the at-risk program was being discontinued, and my services were no longer required. It flattered me a bit to think that he felt he needed the moral support of three assistants to deliver a simple message and perhaps help him deal with my possible reaction. He doodled on a notepad throughout the meeting. As I was leaving, he was transferring a pencil from the paper to his mouth. The next stop was probably his ear; and that's how I will always remember him. A few days later, I did something I had not done before nor since. I took a "mental health" day and went fishing. I did so on a day I was scheduled to supervise the MLC.

I have no idea where the man is today, or where his career path eventually led. Years later I heard that he was teaching a class someplace in the state college system—seemed logical. By now he's probably long retired and living in a planned community in Somewhere, Arizona. In his dotage, he might even be delusional enough to believe that he did some good, and his light was well spent. I hope someday he might read this and recognize himself in the text. I also hope he ultimately rose absolutely as far as his ability and character could take him.

There was a woman hired at the same time as I. She taught the English component of our program. The kids had her crying constantly. She often tried to buy their silence and cooperation with candy and little toys. She ordered pizza for the entire class once. I never knew you could call in and have a food fight delivered right to your classroom! She refused any duty in the MLC and took each of her allotted sick days solely for mental health purposes. At times, I doubled up on classes because she simply couldn't cope anymore. When the program was discontinued, she was hired to teach accelerated English at a different building in the system. Seems her husband was a county commissioner. Really an amazing coincidence.

That summer I worked, went to class, was despondent, and planned a wedding. All except the anxiety were being done on a shoestring. On that, I lavished most of my time and energy. Three or four times I managed to get interviews, and for a day or so I was nearly giddy with hope and relief. When those didn't pan out, I fell to a new level of depression. Finally, two weeks before the wedding, I got lucky and found a job in a small neighboring school district. My assignment would be to teach basic skills to learning-disabled kids. It was what I had been trained for and what I hoped would become my future role as a teacher. I would also be coaching baseball and football. The principal noticed my background in weight training, so if I was interested, I could also supervise the weightroom at 6:00 am every day. Of the dozen or so questions asked during my interview, eight or ten related solely to *coaching*. By this point, I had come to expect that as the norm. Many of my prospective principals didn't know crap about Special Education, but all were determined to hire the best coach available. The principal assured me this would be a great year athletically. My prospective school was expecting good things in most sports. After a long dry spell, athletic notoriety again beckoned. I was going to be part of a local sports *renaissance*. For at least this year, my new principal could probably go to administrative meetings and hold his head high. It's really amazing how much status a principal could glean when their student body included a few outsized kids with violent tendencies. Tall kids were good too.

The interview went well; at least, this guy didn't seem to have any obvious and disgusting personal habits. He seemed a bit stuffy, but at no time did his pencil approach his ear, nose or mouth. Only once was he curious about what I had done in the past year. It does me little credit to say that in answering, I lied like a rug. I told him I had gone to school and subbed a bit. He wondered if I had been in any buildings often enough that someone might give me a reference. "That's probably unlikely," I assured him. "I was in quite a few different buildings, none of them more than a time or two. There were a few teachers who might remember me, but I did nothing long term." This disconcerted the guy a bit, but the references which I brought with me from Eagle River were good, and trying to fill in the one-year gap in my resume would have taken more effort than he really could expend at this point. Besides, it was late in the summer. Hiring should have been done a month ago. By this point in the interview, he had already made up his mind to hire me. He was a baseball guy and was impressed with my baseball credentials and previous record. It surprised me when he asked me where we intended to live. I indicated I really wanted to live within the district where I taught and was surprised when he suggested I think about living elsewhere. He didn't immediately explain himself, and the statement just hung there as he turned back to his desk. As I was leaving, he said in an almost offhanded way that property values out here were really high, and I might do better just down the road. I didn't consider it further. On my way out the main doors, I stopped by the district office and signed a contract. The rest of the summer was a blur. Wedding plans were finalized. Everything considered, it was a beautiful ceremony. No prime rib, but a champagne toast. The photographer we hired took his final picture of us against the backdrop of a beautiful setting sun. Forty-odd years and three fantastic children later, in my memory it has become a rising sun.

There is a very special place in heaven for middle school teachers. Everyone of you is a better person than I.

How good are you at herding cats?
How well can you handle noise?

What's your policy on cell phones?
Because the kids will probably use 'em.

Can you deal with all the giggling,
when the girls discover the boys?

Will it bother you to be ignored,
when you ask the class to lose them?

Are you comfortable with snapping gum?
Can you deal with lots of tears?

That about concludes this interview,
and a decision we have made.

Cuz sometimes kids get difficult,
when they reach their middle years.

You could qualify for sainthood,
or to teach in our seventh grade!

Have you ever dodged a spitball?
Can you cope with funky smells?

Cuz your room is going to have 'em,
when the temperature it swells!

XVII

Jodie

That September was about new beginnings. Newly married, new job, new apartment. We didn't plan it that way, but Mary and I were also going to become new parents right before the end of the school year; a honeymoon pregnancy. More than anything, there were new responsibilities. In all the different aspects of my life, it was time to grow up. The idea of becoming a father terrified me. Soon, I would have a family that needed me to be an adult, and I was in no way sure that I could handle adulting. When I look back on my life, the day that I first held my son was perhaps even more powerful than the day we got married. Now, I truly was a hostage to fate, I had to be better. My experience teaching in a middle school was behind me. Maybe with time there would be perspective, but for now there was only resentment. I carried a sense of failure with me to this job, and that was new for me, too.

The district where I was now to teach seemed to be an especially agreeable place. It was located in a third-ring suburb, but the area still had a rural feel. Horses grazed across the street from the high school, and there was standing corn visible at a few compass points. The town was bisected by the same river that I had often fished as a boy. It was also the same river from which my father had poached and sold walleyes during the Depression. I took this as a good omen. It was a fast-growing community. Only a few years before, I had bow hunted a quarter mile or so from where the high school now stood. The major business enterprise in town was an ancient hardware store built from the bones of an old sawmill. At least four generations of the same family had taken their livelihood from there, one pound of nails at a time. It was a store where you could find almost anything, and all of it was covered in dust. The owners were amazing in their ability to locate almost anything amid this seeming clutter.

Most of the town's citizens commuted a long way to work. The city had no real industry. People lived there because the taxes were low, and you could still afford land enough for horses to graze and letting your dogs run. In a lot of places you could shoot a gun out the back door and no one would notice or care. The roads were more gravel than tar, and most fences were of barbed wire and wore signs which warned you not to trespass or hunt. A lot of the old farmsteads had "shootin' cars" permanently parked on the back forty. These were the rusty crown jewels of impromptu personal junkyards, which also usually included at least one discarded major kitchen appliance and a sixties vintage lawn mower. When I arrived, I thought it to be a poor district, or perhaps the residents simply placed little importance on the usual suburban status symbols. Many houses were small, and the casually maintained yards were large. Only the few homes built in the town proper had city water and sewer, so most of the district's residences were well separated from their neighbors. There were some early signs of suburbanization as some middle-class developments were beginning to sprout up, and two golf courses were in the planning stage. The homes right along the river were beautiful and expensive, with extensive and well-landscaped yards. But everywhere else, crabgrass and sandburs were locked in mortal combat with timothy and rye grasses. A quarter of the district's students lived in trailer homes on rented lots. Most of these were located along the only major highway within the district borders. Overall, the high school was regarded as tough and blue collar. The district itself was located on the most politically conservative side of a very conservative county.

My first glance at the student parking lot was another education. It appeared the official vehicle in this neck of the woods was a Chevy truck. More often than not, the back window of these trucks was festooned with at least one confederate flag and an N.R.A. logo. Bumper stickers warned potential revenuers the occupant of this vehicle would surrender his personal weapon only when their cold dead fingers were pried off the trigger. This was melodramatic as all hell, but still a glimpse into the psyche of my new clientele. They hunted out here. If a creature walked, crawled, trotted, ambled, flew or slithered anywhere within the borders of this district, it was a candidate for meeting an untimely death at the business end of a twelve gauge. Snowmobiling was also huge, and seeing two new sleds parked next to a tumbledown shack or a double wide trailer stopped being a non-sequitur after the first hundred or so times I observed it. I surmised this was a district which might pass an operating levy but once in a generation, and few students aspired to more than tech school or community college upon graduation. This was true when I arrived, but my perception and the reality changed radically over the time I spent teaching there.

Our opening day workshops that year were little different from any of the others I had been forced to attend. First, fire up the troops. An ample woman in floral stretch pants favored us with three a cappella verses of *Hi, Neighbor.* She then droned on for two hours about the role of the school in building community. She kept telling us that she was "gonna get her cows into our pasture." Kind of meaningless to me, but the message was really OK. Still, the song and presentation together sucked most of the air out of the room. The faculty was unimpressed. The old guys slept. Many others openly gossiped. Only the non-tenured teachers paid close attention, lest someone from admin was watching. When she was done, all the new staff got a quick introduction, and we were given an opportunity to say a little something about ourselves. I said as little as possible. After that, we met in smaller groups and discussed *cosmic* educational questions such as, "when should we mark a student as being tardy?" and did students need to be seated by the last tone of the bell, or just in the room?" Hard to believe, but these issues generated a good deal of passion. Voices were raised and a table or two got pounded. We then discussed the issue of hats. Should kids be allowed to wear them? Sadly, these grave questions went unresolved, and after lunch we broke down into even smaller groups to discuss why we couldn't come to any agreement. This required another inane icebreaker. This one involved selecting three items we would take with us on a trip into space, and the things we most feared about the journey. I was less than thrilled, but I hadn't taught there long enough to be a smart ass, so I actually played well with others. I did however say something about my greatest fear being "Klingons" (It's never good when you need to explain an attempt at being clever.) By the end of the day, we agreed we couldn't agree, and the principal should dictate policy. This was of course what was going to happen anyway, but the dimmer bulbs in our little groups walked away feeling newly empowered by the opportunity to offer their weighty and learned input into these thorny issues. Everything considered, it was a waste of time for all involved. As with so many others in attendance, I endured it only as a precondition of being allowed to teach again.

In preparation for my first class, I had read each of my students' Individualized Educational Plans (IEPs) at least twice. Some of the folders were nearly two inches thick, and most chronicled a trail of academic failure stretching back into the student's elementary school years. It occurred to me these were some of the first kids who should have benefited at least a little from the passage of P.L. 94-142. Still, it was evident that some of them had made a painfully small amount of progress during their few years of intensive remediation. The same goals and objectives kept recurring. The targets for reading rates and comprehension levels had shifted slightly upward over the years; this indicated progress. However, even an incurable optimist would have to conclude that many of these kids were still losing ground relative to their non-handicapped peers. If they managed to graduate, they would be farther behind their classmates than they were on the day they entered a Special Education program. For some, their reading and math scores had plateaued. One had actually regressed since seventh grade. I really didn't know how much credence to give these or any other test scores. A kid in the academic mainstream is tested too often, and a kid in a Special Ed. program has to suffer through even more tests. Being that these are no-consequence affairs, many kids don't really give a damn about their scores, and the admonition to "do your best" is a guaranteed eye-roller. Trying to draw valid conclusions from the "data" is really only making an informed guess.

I was assigned to work directly with two experienced female staff members, and either of these ladies could have been easily picked out of a crowd as Special Ed. teachers. Kathy was the younger of the two, and I will always remember she wore lavender cologne. This made her small room smell like a Victorian parlor. She possessed a frail beauty, a characteristic common to many young elementary teachers but seemingly out of place in a high school. Her students loved her. The other lady, Joan, could be anyone's favorite aunt. She smiled well and often. She drove a full-sized Dodge pickup truck, which didn't really fit her persona. She was a former nun who had opinions and causes, and this probably explains why she was a *former* nun. Both were described to me as "real sweethearts," a sexist description, but accurate. Perhaps because I was a man in a feminine domain, they each treated me with a great deal of indulgence and more courtesy than I was due. More than once, they saved my job by helping me become familiar with the required paperwork. I can't begin to express my appreciation for all the help they gave me that year. For the first time, I felt I had mentors. Looking back on my career, I can't stress enough the importance a mentor can play in the development of a young teacher. When I first stood in front of a classroom, I had no real business being there. In time, I believe that I grew into the role of teacher and coach. With a little help, the trip from inept to competent would have been a lot less bumpy for both me and my students.

I was given a specific caseload. Fifteen kids were assigned to me for direct instruction. Of this group, eleven were either freshman or sophomores. The plan was I would be their case manager for the balance of their time in high school. All of these students had been diagnosed as learning-disabled. The remaining four were seniors and no one honestly expected I would accomplish much of anything with them. Whatever I *could* do which might enable them to take a walk on graduation night was acceptable. Frankly speaking, the high school had given up on these kids; and because three of the four had no real intention of getting additional training, this would be the last school to ever do so. Their goals and objectives all involved assignment completion and "survival reading strategies," whatever that meant. None of the four saw graduation as a portal to a better life or a prerequisite to getting additional training. To each, it was only the reason for having a long-promised grad party—something that was probably held out a thousand times as a bribe by desperate parents. If only they could just make it through... then there would be kegs, and there would be gifts. For one night, they would be the center of attention. The relatives would come by, and a parent may even make a public statement of their pride in the child's accomplishment. There might be yard games and friends would stop by. For many of them, this favorable attention would be a first. Somewhere on a table in the garage, they would proudly display their diploma, and it would look identical to those given to their classmates.' Maybe there would be pictures, too. That diploma would likely be the only "trophy" earned in their high school careers, and the crowning achievement of a four-year struggle. That year, three of my seniors eventually got their diploma and their party.

Jodie was my lone female senior student. She was nineteen years old and already twice a mother. The testing we had on her indicated she had an IQ of about ninety, but that test was probably administered on a good day; or at least on a day when she hadn't been working most of the previous night. I doubt anything had ever come easily to her, certainly not school. Her personal hygiene was poor. She had oily skin, terrible teeth and bad breath. For each of these, I pitied her. When I considered the cumulative effects of these and all the other strikes that were counted against her, I marveled that she came to school at all. A hundred times during the year, I thought about how great it would be if someday I could take her to a dentist and direct them to fix all that was decayed or yellowed. Then, she could take her newly brilliant smile and newfound confidence to an interview and secure a job that would pay enough to offer some hope and a future to her kids. Of course, given my finances I would never be able to make it happen, but like many teachers, I think I would have been a damn good rich person. (That's kind of how I rationalized buying Powerball tickets. "Lord, if you let me win I swear that there will be no kids needing dental work left in this entire county.") But, as it was, unless something unexpected happened, Jodie was on her way to becoming a permanent member of the underclass, and all I could really do to ease the trajectory was to buy her an occasional school lunch.

I know that empathy is no real substitute for professionalism, and I never planned on doing so, but that year I completed a lot of her schoolwork for her while she put her head down on her desk and slept. I didn't know what else to do. I did not have the skill, or the time required to fix a lifetime of lost opportunities, so I became a life jacket. What she desperately needed now was a diploma. A piece of paper which might serve as the passport to a better life for her and her family Maybe it could finally give her some options. For that year I could keep her head above water, and even now I refuse to feel any guilt for doing so.

The kid really worked. Her attendance was excellent. She came to my class directly from an overnight cashiers' job at a gas station/ convenience store. As soon as she arrived, she would use my phone to call her mother and ask how her kids were. We then usually went to the IMC to read the help wanted section. She wasn't looking for a different job; she was looking for a second one that would not conflict with school. The balance of our time was spent on homework from her Math and Science classes. Neither teacher was going to cut her any slack because "I have my standards to uphold." Neither of these two had been in the classroom for more than a couple of years. Over time, I was to see both grow into fine teachers. But that was years in the future, and Jodie didn't have the time to let them develop a little empathy.

I read Jodie's tests to her and more than once directed her to the correct answer. I confided as much to one of Jodie's English teachers. She didn't pretend to be shocked. I can still feel her hand on my arm as she thanked me for not making her decide whether or not to fail that "poor kid." Strange thing for her to say because each of us already knew what decision she would have made. Looking backward through a forty-year-old lens, I am proud I once shared a profession with that fantastic woman.

I can say the same thing about many of my colleagues over the years. As willing as I seem to be to excoriate those I considered to be poor teachers, I stand in awe of the charity and kindness daily exhibited by many teachers. The examples are endless. In the days before a girl could simply go to the nurse's office for help, some female faculty members routinely kept feminine hygiene products in their desk drawers for their students to use. Other staff kept protein bars in their desks for kids who hadn't had a square meal that day. I did this for most of my teaching career and was seldom taken advantage of. It's a rare teacher who has never given a kid money for lunch. Coats and boots were commonly donated. Cash was willingly given to buy their students' yearbooks, athletic equipment and school pictures. Fees were waived. A Spanish teacher I worked with provided some after-school day care so one of her students could get to a couple of job interviews. One of our Family and Consumer Science teachers made a prom dress for one of her students. Every time a school-sponsored team or club had a fundraiser, teachers were the first to be asked. In one of my final years, I supported over twenty school-sponsored activities. I was not unique, and many teachers were more charitable than I. Every career teacher will someday retire with closets full of wrapping paper, gold cards, Christmas ornaments, discount coupons, popcorn, candles, and stale band candy. Over the years, they will have discarded many additional items like frozen pizzas, pies, bread braids, and cookie dough—products which might have a suspicious chain of custody. For all of this, they will eventually walk out the door with a fake-gold desk set, a certificate suitable for framing, and their memories—lots of memories! For me, so far that has been enough.

That spring, Jodie graduated. Before she left, I hooked her up with county services. We arranged some day care, and she was set to go to the local technical college to become a nursing assistant. She dropped out after a few weeks, and I have no idea what became of her. After knowing Jodie, I will never consider that I have ever in my life had it tough, and I will always get bitter with people who talk about bootstraps and work ethics. Such people are usually spoiled rotten and do not know the smallest thing about the lives of people who truly have had nothing given to them.

What follows is a political screed and may seem out of place in this narrative. It is however part and parcel of how I feel about the problems confronting kids and education in America. There is real poverty in every school community. For too many years it has been ignored. As I said, I am a liberal. Hell, I might even be considered in some circles to be "woke." Given that this little bit of invective is usually hurled by rednecks as they are losing any argument not based on alternative facts, I will consider being called woke, as a compliment. I am especially liberal when the issues involve kids. Abject poverty in America bothers me deeply, especially among kids. There is no excuse for it. If you are a dyed-in-the wool conservative, you could make a strong argument that Jodie had created most of her own problems and was therefore one of the "undeserving" poor. You might argue that while she probably hadn't exactly chosen to become a mother at age 15, she didn't choose chastity either and had a second child, and after all, "behaviors have consequences." That argument is hollow and usually offered by people who have always had options. It is so easy to become self-righteous and condescending when we examine other people's lives and choices. When I was younger and dumber, I did it myself. Teaching has taught me so much about perspective, empathy, reality, and the convenient lies many people tell themselves.

We all look into our own past and see a mountain of woe which we somehow overcame only by pluck, grit, and hard work. We will happily tell all who will listen, **"Nobody ever gave me anything, I earned what I have."** In most cases, this is such bullshit. There certainly are inspiring stories of people who beat the odds. They worked their tails off, and fortunately for them, in most ways, they were on the right side of the genetic curve. I admire these people and would never try to minimize their accomplishments. I also believe that truly self-made individuals are more inclined towards philanthropy and service than those who inherited their wealth and position. But for every Michael Bloomberg there are a thousand others who had help along the way, refuse to acknowledge it, and really don't intend on paying it forward. Perhaps for most of us, our good fortune was something as simple as coming from a stable home, or having access to a good school, or being born white and middle class. Few people really make it without some spiff. Ann Richards once used a line that I sometimes reflect upon. "He was born on third base and is convinced that he hit a triple." This is especially true for many of the well-to-do. "Yes, my father left me a business, but I worked my butt off to grow it, so nobody ever gave me anything!!" "Yes, I took a job with the family company, but I started at the bottom and *worked* my way up. Nobody ever gave me anything!!" "Yes, my parents loaned me a million dollars to get started, but in ten years I had paid it all back and made a million more besides. Nobody ever gave me anything!!" The attitude is perpetuated when the spawn of some of these unctuous butts make applications to elite colleges and are moved to the head of the line because of legacies or connections. They never had to reach for the brass ring. It was handed to them. Then, they forget, and they now look in the mirror and see only a self-made success who owes nothing to anybody.

For years in America, we had a kind of intergenerational covenant. Each generation was willing to tax itself to provide an education and a future for the next. Schools were built and staffed. Roads and bridges—physical and figurative—were built. This favor was repaid when future generations came to the schoolhouse door and asked for the same. In my years in the classroom, I have seen how this intergenerational understanding has frayed. Each year, I see more of the "I got mine" mentality. Selfishness has become more the norm than the exception, and the rationalizations for cupidity and mean-spiritedness flow like water.

"After all, no one ever gave me anything. I earned everything I have! Besides, if the schools become shit, it will make no difference to me. The schools are failing, and why should I support a failing institution? I think the schools these days are teaching so much stuff I don't want my kids to hear; like this C.R.T. stuff. Mine will have graduated before the roof totally collapses. I am moving to the Sun Belt for six months and a day, each year, when I retire. That way there will

be no state taxes to pay. I will however keep my lake home up here in God's country." Listen fat cat. If you went to a public school in almost any state, you are still on the debit side of the social ledger. This is especially true in Minnesota. Several generations paid for your education and your children's education. Your property and state taxes haven't begun to pay back the debt owed. That statement will still be true when you are eighty. How much of the income which you earned in Minnesota was tax deferred as you built up your retirement accounts? Will this ever be paid back? If you truly had nothing else, education was probably your spiff, credit card, and life raft, without it there would be no second home in God's country. There may not even be a first home. Please ponder that thought when you rush out to vote against your district's next operating levy.

In my second year in the new district, the school board got up the courage to ask the local residents to approve a bond levy. The funds raised would be used to perform overdue maintenance on district buildings, plus purchase a modest number of computers for classroom use. This levy was sorely needed. Our chances for success were meager at best. As the day for the vote neared, a group of us teachers volunteered to do some door knocking in hopes of garnering support. The proposal would have cost the average district household about nine dollars a month. At most of the homes I visited, people were generally polite but uninterested. A few were rude and quite willing to share their opinions about "what a bad district this is," and how "the goddamn administration is already wasting money by the bale, and why should I give them some more to piss away?" One of the houses I stopped at was a two-story colonial with a brick facade and a three-car garage. The driveway was circular, and it enclosed beautiful beds of perennials, and a small fountain. The owner told me that he had no interest in providing additional support for the local schools; he open-enrolled his kids in an adjoining district, and he didn't give a damn about this one. As I left, I thought that this guy really needs to buy a statue of a black jockey with its fist out stretched for the front to really complete the look. Never have I so wanted to give someone the finger.

Towards the end of my evening, I knocked on the door of an older three-bedroom rambler. It was cheaply built, and the Masonite siding was swollen and rotting off in spots. The roof had seen better days and the door on the detached garage needed replacing. There were a variety of riding toys in the front yard, so there were children in the home. A man answered my knock and by his dress and demeanor, I judged he was just finished with a long day. I introduced myself and my purpose, and totally expected another full-throated protest that his taxes were already too high and where the hell did I get off coming around with my hand out asking for more. Instead, he listened carefully, he asked questions, and then he agreed the district schools could use a few upgrades. I guessed that nine dollars a month probably meant something to him, but obviously not as much as his kids' futures. He even wondered if he could speak to the issue at his church next week? I thanked him profusely for the offer.

I left, amazed at the generosity of the man's spirit. I'm guessing he wasn't born into a huge amount of privilege, but he was willing to help his kids, all kids, do a little better. He was a man of character. I went home feeling more positive and upbeat than I had in months. A few weeks later the referendum actually passed.

When I taught in Eagle River, I had a lot of students who, much like this man, weren't born on third base, but in most cases, they had something to cling to. Most had values. Maybe their best possible future was to take over the family farm and continue to eke out a meager living from the land. Maybe they had a strong back and were fortunate to have been born in an era when that alone could shield a person or a family from becoming destitute. Perhaps it was nothing more than being a part of a large family that was willing to look after its own. But very few of those kids were dealt hands that were pretty much unplayable. Now that I was teaching in Special Ed, I daily worked with kids who had few choices, and the cards they held stunk. Jodie and others like her had few *real* options. The most consequential choices in their lives had been made for them. Jodie never chose to be raised by a single mother. She never chose to be physically abused and raped by Mom's boyfriend. She never made a conscious decision to have a learning disability or get involved in the meth trade. All teachers occasionally see things which trouble them deeply. Special Ed. teachers do so daily, and it's one of the major reasons why teacher turnover rates in Special Ed. departments are so high. The other major reason will be discussed in a later chapter.

My three senior boys were generally self-sufficient. One had as his most prized possession a chainsaw. It was a much different time, and he once brought it to class to show me. He also used it in an English class to give an explanatory speech about the superiority of STIHL products. When he graduated, he was going to continue working with his father in a firewood business. A second was really quite skilled at carpentry, and in the fall, he was scheduled to begin a construction trades apprenticeship program. The third simply wanted to bum around the country for a few years. When he had satisfied his wanderlust, he was going into the carpet cleaning business. Somebody had convinced him the job was well-paid and in high demand. He invited me to his graduation party with the understanding I would leave before the first keg was tapped. I obliged him on both counts. He sent me a letter a few years after he graduated. It was close to National Teacher Appreciation day, so I assumed that to be his motivation. The entire letter read:

McLean,

Just a little note to thank you for putting up with me. I'm doing good, got to see a few things after I left high school, and I am now living in Wisconsin. I hope you are good and still teaching.

Allen had always been a man of few words. There have been many days when I questioned my decision to become a teacher. That day was not one of them.

For the freshmen and sophomores on my caseload, I was primarily charged with reading instruction and helping them stay current with their mainstream assignments. On the face of it, things seemed pretty straight forward. No more than four students were assigned to me at any one time, and each had specific goals and objectives which had been decided upon at a staffing the previous spring. They had also been retested last spring, so I had a reasonably current performance level on each. However, as the testing was done in May and this was September, it was probably a lock that each of the kids on my caseload had regressed. Summer break is detrimental to the educational development of most students, but to a kid with learning disabilities it is deadly. Each of my students was already at least three grade levels behind their peers in their reading and math proficiency.

I was determined to change that. During my graduate work, my professors had done a very good job explaining to me the *science* of reading. I now attempted to master the *art of teaching* reading. I came to realize they were not the same thing. There are skills which can be taught to a young child rather easily and systematically. I think that reading may be one of these. Unfortunately, reading instruction gets progressively more challenging as a child ages. By the time a student shows up on a school's radar screen as being significantly below grade level, remediation is already difficult; by the time the same student gets to high school, remediation to grade level may be impossible. I don't know why this is true. Perhaps after a hundred failures, kids become hard-wired to fail and dismissive of the possibility for success. Also, some kids become masters of surviving school without the ability to read; this is especially true for girls. They develop enough teacher-pleasing behaviors that they are promoted more or less automatically. Several of the girls on my caseload were ultimately given diplomas because they smiled appropriately and didn't become discipline problems. This was also true for many girls in mainstream classes. Boys were usually more "in your face." They expressed their frustration by acting out or wearing a facade of indifference. Assignments were seldom done, and when they were completed, they often 'forgot' to turn them in. It is very easy to accept failure if you can convince yourself that you didn't really try or care. It's much harder to admit you couldn't read or understand.

At some level, my learning-disabled kids knew that school was important, and reading was a critical skill; the motivation to succeed was there. I think the fact I was trying different strategies than their previous teachers was encouraging to them, but looking back on those years, I still feel a frustration that has been little abated by time. Weekly I took oral reading samples, and the results were unimpressive. Progress was painfully slow. I began to review the current literature for anything which might facilitate their learning and found precious little that really worked. Each strategy was somewhat effective for a time, but each failed in the long run. I discovered there were things which I could do which would get me a temporary spike in certain aspects of reading. Vocabulary could be drilled and improved. Reading rate and fluency could be increased. But reading comprehension was the key, and that remained a rock that consistently shattered my best efforts. During the course of my time as a Special Ed. teacher, nothing I tried significantly improved a student's reading comprehension. I still remember kids who came to me intimidated by the printed word, and I think many left feeling pretty much the same way. It's a painful admission, but I failed them miserably.

The kids I was working with were usually so deficient in background information they could not fit new learning into any kind of meaningful whole. In terms of reading, all of them got better at decoding text, but that by itself didn't help them extract meaning from the text. The factoids may have been there, but drawing conclusions and making assumptions is dependent upon a base of prior learning, and they simply didn't have enough. As school became more complex, the cumulative effects of their deficits became greater and their deficiencies more obvious. The students internalized their lack of success and concluded, "I'm stupid." During my time in the classroom, I have had dozens of students make this statement to me. Usually, they were telling me they didn't get something, or they simply hadn't done something, or it was a sympathy play and they needed reassurance. But kids with healthy egos do not look at you and in a matter-of-fact way tell you they are stupid. Over the course of their academic careers, my students had accepted the message and the snowball just kept rolling downhill. Many times, it became an excuse not to try, or to limit their dreams.

Gina and Curt were probably two of the best examples I encountered of negative self-perception. They were both on my caseload and absolutely smitten with each other. Both were bright, friendly kids who accepted in a rather matter-of-fact way that they were stupid. They made self-deprecating jokes about being dumb. (God but I hated that.) Gina was especially heart-rending in this regard. She tried so hard and cared so much. At conferences, her mother told me that Gina did at least two hours of homework a night, and I believed her. Curt had stopped trying years ago.

One day, Gina asked if she could come to my room after school and talk to me. That Curt came too was no surprise, as I expected he would. Almost immediately, Gina began to cry. It seemed there was to be a new coffee shop in town. A small place, but they would be hiring seven or eight employees. Between sobs, she managed to choke out that she really wanted to work there. Her family could use the money, and perhaps she could save a little bit for some training after she graduated. In what must have been a tremendous act of courage, she went to the storefront where the shop would be opening and asked for an application from the person apparently in charge. She took it home and soon realized that neither she nor her mother, nor Curt, could completely fill it out. She could write her personal information, probably from years of practice. However, the simple question, "Why do you want to work here?" completely defeated her. She could have done a hundred things. One of her friends could have helped her. Certainly, one of her teachers, myself included, would have helped her. However, she ripped up the application, threw it in the trash, and refused to get another. Curt went and got another for her, but it was still in her backpack. She kept it more to humor him than to complete later.

"Why am I so stupid, McLean? You know no one will ever hire me, and I can do that job, McLean. I've run cash registers. I can clean. I think that I am trustworthy." It took a few minutes before the tears stopped, and a cup of coffee before she was composed enough to listen. I told her I had been teaching for quite a while, and I absolutely knew she was intelligent enough to accomplish anything she was determined to accomplish. We talked a little bit about the nature of learning disabilities and schools that would help her once she graduated. We set up an appointment with her counselor, and a couple of weeks and a few calls later she was employed. She and Curt graduated and went to a local community college which had a resource center for learning-disabled students. Curt finished a program in auto body repair. Today, he and two classmates own a small shop. Gina finished a program in cosmetology and today she works for a major hair cutting chain. They got married four years after graduation, and to my knowledge, have two kids and a home on a pretty plot of land just outside of town.

During my years in the classroom, I learned how fragile the adolescent psyche is, especially today, when cruelty can be endlessly multiplied with a mouse click, and egos can be shattered with a thumbs down icon. I learned that most kids in the school feel themselves to be in a type of academic competition. It has poorly defined rules but definite winners and losers. In such an environment, it's easy to understand why kids internalize their failures and become "stupid." Many times, I tried to explain to my students that if they were diagnosed with a learning disability, it was proof they were at least within the range of average intelligence, and some were much higher than that. A student is placed in a program for the learning-disabled only if their academic achievement significantly lags what might be expected from their IQ scores.

Despite their learning disability, some of my kids displayed a real facility in some non-academic parts of their lives. Some displayed mechanical aptitude and did well on non-paper and pencil tasks. One student of mine could take apart an entire automobile engine, diagnose a problem, fix it, and reassemble it in running order. Many of his friends trusted him to do their mechanical work. Another designed and sewed most of her own clothing, and she did it well. A couple of them seemed to command a real wealth of trivia in certain discrete areas. One boy in particular knew as much about the Second World War as a couple of our history teachers. He was really into tanks and fighter planes. During free reading periods, he stared at pictures of P-51 Mustangs and the main battle tanks of the allied and axis combatants. About every week he wanted to play a game he called, "Who beats?" "Hey McLean, a Russian T-34 battles an American Sherman, who beats?" "Hey McLean, a British Spitfire gets in a dog fight with an American P-38, who beats?" Then he wanted to argue with my answer. Once, we were reading aloud a story about a boy who dove into a well to save a child who had fallen in. When it was his turn to read, he piped up with. "Those Japanese tanks really sucked." Originally, I saw this as kind of precocious. His mother did also, and at conferences she pointed to this behavior as clear evidence that her child was really bright and that the school simply failed to draw it out of him. "Mr. McLean, if he knows all these things, why isn't he doing better in school?" I had no answers for her then and would have few now. Looking back, I think that the kid was clearly somewhere on the spectrum. We knew so little about autism then. I can't remember that it was ever discussed in my graduate education programs. Or if it was, the kids discussed were clearly and profoundly handicapped. These students were sometimes fitted with helmets so as to avoid injury if they threw themselves to the floor or against a wall. They were assigned a fulltime aide. In the years since, I've had a few kids in my classes diagnosed with Asperger's syndrome; some were a pure delight, others were disruptive to the degree they had no business being there and compromising the educational opportunities of every other kid in the room.

By this point, legislation had been passed which required that, regardless of disability, a student be educated in the "least restrictive environment." This concept was never clearly defined, and in practice will always be a subjective placement for the handicapped student. This is great in theory, but in practice it has become a duel of competing rights. As with educational funding, many times it pits the handicapped kid against their non-handicapped classmates. It also pits teachers against each other. It seemed that as a Special Ed. teacher, I wasn't really a part of the larger faculty. To the mainstream, we were often viewed as glorified teacher's aides. This was especially so when it was decided that the best use of Special Ed. staff was to have them team teach with a mainstream instructor. On the surface, this looked like a workable way to provide a somewhat modified classroom situation to the handicapped student within the mainstream. In some situations, this worked out well, but more commonly, it didn't. If Special Ed. teachers advocated for their students, they were seen as pushy. If we expected mainstream teachers would make meaningful accommodations, we were asking them to do more work. None of this helped to develop the type of educational team which might better serve the needs of the handicapped. In these situations, the Special Ed. teacher was usually relegated to taking attendance, making copies, passing things out, or a dozen other classroom management chores better handled by a teacher's aide. This was demeaning for the Special Ed. Staff. It was also a poor use of resources. I know that at times my relationship with a few teachers was more antagonistic than collegial—to a lesser extent I hope; but this may still be true in many classrooms.

She probably closed the store last night.
Which wasn't really legal.
Which wasn't really right.
She had very little time for sleep.
So it wasn't very long.
So it wasn't very deep.
Yet still she drags herself to class.
She tries to learn.
She tries to pass,

But her family needs the hours she fills.
To help with rent.
To help with bills.
Her homework is of course undone.
No time for that.
No time for fun.
The price she pays; so steep it seems,
She's forfeiting her childhood.
She's forfeiting her dreams.

Almost every day I taught, I saw at least one of these kids. They were hanging on by their fingernails in the hope of something better happening for them if they could only make it to graduation. Now, tell me about how tough **you** *had it.*

XVIII

Who Benefits?

When I began the coursework required to teach Special Ed, I was only vaguely aware of the different levels of service offered or the variety of handicapping conditions being addressed. The two ladies I've described and I were teachers of the learning-disabled. This was the largest segment of our special needs population. We had two additional teachers who were certified as instructors of the moderately mentally handicapped, then termed MMH These students were labeled based primarily on IQ scores. There was also a separate component for the emotionally and behaviorally disordered or EBD students. By law, all of these kids needed to spend a certain amount of class time interacting with the mainstream student population. For the students on my caseload, this was usually not difficult. Most were pretty well-behaved, and by having them with me in a study hall, they could stay current with most classroom assignments. Back then, mainstream teachers were required to make only minimal modifications to accommodate handicapped students. Over the course of my career this changed radically, but in the early eighties, modifications to testing and curriculum were made by the Special Education teacher, and then only with the acquiescence of the mainstream instructor. There were situations where it was simply not "appropriate" (I put quote marks here because "appropriate" is the single most overused word in all of education) to place some students in general classes. One truly conduct-disordered student could effectively destroy the learning environment for thirty other kids and little could be done to prevent it. I have seen this happen, especially in elementary classrooms. Parents have every right to complain when the classroom environment becomes so chaotic that the educational opportunities for their own children are compromised. This is not supposed to happen, that it does is an unresolved issue which few districts have effectively addressed.

Adam was the single most disruptive student I'd seen up to this point in my career. His behavior issues began in kindergarten and became almost exponentially worse during his time in elementary school. By junior high school, he was assigned a full-time aide to walk with him in the halls and sit with him in classes. He had a history of running away from the poor woman and hiding in different spots in the building. In P.E. class, he once tried to choke another student with a shoelace. Nothing came of the incident because he maintained it was a joke, and he had no intention of really hurting the kid. There was a brief suspension and then the district pretty much papered over the assault. There was a restraining order filed by the parents of Adam's intended victim, but he suffered no real consequences.

By the time he got to high school, Adam was out of control. He was by no means stupid; he was a bright kid, but I would also describe him as cunning. He always managed to take things right to the edge, then backed off before there was any reason for police involvement. Over the years, his parents became expert in contorting the laws governing Special Ed. to make constant, impractical demands upon the school district. Many of these suggested accommodations involved litigation, and the expense to the district was staggering. Because they usually won, in time the district simply threw in the sponge and gave them whatever they demanded. This included the *on-call* services of a behavior modification specialist. This gentleman was paid to come to all meetings regarding Adam's IEP. He also had to observe Adam on a weekly basis and meet with him for therapy and counseling. Once, while being observed during a class, Adam lost it completely! The profanity and volume of Adam's tirade was stunning. The classroom teacher was totally powerless. He *pleaded* for the specialist to, "Do something!!" The high-priced consultant merely replied, "Control is not my thing," and calmly continued taking notes. (Ever hear an expression describing the utility of mammary glands on a male cow?) These "expert" services *plus* the cost of a part time anger management aide were borne almost entirely by the district.

The plans generated to accommodate Adam's special needs were beyond bizarre. He was given release time every day to go work in the school's greenhouse. He was given his own office in which to do his class work. Because we were cramped for space, the dean of students had to relinquish his own office for a couple of hours a day. Adam now essentially ran the school. The bitterness this caused was probably the main reason the dean resigned two years later.

Adam was the only student in the building who had a recess. Daily, he was allowed to wander the school grounds, even the town. His case manager was required to go with him. This went on for almost two years. Finally, after his third physical altercation with a staff member, the school at last managed to get Adam placed in a more restrictive setting. I recall he eventually graduated, and the last I heard, he had started a business and was doing well.

Adam may have been the most disruptive young man we dealt with, but he was not an isolated case. We were required to make extensive modifications and provide services for several belligerent and potentially violent students. Much of their anger was directed towards staff. This was not unique to our district. I cannot validate this with statistics, but at the junior-high and high-school levels, there are very few Special Ed. teachers who have not been threatened with violence or verbally harassed. Many have had physical confrontations initiated by students. During my career, I had two. I can't begin to count how many times a student suggested that I do something which was both impossible and unnatural. Once I had to intervene when an especially large young man tried to choke a para-professional. The assailant was seriously disabled. In truth, I can assign no blame to the student.

The problem was with his initial placement. He never should have been in a public high school. The assault occurred in an empty classroom located in a far corner of the building. I pulled him off the woman and got him to the police liaison office. When I reported the incident to the principal, I was told that because the kid was on an IEP, the school would try to deal with it internally. I was also threatened with having a disciplinary letter put in my file because I had used some force to get the kid's hands off the woman's neck. Apparently, I should have been able to de-escalate the situation *before* it got to that stage. Being that I wasn't in the room before the incident *occurred*, I think *that* particular scenario was a tad bit unlikely. The lady involved never set foot in the building again, and I was a coward for not pursuing it further. Incidents like these partially account for the high turnover rate among special ed staff, but the *primary* reason has little to do with kids and everything to do with paperwork.

When I began teaching in the field, an Individual Education Plan was usually seven to ten pages long. The document was a proposed course of instruction and included goals, objectives, and accommodations, agreed upon by the Special Ed. teacher, administration, mainstream staff, and the parents. In time, transitioning to the world of work and related training goals were included. Because of the number of meetings required and the different people who needed to be in attendance, the process was involved and could be lengthy. This was in the mid-eighties, and each year the amount of paperwork required to be in compliance kept expanding. A third of the Special Ed. teacher's day might now be spent developing and maintaining these IEPs. A teacher might be terminated if IEPs were not done in a correct and timely manner, no excuses. During my time as a teacher, I saw three of my colleagues dismissed for poor or incomplete paperwork. Two of them were *damn good* teachers who were overwhelmed by bureaucratic demands. I have no idea how I escaped a similar fate. Objectively, my paperwork sucked, and it wasn't for a lack of effort. Hours when I should have been teaching were spent perseverating over forms. The stress this placed on me and other staff was almost paralyzing. On more than one occasion, I saw colleagues in tears after a particularly scathing review and a thinly veiled threat that, "your paperwork better improve…" To cover their asses against lawsuits or disciplinary action, Special Ed. staff documented everything they did. All direct instruction of assigned students, all parental contacts made or attempted, and all meetings with mainstream teachers. This was done whether the paperwork was legally mandated, or just for self-protection. The amount of time it consumed detracted from the quantity and quality of instruction.

The hurdles for Special Ed. teachers increased, and the money-pit got deeper when the district saw fit to hire quasi-administrators to directly monitor the teacher's efforts at compliance. When I first became a Special Education teacher in the early '80s, the entire Special Ed. program consumed about 10% of the district's budget. In the six years I served in that capacity, the amount had grown to about 15%. I have no idea what that percentage is today. However, I can say with certainty that in many buildings, the Special Education department is the largest and most extensively staffed.

This expansion of services while unsustainable might be justified if the targeted population actually benefited from the proposed intensive remediation. Some students do, no doubt, but even the best programs fall well short of the success envisioned by the authors of P.L. 94-142.

As the administrivia associated with Special Education was metastasizing, I was spending less and less time as a reading teacher. I was becoming a full-time case manager and hating it. I began to look for opportunities to get back into the mainstream as a Social Studies teacher. For the first time in my career, I began to dread going to school. Actual teaching had almost become secondary, and much of my time was spent doing endless paperwork and modifying mainstream coursework for the students on my caseload. Which is to say I was often watering down the curriculum. This is a terrible admission and will probably draw a scathing reaction from most Special Ed. teachers, but from my perspective it was, and is, true. I say this anecdotally, but I am reasonably certain that a very high percentage of mainstream staff would agree with me.

Certainly, some modification to the curriculum is valid and necessary. Allowing students additional time to complete assignments is common sense. Allowing a student to use a resource room to take tests or do class work is also a very common-sense accommodation. Allowing a student to have a test read to them is a valid way to assess. But deconstructing tests in a way that renders them almost meaningless is a disservice to the student. Examples: On four item multiple choice tests, the instructor will eliminate one of the incorrect choices. No test will require written responses or short answers. No essay tests. On all tests, students will be graded pass-fail. The student will have the option of retaking any failed test. Students may eliminate or cross off a certain percentage of the questions. There are more examples, but the point has been belabored enough. Modifications made to daily assignments were often more extensive. Once, a science teacher I was working with observed the proposed modifications and suggested that perhaps the best thing he could do was to put the student in a sunny corner and water him occasionally. For this, I can't blame the individual Special Ed. teacher, nor realistically can I blame individual districts. Sometimes, simply getting the student to graduation is in the best interest of the child. But for most students, disabled or not, a high-school diploma should indicate a certain level of achievement. Sadly, this is often not the case. I have no doubt there are schools that offer excellent Special Education programming, and their kids are truly ready to succeed in a job or move on to additional training. I am equally sure that many school districts have neither the resources nor expertise to offer this type of consistently high-quality programming.

Recently, these inequalities have been somewhat addressed with legislation designed to target additional funding to less affluent districts. But still there is no real parity in funding. Richer districts with a large property tax base can offer services that poorer districts cannot. This is true for Special Education and every other program a school district might offer. The problem has been exacerbated by open enrollment. If a parent can opt out of their home district and send their child to one they see as better performing, they often make the move. In Minnesota, state funding follows the student. There is an incentive for schools to compete for high-performing kids. They do so by offering better facilities and enhanced opportunities. Programs for the gifted-and-talented have proliferated. Language immersion programs are now commonplace, and International Baccalaureate and AP classes are often available. Offering concurrent enrollment programs makes it possible for students to graduate with most of their college general ed. requirements completed. This is a huge benefit to many kids and their families. They are also expensive and require funding. Opportunities for competition in athletics have expanded, and I think it fair to say that poor districts cannot offer lacrosse. Richer districts can afford this educational arms race. Less affluent ones cannot. Certainly, districts *do not* actively compete for special needs students, especially those kids who require a laundry list of services. The cost of providing these services can be overwhelming. This concentrates student populations on both ends of the achievement spectrum. Over the course of my career, I have seen these disparities get incrementally worse and there seems to be no real solution, or at least not a solution that is politically feasible. In fact, a more likely possibility is that the situation will become much worse.

Today, many states are trying to implement some type of voucher program. This will give parents an opportunity to opt out of the public education system entirely. (I will discuss this at some length later in this narrative.) Perhaps, some parents and students from less-privileged backgrounds will use vouchers as an opportunity to escape grossly underperforming schools. This could be one positive scenario and has happened on occasion. A more likely outcome is that more affluent families will use their voucher to pay a portion of the tuition at private schools. Most of these parents will be white, and many are middle- or upper-class. Most of the private schools opted into do not have Special Ed. programs, nor a requirement that they accept any student who chooses to make an application. The use of vouchers may well re-segregate many school districts, and further exacerbate the economic divisions between schools. This does not bode well for public education nor for democracy itself.

If you are a teacher reading this, you understand this situation with the clarity of a thunderclap. Every day, in many classrooms it has become a battle of competing rights. Many handicapped students have benefited greatly from inclusion in mainstream classes. At times however, this hasn't worked for their non-handicapped peers. For this situation, I see no clear or easy solution. My own daughter is a teacher; and I believe a darn good one. She believes the two years of Covid Closures have exacerbated the behavior issues for all students. It has also put Special Ed. kids especially, further behind the eightball. Kids, all kids, have lost almost two years of learning and socialization. Hindsight is 20/20, but we should have found a way to keep the schools open.

Part III

XIX

Almost a Bad Banker

By my sixth year as a Special Ed. teacher, I had become completely disillusioned with the direction my district and the state were going in providing services to handicapped students. Most of this was dictated by the economics of education, new state mandates, and the persistent threat of litigation. When I left Eagle River, I thought that my best possible purpose might be to teach kids to read. I still felt that way, but daily I was spending more and more time on secretarial functions. There was still the occasional kid who I really believed I could help, but not in the way I envisioned when I undertook the coursework for my Special Ed. licensure. Many students with special needs do not have regular or positive interactions with mainstream staff. However, these same kids will often open up to their case manager. Much of the best work I did in Special Ed. was just providing a sympathetic ear to students on my caseload. These kids had some unique problems, but they were still kids. They needed adults to talk to. They desperately needed praise and reinforcement, and they needed someone to look for reasons to praise, and behaviors to reinforce. I'm convinced the best Special Ed. staff are first and foremost world-class listeners. They are also patient, empathetic, and kind. Many of the Special Ed. teachers I worked with were truly remarkable people. Sadly, a good number of them are also in the process of burning out. I know I was. Bit by bit, I became over-invested in my kids. Many of them were on my caseload for all four years of high school. Over the course of time, I learned way too much about them. I knew about young ladies with anorexia. I knew about probable drug and alcohol abuse. I could tell if my kids were high, I recognized when they were unnaturally depressed. Abuse, physical, emotional, and sexual, was not uncommon. As a mandated reporter, I followed up most of my suspicions with a referral to the nurse's office or guidance, or admin. In some cases, these ultimately found their way to county social services. Once or twice, they got to the police. These agencies responded as well as their limited resources allowed. A couple of times the only response I got was an angry call from a parent suggesting they knew it was me generating the referral and I should go fuck myself. Once there was a threat of retaliation. My own family suffered. My mood was terrible. I constantly worried I had screwed up somewhere on a tranche of paperwork. After six years as a special Ed. teacher, I was faced with a rather stark choice, either quit being a Special Ed. teacher, or quit teaching—period. I was at a mid-career crisis and really saw no good alternatives.

The ultimate decision was precipitated by paperwork. Through a series of unfortunate, and in my opinion unavoidable, circumstances, my spring paperwork was incomplete and deemed to be deficient by administration. If you are familiar with the IEP process, you understand the myriad ways this can happen. If not, suffice it to say that God was unavailable when I really needed her to countersign a couple of required forms. I was told in no uncertain terms I was a liability to the district and replaceable. No explanations on my part were considered, no excuses accepted. For the second time in my career, I tolerated being berated for something which even in hindsight I saw as beyond my control. This time the humiliation was worse and more long-lasting because the woman dressing me down was a thirty-something who never once had taught a class or managed a caseload. By this point in my career, I had been selected as a Teacher of the Year in two different school districts and had received a similar nomination at the state level. I had received commendations from two school boards. No administrator had ever expressed the smallest concern with my teaching. This all amounted to nothing when compared with the egregious sin of having incomplete paperwork. By this time, Mary and I were expecting our third child. Quitting to find another position would have put too much strain on my family. A thousand times since that day, I have replayed the incident in my mind. Each time I did, I came up with a different and pithy way to tell the lady what she might do with the job, the district, her paperwork and her pretensions. But I *needed* this job. With a mortgage and two kids who needed the occasional pair of shoes, keeping my self-respect wasn't an option; and open teaching positions were scarce. This was especially true if I wanted to get back into Social Studies. Were I a Math or Science teacher, there were opportunities and options in several neighboring districts. But there's never been a real shortage of history teachers. If you shake a tree, two or three fall out. Still, I sent applications to every district within fifty miles and hoped.

By July, I had pretty much given up on anything opening up for me. I had not so much as an interview. This was no surprise. It was late in the hiring season, and by now I was a reasonably high-priced potential employee. With an advanced degree and experience, I would command a pretty decent salary; for a teacher that is. I had yet to resign my Special Ed. position, but I knew that chapter of my life was probably over. With great reluctance, I accepted a job at a local branch of a large national bank. I would start out as one of those guys who inhabit a desk in a small kiosk, usually located near a big box grocery store or major retailer. During the interview, I gathered that my primary function would involve flagging people down and convincing them they could not survive another day without some overpriced, exotic financial product which only this particular bank could provide. There would also be some cold calling. During the interview, it was not so subtly suggested that I was a little old to be looking for an entry level position. I really didn't need to hear that. I was to start in two weeks. Fourteen days to hope for a minor miracle.

Looking back, I'm extremely confident I would have reeked at the job. Thank God, I never found out. A few days later, a guy I taught with called me to let me know a senior member of the Social Studies department had decided to retire due to poor health. The department was taking this as an opportunity to reorder their sections and create classes for at-risk students and some Special Ed. kids. It wasn't a bad idea. It would be good for students, and also make life easier for every other teacher in the department. My colleague thought I might be interested. I was thrilled! As a tenured teacher with the appropriate licensure, I was entitled to request a transfer to the open position in Social Studies. My new assignment would require me to teach two sections of freshman civics, two sections of sophomore American History and a section each of Economics, Geography, and Senior Social. The kids placed in these classes would not be good students, many had behavior issues, many were poor readers, and few of them wanted to be in school. All things I was familiar with, except now I wouldn't be hampered by the kingdom's bureaucracy and endless paperwork. One of the unstated goals of the new program was to keep these kids from dropping out and going to the alternative learning center in a neighboring district. Again, it was a decision based on money as well as pedagogy. Dollars follow the kid, after all. For the first time in my career, I was assigned a teacher's aide. She would handle any required paperwork, plus classroom management tasks. She was a godsend! Cheryl truly was one of the great people I have ever worked with. In the five years I taught within this framework, I was able to learn more about teaching than I had in the previous ten. She made it possible for me to concentrate completely on my craft and on the kids assigned to me. Should she ever read this, I believe she will recognize herself in this narrative. I hope she knows much of the success I had in those classes was hers. Putting a woman in the room made a fantastic difference. My female students came to see her as a confidante in a way that I never could have been. She also moderated the behavior of the boys. At five feet even and maybe 100 lbs, I think she was a more effective disciplinarian than I. She helped me escape the Kingdom of Spec Ed., and I will be forever in her debt. My only regret was leaving a truly dedicated cadre of teachers. Folks who daily tried to serve the educational and emotional needs of the most challenging portion of the student body. These committed professionals deserve all the praise and props which might come their way. Regrettably, few will ever be recognized for their contributions to the most needy and vulnerable part of any student body. I do *recognize and respect* them. As my career progressed, not a day passed that my mainstream students didn't benefit from the insights I gained as a Special Ed. teacher, or the skills I developed teaching alongside my former colleagues in the kingdom. I resigned from a bank job I never started and began to prepare for my new position.

I'm done with endless worrying,
about forms I may have missed.

I'm done with endless scurrying,
so the admin. won't get pissed.

I'm done with all the staffings,
and I'm done with IEPs.
I'm done with all the shit I take,
If the parents I don't please.

I'm done with keeping phone notes,
for every call I make.

I'm done with all the mainstream staff,
who see my job as cake.

I'm done with modifying,
all the work my kids should do.
I'm done with justifying.
*Today **I quit,** I'm **through.***

XX

Best Memories

The classes I was assigned to teach were for kids who had experienced little success in school. Some were Special Ed. students, and my classes would serve as part of their required mainstream inclusion. Most of the rest were simply described as "at-risk." This could mean almost anything. Some had experience with the juvenile justice system. A few others had attendance or behavior issues. The rest simply had failed multiple courses and needed to succeed and perhaps stay on track for graduation. None of them was a real viable candidate for National Honor Society. To the credit of the building administration, I was given a remarkable amount of flexibility to create a curriculum which at least loosely met the state standards and also kept the kids in school. At the time, the basic aid formula from the state was around $1600 per pupil unit, half again as much for high-school students. If a kid dropped out or went to an alternative school, real dollars went with them.

The classroom I was given was a pit. Once a storeroom, no one had taken care of it in years; it didn't show up on any custodian's cleaning schedule, so it was filthy! The wallboard was breached in several places where someone had been careless with a two-wheel hand truck, likely while moving spare desks or file cabinets in and out. Kind of like man-made mouse holes, and judging by the droppings surrounding them, they had served as such. The carpet was threadbare and patched together from remnants. A good number of the suspended ceiling tiles had been removed to be used as replacements in other rooms around the building. There was a clock, but it hung from the wall by its electrical connections, like a spent jack-in-the-box, and perpetually read ten minutes to nine. In the middle of the room were two support pillars. The room had been deemed to be unsuitable as a classroom a long time ago. I had been in the building for six years and had never seen the inside of this space. The Social Studies department chairperson told me it was the only room available. Our building had become overcrowded due to a welcome influx of families moving to the district, and "of course it would be cleaned before I held my first class." He told me that if I was totally put off by the classroom, I had the choice of becoming itinerant staff. This meant I would put my teaching materials on a cart and move between open classrooms when other teachers had their prep periods. This was *not* a good option, by any means. Teachers, especially the more senior ones, become proprietary where their rooms are concerned; and I didn't blame them. As a teacher ages, a good part of their life gets transferred to their classroom. There are books, pictures, and file cabinets full of things which haven't been looked at in years. Perhaps there is a "brag wall" decorated with degrees, certificates, or any proof of achievement or excellence. Most importantly, memories sit in each desk. Six times a day, I would have felt like an intruder. Not to mention the hell I'd catch if things were out of place or missing.

I wanted my own room, and despite its obvious flaws, I wanted this room. It had two large windows which I really liked, and perhaps the only remaining blackboards in the building. I've always liked chalkboards. Some of my best memories of school were made in rooms with enormous blackboards, and erasers that you could clap and create a cloud of dust. When I was in elementary school, we competed for the honor of doing so. Blackboards were places where kids could play a game of hangman during study hall or draw when they had a few stray minutes. Most importantly, *my* room was somewhat removed from any other classroom, so I was free to make a little noise, and I intended to make noise. We were going to sing. I didn't know it at the time, but that room was to become the greatest teaching tool I have ever had.

That fall, as my first class filed in, each kid reflexively stopped in the doorway and glanced around the room. One of the young men pretty much summed up the consensus of his classmates when he muttered, "This is a piece of shit." He was a bit surprised when I responded, "Glad you weren't looking at me." I also told him we would fix it. Day one of my first class, I asked the kids to bring in every partially full can of light-colored latex paint they had around the house. All were curious, and five or six kids complied. That weekend I came back to school, mixed all the donated paint together, and covered the walls with the result. The color wasn't as terrible as I thought it might be. It was a kind of light gray-green and would prove to be a good background for my kids to draw on. The wall panels I divided into decades, each labeled. We began in the 1800s and went up to 2020. Some decades were allotted more than one panel, but my goal was that when complete, no matter where you looked in my room, there would be a history lesson. Every student who had a class with me from that day until the day I retired was required to leave something on the walls and to sign their work. The drawings had to be of things "historically significant." This is subjective as all hell, but the kids got it. The drawings were to be placed in the correct historical period and I had to pre-approve the subject. If a student felt her or his artistic ability deserved a grander venue, I would haul down a ceiling panel and let them decorate it. In these cases, the subjects were to be of my choosing, and when complete the ceiling would represent a pictorial timeline of American history. Every kid in that class was to sign the back of the newly decorated panel. I had already decided the first ceiling tile was to be an illustration of the land bridge between Alaska and Asia; the second a Viking ship; the last, a drawing of me walking out the door with a fishing rod over my shoulder. There were 180 ceiling tiles in the room, and ultimately 179 were filled. The last one never was done. In time, my teaching load expanded beyond at-risk students. But, I kept the room, and the drawings multiplied.

Dealing with my assigned segment of the student population taught me an incredible lesson. All kids really do want to learn. Even the biggest pain in the ass that walks into your room wants to learn. But often they don't want to learn in the way teachers most often want to teach. In one of my at-risk geography classes, a young lady once looked at me and said, "McLean, can I ask you a question about something I've wondered about for a couple of years? I assured her that answering questions was my job. "Are the girls in Africa like us?" I told her that except for more melanin in their skin, yes, they were exactly like American girls, but usually not as well nourished, and they didn't obsess over boy bands and glittery make-up. My attempt at humor flopped, and she went right on with her inquiry. "OK, McLean, then what do they do when they get their *deely bop*?" At once, another young lady chimed in, "Ya, McLean, I've thought about that, too; it's not like they can run to Walmart and buy pads!" I explained that perhaps I was not the *best* source to ask, but I did tell them where they might get the information. Then I let it drop. Two days later, the first young lady came into class smiling and proudly told me she had found the answer. She also found a bunch of information on several things kind of related, like how women in less developed cultures handled childbirth and birth control. That was impressive, and I told her so.

These kids could be taught, of that I was sure. No matter what they had been conditioned to believe, they were not stupid or unmotivated or a dozen other negative descriptors. If I came up empty on ideas for a really creative lesson plan, I often simply read to them. They looked forward to it. Sometimes I told them to put their heads down on their desks and just concentrate on the language. As with my other at-risk group, we read *Night* and *A Day No Pigs Would Die*, This was kind of a coming of age story about a boy forced into adulthood when his father dies by Robert Newton Peck. We read *Hatchet*, Gary Paulsen's novel about a teenager's struggle to survive after a plane crash, and a few others. They loved *Walk About,* and it became the basis for a journaling assignment. They enjoyed the discussions which followed and being on a more-or-less equal footing with every other kid in the class. A class without superstars can be a great thing.

They loved doing hands-on things. To learn a little archeology, we once grabbed some metal rebars, but on boots and went into a boggy area near school and used the rebar to probe a short way down in the peat. At heart I am an optimist so when we hit something solid, we took a shovel and dug it up. Usually, all we did was liberate a long-buried tree branch. Once an old bleach bottle, but there was always an initial bit of excitement and anticipation that this time it just might be the skull of a long extinct bison. One of my autistic kids fixated on dinosaurs, T. Rex especially. The boy was an incurable dreamer. Of course, he never found a T-Rex skull, but not for lack of trying. We made primitive tools, and some were ingenious. There were stone hammers and wooden spears, but once one of my kids did a bit of research and made a functioning atlatl. That remained in my room until I retired. It was a reminder to myself that the labels we put on kids like **at-risk,** do not really *define* them. These labels do, however, often *describe* them. For surely this group was at risk of being so turned off by their entire school experience that they would drop out and by doing so, cut themselves off from a million potential opportunities.

To celebrate the Lewis and Clark bicentennial, we went orienteering. One of my colleagues had been a U.S. Army Ranger, and he was willing to give my kids a quick course on the use of a compass and topographic map. He helped me set up a short orienteering course and was spry enough to put a couple of the flags up in some trees. The kids who found them bragged about their keen eyesight and climbing skills for weeks.

Lewis and Clark took an extremely powerful air rifle with them on their journey of discovery. So, I decided that we *were* going to have an air rifle shooting contest but was told by the principal under no circumstances was that going to happen. In hindsight, it was really one of my more boneheaded ideas and rightfully rejected, but it would have been cool.

We did other hands-on things, but one especially stands out. In each class, we had a day designated "To build a fire," an obvious take-off on Jack London's short story by the same name. In teams, the kids were to find a way to build a fire without using any current technologies. I also banned flint and steel, and magnifying glasses. "Too easy." We never got one going, but one team gained some celebrity by getting a bit of smoke using a fire drill and a bow. Another thing I discovered was that these kids began to like each other. The dynamic in the room was really positive. If someone missed a couple days in a row, there was genuine concern expressed. We celebrated birthdays. I brought in a couple of hot plates and cooked them breakfast once.

As many schools do, we had a canned goods collection right before Thanksgiving to help restock the local food shelves. Classrooms were to compete, and the prize was a four-foot sub sandwich. We resolved to win it. I told the kids I would match their contributions item for item. While this might seem overly generous on my part, I really didn't expect I would be on the hook for much. I thought my group would go home and search the pantry for items like canned asparagus or some nasty variations on obscure root vegetables. Again, I underestimated them. The cans poured in. We had some good, worthwhile contributions. I kept my word and matched the class, but I have to admit it pinched a bit. There were also a few more packs of ramen noodles and mac and cheese than I was intending, but the rest of the building was doing likewise, so "when in Rome." There were some oddball contributions, too. One of my students hauled in a case of fresh bok choy. I thought this to be strange. But all twelve bunches were added to our tally and helped us win. We had a great celebration and shared a sense of accomplishment. I later found out that one of my kids worked at a Chinese restaurant and the bok choy contribution may have been a little sullied. I never asked him how he got it. I choose to believe his employer made a donation. The most remarkable thing donated was a gallon can of garbanzo beans. This monster must have been World War II vintage. Costco wasn't a thing yet, so something that out-sized was unusual. I was a little worried about the safety and age of the contents, so instead of donating it, I kept it as a traveling trophy, awarded to the high scorers on tests. They were allowed to sign it and return it to a spot of honor on my bookshelf.

This class served as a mainstream intervention for inclusion purposes for many of our Special Ed. students. I had a young lady with Down syndrome who was with me for part of the day during much of her high-school career. She first came to me as a sophomore. She was so shy. Her aide was a fantastic lady who treated Caroline as she would a beloved grandchild. She brought books for Caroline to look at and tapes for her to listen to during class. Caroline always had headphones on, and her head was usually down on the desk. I think it took until October before she actually looked at me; or rather, at the plant I was carrying.

My wife had a hibiscus she wanted to try to keep alive over the winter. She knew I had two large south-facing windows in my classroom. I had no idea if the sunlight would be sufficient to keep the plant alive, but I was willing to try. With Caroline watching, I put the plant in a spot where it would catch the most sunshine. The plant had only a single blossom, but two large buds were beginning to swell, and shortly would be beautiful flowers. Class was starting soon and as I was making final preparations, Caroline's aide came and asked me if Caroline could come and smell the flower. I walked to the plant, removed the flower, and went back and gave it to Caroline; or tried to. It took several assurances from her aide that it was alright before she finally accepted it. We all have things that are indelible in our memory. As a parent and grandparent, I carry almost fifty years of memories of my kids and grandkids with me at all times. As a teacher, I carry a similar mental album of my students. The smile that slowly spread over Caroline's face was instantly and permanently etched, and a dam had been broken. When her aide took the flower and placed it behind her ear, Caroline looked at me and said, "I'm beautiful now." All I could think to say was, "You always have been, darlin'." From then on, when I saw her each morning, I *usually* got the same smile and a wave. There were mornings she was sullen and petulant, but she was after all still a teenager. I put her in charge of the plant, and daily she watered it and broke off any diseased looking leaves. She was also in charge of distributing any new flowers that appeared to the other kids in the class; she had a waiting list for blossoms no single plant could ever accommodate.

Her aide figured out that if the plant was to get the maximum sunshine, it had to be moved oc-casionally. Caroline did this. One morning I came to my class and found a very sullen Caroline with her aide hovering over her. She had her head down on the desk, and I think she was crying. Her aide explained that when the custodian vacuumed last night, he moved the potted flower a long way from where Caroline placed it the day before. When the sun came up, we rectified the situation, and to make sure that it never happened again, we marked the proper spot on the carpet with some tape. The plant responded well at first. But as winter wore on, there were fewer and fewer flowers. The plant became kind of infested with small flying insects. The infestation never diminished Caroline's care and attention for what surely had to be the best loved hibiscus in Minnesota. In the spring, right before the summer break, Caroline came to my desk and gave me a small stuffed bear. I had it on my desk all the years I taught after that. Now it's on my desk at home, I am glancing at it occasionally now as I write this account. It is a wonderful memory. Between the tiny bruin and her smile, I will never forget her. That little girl showed me almost daily the joy that can be taken from simple things. She was one of the best teachers I ever had.

Several students were with me for four years. As they progressed from freshman to senior, I was their only Social Studies teacher. Perhaps this was not healthy. But I have never been able to know any students so well as I did my at-risk kids. This was made all the better because now I didn't have the stressors I experienced as a Special Ed. teacher. In this class, it was almost as if we had managed to recreate the best parts of an elementary classroom. Unfortunately, district finances made it impossible to maintain the program. I was disappointed and saddened by this decision. In transitioning to an all-mainstream class load, I arranged to keep as many of my at-risk kids as I could in my regular classes. Some of my former "at-riskers" still drop me a line on occasion. Recently, I saw four of them packing food together at a nonprofit where I work on occasion- *Feed My Starving Children.* It took a while before they were sure it was me, and one of them quipped that ,"You look so different without hair, McLean!" But they were happy to see me and remembered me well. I will remember them always.

Opening up my classes to the general student population proved to be a good thing. Like my at-risk charges, the mainstream kids almost immediately took ownership of the room and began to see it as their space. Throughout my career, I never had a group that didn't enjoy decorating. When I first began letting the kids adorn the walls with their history-themed artwork, I had some concerns my panels would be an open invitation to vandals, but this never really happened. Once I had to erase a joint that some kid had drawn in George Washington's mouth. On another occasion, one of my immature freshmen thought that it would be clever to give a drawing of Sandra Day O'Connor a penis. Not one of proportional scale, but a truly huge unit. (Why is it that the height of freshman cleverness often involves drawing a penis on something?) Heart shapes with initials inside proclaiming true and eternal love appeared occasionally. However, the things I most feared like racial slurs or homophobic screeds seldom happened. Overall, I was pleased with how the kids respected each other's artwork. As the years accumulated, it became the artwork of many previous classes of students. I eventually taught several children of my classroom's former "artists." I stood open-mouthed in disbelief the first time

I heard a kid tell me, "You had my father as a student." I spent about a week afterward sitting in my basement, reflecting on my own mortality. But after a while, it became fairly common for me to show some kid what their mother or father had drawn "back in the day."

Over the years, I needed to buy more ceiling tiles and art supplies. On more than one occasion, I needed to defend my space against an overzealous administrator bound and determined to "get rid of that eyesore" and relocate me into one of the sterile boxes which became available as our enrollment started to shrink. Once I had to enlist the support of one-time students, now adult members of the school board. It took very little pleading to get them to see the room as a kind of school institution worth preserving.

Former students occasionally returned after school hours to see how the walls and ceiling were progressing. Some brought their own children, eager to point out what mom or dad had drawn when they were in high school. One of the best memories I carry from my years in that room was of a student I had early on in the at-risk program.

It was December, shortly before Christmas break. It began snowing about noon that day, and while certainly not a blizzard, enough had fallen to make the roads interesting. It was getting dark and though I didn't consider myself to be an "old" man by any stretch, the beginnings of cataracts made night driving a little interesting for me. Besides, my route home was lousy with deer, and I had already thinned the herd twice that year. I was putting on my coat to leave when a short man in his mid-thirties with bright orange hair knocked quietly on the frame of my open door. He had two children with him, a boy and a girl. They were perhaps both in early elementary school, and each had inherited dad's hair color. He appeared hesitant to come in at first. The children were less so, and quickly moved closer to the walls to get a better look at several of the Disney characters recently drawn. They also found Fred Flintstone and Barney Rubble, along with a dozen other cartoon figures and Muppets. The little girl beckoned to her father to "come look, Daddy, this must have been such a fun room." Slowly the man moved to his daughter's side and told her, "It was honey, I wasn't here for very long, but it was fun."

The entire time this tableau was playing out in front of me, I was frantically searching my memory for a name, and for one of the few times in my career, nothing came to me. "For Christ's sake, how had I forgotten that hair?" He must have recognized my discomfort, for he quickly put me at ease by telling me that he would have been amazed had I actually remembered him. Moving toward me with hand extended, he introduced himself. "Hi, Mr. McLean, my name is Ron. I was in your class for a couple of weeks about 17 or 18 years ago. I shouldn't have done it, but then I dropped out, eventually got my G.E.D., and joined the army. I just got back from Kosovo and for some reason I wanted to show my kids this room. Rather, I wanted to show them some evidence that I had actually been a student here. That I had actually been a student at all." With a little bit of searching, we soon found the Tonka truck he had so painstakingly drawn all those years ago. His name underneath it, an indisputable proof of ownership. His son was mightily impressed with his father's artistic ability and loudly proclaimed his dad's drawing to be, "the best one in the whole room!" Ron smiled for the first time since he appeared at my door. He imagined aloud that I must have thought him a dumb shit for dropping out, but he hated school with a passion. That "nothing me or anyone else might have done would have kept him in school, and quitting had really worked out well for him." Seems the Army found him to be a young man of high intelligence. He was placed in psy-ops and advanced through the ranks quickly, eventually becoming a Master Sergeant. His duties involved important and often classified work related to national security.

He was recently discharged and took a responsible position with a Fortune 500 company based in Minneapolis. He and his wife were happy. But nostalgia is a powerful thing, and lately he was thinking more and more about paths not taken, friends long forgotten, and a diploma never received. He was wondering if I could locate the ceiling tile other members of that class had signed. He had no yearbook to help him put names to memories, and now he wanted to remember. By this point in my tenure, I had perhaps eighty of the tiles decorated and could only approximate where the one he wanted might be. I gave his kids a set of colored magic markers and indicated a couple of spots where they might wish to add to my collection. Both leapt at the opportunity, and Ron and I climbed up on a couple of desks and started to take down ceiling tiles. By the fifth one, we had it. Even the accumulated dust of a decade and a half couldn't obscure the names so carefully signed by Ron's sophomore American History classmates. I pointed to a few of the names and shared what I remembered about them, or what had become of them. One young man we both remembered fondly had died in a traffic accident only three years ago. Another was in prison, which surprised neither of us. One was a sheriff's deputy, which amazed both of us. Many were still in the area, doing basically what he was doing: raising a family and being productive citizens. Ron took down a few names and started to replace the tile. I stopped him and asked if he wanted to sign it. "But I didn't graduate, Mr. McLean," I told him none of his classmates would object to his inclusion and that I was proud to have once been his teacher. Even if it was for no longer than it took to draw a Tonka truck on a classroom wall. He smiled and signed his name with a flourish. All three thanked me as they turned to go. The room they left, now made better by the addition of the red Power Ranger and Bat Man's cowl. All three were laughing as they walked through the snow to their car.

That night, I learned how important it is for kids to leave a wake on their journey to adulthood. If they're lucky or talented, it might be a series of achievements, or perhaps nothing more than their handprints pressed in wet cement, or a jersey number scratched into hot tar. Maybe only a memory attached to their name. Once at a Chinese takeout place, my bill wasn't right. I told the cashier I owed about another five dollars. She said the bill was correct, that one of the guys in the back had given me his employee discount. I asked who, while craning my neck to look into the kitchen. Right away I recognized a former student working a fryer. He glanced at me and, while still focused on his work, he simply said. "Because the last time you were in, you remembered my name." As we age, we all occasionally go back to places that are laden with the artifacts of our childhood and adolescence. To look at something tangible, something we can pretend is permanent. The things in our lives we once thought to be important and hope they will remain. Places and things that were a huge part of our growing up and are now stitched into the fabric of our hearts. Distant, but never completely forgotten. An old stone arch bridge, or maybe a huge rock on the riverbank, where we always used to fish. A tree that was, and still is, impossibly gnarled. Something that memory has given us title to. Or perhaps nothing more than a signature on a ceiling tile, and a drawing of a Tonka truck.

Over the years, the art appearing on my classroom canvas changed. The kids wanted to draw people I never heard of. Images of rappers and athletes appeared. Heavy metal bands I would never listen to, and iconic characters from video games I would never play, became common. Unfortunately, so did place names where mass shootings had occurred, or hurricanes and earthquakes had left grim reminders of human frailty.

Only once in my career was I accused of being a racist. A black student of mine wanted to draw a likeness of Tupac Shakur on a prominent spot on the wall. Now, I was (am) about the least "hip" person there is. I had no idea who Tupac was, so I said I'd need to look up Tupac first. He just went off on me! Accused me of being a bigot and worse. I was dumbstruck! Before I could respond, he stormed out of the room. Still in shock, I asked a stunned class who Tupac was. Now *they* were truly amazed, this time by my ignorance: "*Who* was *Tupac*?? McLean!!" I sent another student out to find my accuser. When he returned, I explained to him and the class that most of the time, bigots are indeed stupid. But, all stupid people aren't bigots. He accepted that, and he apologized for the accusation. The next day, he apologized again, but this time with a bit of a jab. He said, "McLean, I think that you are really cool, but in some ways you are the *whitest* person I have ever met." I asked him about it a few times, but he never really explained to me what he meant. In time, I've come to understand, somewhat … but, I'm still not very "hip" and probably never will be. I expect that I'll blunder through the rest of my life blissfully unaware of a lot of popular culture.

I was pleased when a class decided we should include a memorial to the victims of 9/11. We built a floor-to-ceiling framework of the Twin Towers using two by fours. We covered the superstructure in blue linoleum tile squares and around the base we used chicken wire, paper-mâché and spray paint to create a facsimile of a gray dust cloud. We cut the likenesses of the Pentagon and the state of Pennsylvania from a sheet of plywood, and painted them. These were mounted between the towers. The names of the victims, almost 3000 souls, were inscribed where they had died. The class named the Memorial, REMEMBERING THE FALLEN. A young lady won five dollars for suggesting the title. Looking back, the memorial was the best thing we did. It also assured the room would remain untouchable. No administrator was going to take ownership of eliminating the Memorial.

There were other class projects. Once in summer school, while studying sweatshops, we hand-sewed together a huge U.S. flag made entirely from the kids' discarded jeans and sweatshirts. I enjoyed watching a couple of the class "bad asses" sitting in a circle, hand stitching that flag. One, acting as the self-proclaimed foreman of the project, started to bitch at the others that their stitches were too big. Other embellishments included, a functioning lighthouse, a pretty fair-sized guillotine (with a *non-le-thal* plywood blade), a totem pole and a TARDIS—more about that later. But when I think of my old room, *the Memorial* still stands out.

In the 31 years I was there, my goal was to create a space which belonged uniquely to the kids. Few teachers get the chance to do anything like it, and I am thankful I had the opportunity. Long term, I hoped when I retired, some bright and ambitious young teacher would get my room, paint over the walls, throw out the clutter, and start again. Unfortunately, this wasn't to be. But every teacher on every level should try to make their room a space that belongs to their students. Good elementary teachers do it every fall. I would encourage all teachers to push the envelope. I freely accept that I was given lemons, and the administration turned a blind eye as I made what I thought to be lemonade. But I doubt anyone has ever been fired for painting things like the Starship Enterprise going into warp on their door. I know; I did it. Get paper, huge sheets of paper. Get your kids to draw a seven-foot-high Frederick Douglass, or M.L.K. or Caesar Chavez, or all three. Outside my door, I had a five-foot picture of Yoda swinging a green lightsaber. He was drawn to bear a remarkable resemblance to the room's occupant. Written over the picture was the inscription: "If knowledge you seek: Teach you I will" At the end of the hall, my class drew a huge picture of Mt. Rushmore. At the top, the legend read, "The Other Founders" the customary likenesses of Washington, Lincoln, Jefferson and Roosevelt were replaced by images of MLK, Tecumseh, Harriet Tubman, and Caesar Chavez. I don't know if I could get away with that in today's political climate. It seems it is alright to build monuments to traitors and defend them as part of our history and heritage, but honoring other heroes in such a venue just may be too "woke."

One day, a student presented me with two street signs that read McLean St. I thanked him pro-fusely for having them made up, and I put them on either side of my door. I was now the official owner of the social studies hallway. Two years later, right before he graduated, the street sign donor came to see me after school. Rocking back and forth, with hands stuffed in his pockets, he sheepishly con-fessed to stealing the signs from a street corner in Pease, Minnesota. The signs were weather-beaten when he took them, so he sanded them down and repainted them. There was a brief "What the hell" silence before I started to laugh. I scolded him, just a bit. Told him that while he was a criminal, I still intended to go to his graduation open house and wished him luck on his finals. I also gave him my email address and told him to let me know if I could help him in any way when he got to college. (A note to people who teach seniors, do likewise, nothing I've ever done was more appreciated.) Today, in retirement, those signs hang on my inside garage wall, and I smile each time I see them.

A few years before I retired, my principal stopped by to chat. He told me when he was interviewing new teachers, he always stopped by my room to show them "We respect and encourage creativity in this building!" He thanked me for, in a sense, giving every teacher in the building permission to be a *little* off the wall. "Every school should have someone like you on staff," he said, "but no one should have two." I still smile at the earnest way he said, "but no one should have *two*." If I could give any advice to a new teacher, it would be this: do your best to be a *little* different. Have a thing or two that is uniquely yours. Have a bit of a schtick. I was amazingly fortunate that in my career I was given permission to do so many of the things I have described. I know that throughout this narrative I have excoriated principals, collectively, and at times individually. What I wanted most from administration was simply to be left alone, and most of the time, I was. In some cases, I had administrators who were *incredibly* helpful and considerate. I had a principal who once came to the ceremony where I was being given an award. That meant something to me. With one exception, everywhere I taught, I found at least one administrator who believed that, while many of the things I did were a little unique, my agenda was about kids and trying to create a school climate that made our building a better place for them to be. They mostly allowed me to occasionally color outside the lines. I know that much of the success I enjoyed in the classroom was directly attributable to administrative flexibility and tolerance.

Think about the most cherished memories you have of your own school years. Think of the teachers who seemed to truly love their work. For me, many times, it was their classes that got me through the day. These teachers were oftentimes a little eccentric, and they weren't afraid to laugh. I think they cared about their students. This was perhaps no more than ten percent of the faculty, but they taught me about ninety percent of what I really learned in high school.

XXI

The Madison and Making Noise

Before you read this section, I feel it necessary to assure you I did not go to school every day with a fake red nose and big floppy shoes. In most respects, I think I am a serious student of certain periods in American history.

While I was blithely sloshing paint all over the walls, and building time machines, I applied for, and won, a James Madison Graduate Fellowship. The program was established by Congress in 1986, to advance the teaching of the roots, development, and principles of the Constitution of the United States. Each year, the Fellowship Foundation conducts a nationwide competition to choose new Fellows. One Fellowship is awarded per state and the U.S. Territories per year. Fellowships financially support teachers in summer and evening graduate programs leading to a Master's degree in American History or government. These grant opportunities have been expanded to include an education degree with an emphasis in constitutional studies. Each program must have a large dose of coursework on the history, interpretation, and development of the Constitution and Bill of Rights Fellowship; financial assistance is renewable for up to five years. During the summer following their first year of graduate study, all Fellows are required to attend the five-week Madison Summer Institute held at Georgetown University. This was one of the greatest learning experiences of my life. The Foundation provided me with a way to complete a Master's degree in American History, and most of a second in Political Philosophy. By this point in my life, I had been blessed with three children. Without the fellowship, I never would have been able to afford the tuition for the classes required to complete an advanced degree in either. I will never stop being grateful to the Madison Foundation. They gave me the funds to achieve a personal goal which I thought to be forever out of my reach. Participation in the summer institute also opened my eyes to a world of scholarship that added greatly to the authenticity of my classroom presentations. If you are a Social Studies teacher reading this and wish to pursue an advanced degree in American History or Political Science, please consider making an application. If not, please think about applying for one or several of the institutes and programs available to you through programs like The National Endowment for the Humanities, Gilder Lehrman Institute of American History, The USS Midway Institute for Teachers, The National World War II Museum and literally dozens of others. I have taken part in several, and enjoyed and profited from each. Much of my graduate education was directed towards learning how to better teach. If you are a teacher, I assume that to be true for you also. However, many of the programs I mentioned will help you better understand the content of your discipline and help you to determine *what* to teach. This is the other half of the walnut. It is especially important in today's world. There are no *alternative* facts, just facts. Truth does not have a political ideology, and history poorly taught is little different from propaganda. (Think of the pseudo-history crap currently being peddled in Florida) Somewhere within the scope of our curricula, we must be more inclusive. The old narratives don't work anymore. At one time we as Americans thought we shared a single and heroic narrative of our national history. This became accepted as true and was seen as part of our common heritage. As history teachers we should now be challenging the self-congratulatory story that has been taught for years. We need to reexamine our cherished beliefs about the past. Mary Douglas once suggested that we needed a common and celebratory history. It was once believed that as a nation, we might only keep our shape by building shared traditions. This helped to create a culture of patriotic slogans, sound bites and glorious imagery, but not real patriotism. Generalizations and groupthink are easy—truth; not so much. If you continue to tell America's story in a traditional way you will reinforce in your students a set of values that are white in color, male in gender, and Protestant in cultural orientation. We would then perhaps point to our good and great nation as a *prima facie* validation of our own narrow definitions of truth and divine favor. I am NOT a revisionist! We have a right to be proud of the American story. But adding other facets to our national mosaic only enhances the beauty of the whole.

The longer I taught the more I realized that history had a power which was owned by no other discipline. In a political sense one of the hallmarks of a totalitarian society is the blatant attempt to manipulate the past. Or as is more true today, to ignore the past of other groups that have a different truth. Democracy and history have always existed in a state of tension. But the study of history must always try to serve the truth. People may be uncomfortable with the truth—the facts—but if you teach, much depends upon the accuracy and inclusiveness of the interpretations you offer your students. These content-based programs will help. They will also pique your personal scholarship. I think the idea of having teachers/scholars is central to school improvement. I hope that long after I retire, I will be remembered as an historian who also taught history.

Many of the things I now mention may seem a bit unique, but I have learned over time, before you have achievement you need your students to engage with the subject. For example, I found my kids were willing to put up with a lot of lecturing on the Civil War when they found out that the next day, we were going to reenact the charge up Marye's Heights and the Battle of Fredericksburg. When the "battle" was over, there was always a fire and s'mores. Amazing what a kid will do for a little fellowship around a campfire and a s'more. Occasionally, I even favored them with a few verses of "Dixie" and the "Battle Hymn of the Republic."

I think that I became a better teacher when I lost most of my inhibitions, at least in the classroom. I said earlier that I am, and always will be, a shy and private person. In most instances, I detest being the center of attention. I am almost incapable of public speaking, and I live in dread of the day my daughter gets married and I have to offer a toast. I will so be a blubbering pile, and I am an ugly-faced, squeaky voiced crier. Lord how I wish that I was one of those stoic individuals who can speak with incredible clarity as dignified tears slowly roll down their cheeks. I have decided that I will be cremated, and my ashes will be scattered as soon as the embers stop glowing. That way I don't have to be the center of attention at a wake. However, in school, I often sang while walking through the halls. Sometimes I recited poetry at a pretty high decibel level. I love Robert Service, and *The Cremation of Sam McGee,* especially on cold snowy days. *"There are strange things done in the midnight sun by the men who moil for gold..."* Tennyson was good, too. If you're a teacher reading this right now, mentally march to your classroom reciting this.

> *Half a league, half a league*
> *Half a league onward,*
> *All in the valley of Death.*
> *Rode the six hundred.*
> *Forward, the Light Brigade!*
> *Charge the guns! he said.*
> *into the valley of Death*
> *Rode the six hundred.*

Stanza two is also great, especially the "Reason why and do and die" part. This is really stirring stuff, so recite it loudly. If you're an English teacher, you should be nearly *shouting!* This is an aside, but I developed a grading system based on this verse and the annoying habit that kids have of turning things in late. "Half a grade, Half a grade, Half a grade downward. All in the valley of F rides your assignment." You put in the time increments.

The first few times you do this, several kids will assume that you have a screw loose. Some of your colleagues might be a bit upset with your apparent lack of professional dignity, but most kids you walk past will be smiling, and the rest will get used to it. **Let them know that you are happy to be here.** How in the hell do you expect the kids to enjoy school if you walk around looking constipated! Kids should have no doubt you truly enjoy what you do. About twice a week, I paraded around the halls near my room wearing a sandwich board that proclaimed in large letters on both sides: **Free History Lessons: Follow Me.** This magnificent offer really needed to be shouted. Sometimes I rang a bell. Usually, I could get at least a couple of kids to tag along for a few steps, asking me some history-related questions. Once or twice a kid actually followed me to my room, sat down, and stayed until nearly the end of the class period. I always took attendance at the end of the period, and I am kind of oblivious anyway, so I didn't notice. When I finally figured it out, one of them asked me for a pass to class because he was only following my orders to "Follow Me." When I laughed at him, he put on a great show of being indigent. His acting was superb, his chutzpah enviable, his punishment—detention. Later in the day, I walked past a Spanish teacher in the hall. She was muttering something about "That damn sign." Fair warning, you will ruffle feathers occasionally.

I set up a philosophy booth. This I thought to be one of my more inspired bits of schtick. I found a large box that had been used to deliver a freezer to the Family and Consumer Sciences room—opportunity beckoned! In a real shameless rip off of Charles Schultz, I made a booth out of it, papered over everything and wrote "Philosophy" across the front. I added something like, "Aristotle spoken here." I got a stringy white wig and beard, found a cheap shower curtain with a blue stripe which worked for a toga, and set up shop. Between classes as the kids walked by, I demanded of them, "Young student, seek you wisdom or seek you knowledge?" Depending upon their answer, I handed them a slip of paper on which I had written down a few simple quotes that meant something to me, and I thought might profit them. I found a few of these quotes littering the halls on occasion, but I think most kids at least thought about them. I did get some negative feedback. A couple of parents thought I was getting "too political" with a few quotes that referenced "truth." Seems they thought I was criticizing certain politicians and their use of "alternative facts." *Of course,* nothing could be further from the truth!

I may have been one of the few teachers in America who had a functioning TARDIS in their classroom. If you're not a Dr. Who fan, you may be unimpressed, but if you are, you must clearly see the benefit to a history teacher having a functioning time machine. Long before it became a TARDIS, the device served as a book cabinet with double doors on each side for easy access. To make the conversion, I took the shelves out, I painted it appropriately and on top I installed a yellow light which flashed when I flipped a switch. I had a tape recording of the TARDIS going in and out of phase, which I operated manually and loudly! When a kid posed a question that was perhaps a little challenging, I donned a long scarf and a hat which resembled those worn by Tom Baker, who all good Whovians know as the fourth doctor. Music plays, lights flash, I climb in, "travel" back to the date of the event in question and emerge with an answer. Sometimes I first threw out a small stuffed dinosaur and screamed that someone had been screwing around with the controls! The kids loved it and remembered both the question and the performance. Alas, after a few years of successful operation, the fire department got wind of my time travel device and determined the jerry-rigged wiring was not up to code. Besides, the flux capacitor was out of warranty. They also had a few things to say about the cans of paint I stored in a couple of spots in my room. No doubt, they were agents of the eternally malevolent rogue Time Lord, known as "The Master." I really loved that little bit of schtick. By the way, **T**ime **A**nd **R**elative **D**imensions **I**n **S**pace.

If you have any musical ability, use it. Some of the best teachers I know bring instruments to class. An English teacher I respect as a very good instructor occasionally plays a banjo during passing time. I really wish I had learned to play the guitar—"damn my fat fingers and left-handedness." I would have loved to just once have been able to sing Bob Dylan or Joan Baez or a dozen other social activists during my units on the '60s. I tried to put a good deal of my class content to music. It really is a good mnemonic device. While the topic can be sophisticated, the more simple the tune the better. I used *Jingle Bells* often. Sometimes at the beginning of class I asked kids to give me a topic just to see if I could turn it into a song by the end of the period. The example which follows is from a Political Science class. The eternally peevish Mr. Hobbes would spin in his grave if he knew his political philosophy was being reduced to a few verses of a Christmas song

Thomas Hobbes, a "sing along" (to the tune of Jingle Bells)

Dashing to and fro,
In a constant state of war.
Man does not trust man,
There's blood and guts galore.
Dominion over all,
becomes our only goal,
we live as individuals,
At battle with the whole

OHHH, Thomas Hobbes, Thomas Hobbes
We need your guiding light!
How much fun
We all would have
Without the need to fight

OHHH, Thomas Hobbes, Thomas Hobbes
A contract we will share.
This constant war

Of all on all is
More than we can bear.

It goes on for six additional stanzas. I want to share one last verse because it captures the essence of Hobbes.

We need stability
Warfare we must shun
We'll build a safe and stable state,
The new Leviathan!

This state must have some power,
It's called coercive force.
Cuz government without this thing,
Is a sleigh without a horse

I freely admit that I am more often corny than clever; but damn!! I think that last verse is clever. I also did Locke, J.S. Mill, and most of the Greeks. Great way to review, and even the biggest grump in the room will sing along. My favorite history tune was *The Seven Major Causes of World War I,* sung to Peter, Paul and Mary's *Puff the Magic Dragon.* Lest you think I am fabricating; here are verses one two and three.

The Seven Major Causes of World I

The British Royal Navy controlled the whole darn sea
their empire stretched from India to far-flung Galilee!
But Little Will the Kaiser, their fleet he did envy,
so he built some ships to challenge their naval hegemony!

Oh, the French, they still were smartin'
from the Franco-Prussian War.
The Huns had often kicked their tails,
and they couldn't take no more.

So they spent big bucks on weapons,
and to everyone's surprise'
then they went and got themselves,
a bunch of new allies.

The Russian royal army,
Was of tremendous size.
But those backwards folks were the butt of jokes
For how slow they mobilized.

It goes on for five additional verses. These two are out of sequence, but I really like them …

With Europe locked and loaded, there came the big event.
The Duke of Austro-Hungary, to Serbia he went.
The trip was diplomatic, but what he hadn't planned,
Was he and his wife Sophia being shot by the Black Hand.

There came an ultimatum, and everyone agreed.
But mighty Austro- Hungary it still was pretty peeved
So shortly they invaded, and no one knew what for,
But by August, 1914, the world it was at war.

As a companion benefit, the young barbarians in my class were now being exposed to the classic and wholesome music of my generation. Not that druggie stuff they pollute their minds with constantly nowadays. Once, we plagiarized the score from *The Sound of Music* and turned the French Revolution into a musical. The kids wrote most of the lyrics. This was part of a solo sung by someone dressed as *Louis XVI*. The tune was:

Doe Re Me
Dough! is dear,
We got none here
Pay! is what the peasants do!!
Marie! my Queen,

She shops so much!
What's a husband gonna do?

We stormed the Bastille to a modified *Battle Hymn of the Republic*.

Come on you angry Frenchmen, let's go smash down the Bastille.
We are sick of old king Louis, so let's show him how we feel.
We are tired of being hungry, We all need a better deal,
Let's smash down the Bastille!!

Louis, Louis we all hate you
Louis we so underrate you.
You and your pretty queen
Are both gonna leave the scene.
Lets smash down the Bastille!!

When it was time for Marie to meet her unjustified end, we slipped in some Sinatra and marched her to the guillotine to a modified version of *My Way*, followed by Queen's *Another One Bites the Dust*.

I love reenactments, and my high school was perfectly situated for a bunch of them. I had the river nearby as well as the county park system; both offered endless opportunities to do what I came to refer to as "historically significant" group activities. I mentioned the Battle of Fredericksburg. We also did Pickett's Charge. The period of the American Revolution offered lots of possibilities. The Boston Massacre, complete with snowballs, taunts and flirtatious young ladies. The Boston Tea Party, complete with throwing tea into the river and railing against the king. (This was my favorite taunt hurled at King George III: "*Your wife prefers Frenchmen!*") We burned the king in effigy and sang a few choruses of Yankee Doodle. We made ship's biscuits and hardtack, to taste what the basic rations in the U.S. Army and Navy were during the Revolutionary, and later the Civil War. The kids wrote some pretty good skits based upon the Constitutional Convention. I was of course cast as Washington. During the War of 1812, the reenactment of the bombardment of Fort McHenry didn't go so well. I had a kid in the background throwing little jumping jack firecrackers. These were completely legal, but hence forward completely banned from all future reenactments. Seems that a couple of parents heard the word "firecracker" and complained to the office rather strenuously. When we studied the 1950s, we set up a coffee house in my classroom and attempted some beat poetry, complete with bongo drums and finger snaps.

Taking a class outside can be a risky proposition, I know that. To do a couple of my favorite recreations, we had to cross a semi-busy county road. Maintaining close supervision of 35 teenagers on the move is difficult. When trying to lecture at the same time, it becomes nearly impossible. I had to trust my kids, and *most* of the time they were completely trustworthy. On a couple of occasions, they weren't. The local terrain was ideal for reenacting events, but it also helped some kids get away with things. Twice I caught two of my students doing one-hitters behind an especially wide cottonwood tree. Once, one young man was screwing around and fell into the river. Fortunately, the water wasn't very deep, so I wasn't called upon to be heroic. Admittedly, it is a nervous proposition doing many of the things I have discussed. When I was younger, I just didn't think much about it. When I got older, I prayed a lot and asked the Lord if she would protect me and the kids just one more time. In my own risk-benefit analysis, I always thought the trips to be worth it. For a couple of these ninety-minute "historically significant" group activities, I know darn well, they were.

I have two recreations which became my personal favorites. The culminating activity for a unit about the Great Depression was setting up a hobo jungle down by the river. Each kid brought a can of something to cook and share. We combined them in a large pot and put it over a fire. The rules for contributions to the common feast were simple. One can of Spam was required as well as a raw potato or two. No fruit, no tuna, nothing sweet and no bizarre vegetables you wouldn't eat yourself. Most importantly, no hot peppers that you want to throw in just because you know I'm a spice wimp!! While the stew was being brought to a boil, we created a long narrative song, with each kid singing a verse which explained how they had been brought to this mean estate. These were to be written beforehand. All of their verses needed to be based on the Gene Austin song, *I'm Going on Down the Road Feeling Bad.* The creativity displayed was amazing. Very few refused to sing. This was incredible compliance from a group of teenagers. With the stew, we also made some fried dough using flour, cornmeal and water. We rolled it into ropes and baked it over the fire wrapped around a stick. It turned out burned black on the outside, barely cooked on the inside. If I wanted to be really authentic, we would have eaten the stew using a can for a bowl, but liability issues made that a potentially bad decision. We used Styrofoam cups, and the bread we ate with blackstrap molasses. This stuff is really bitter but healthy as all get out. In a couple dozen years of doing this, I never had a kid refuse to at least try the bread and stew. Most of the time it was pretty good. Each kid was also to bring a can of something for the local food shelf; so perhaps another lesson learned. I also learned something. When building large outdoor fires, watch out for your coat sleeves. I started myself on fire once. The kids laughed, I screamed, did a fast stop drop and roll, and caught hell from my wife when I got home.

The last reenactment I will describe involved whaling. I took several classes on "whaling expeditions" on the Rum River. Now, you're probably thinking there are no whales in the Rum, or any other river in Minnesota. Darn skippy, there aren't! Not anymore! The *whales* were plastic milk jugs partially filled with water and some red food coloring. Our harpoon was an old spear I had used in my youth to terrorize suckers and carp in Elm Creek. Using my best Gregory Peck imitation, (which, by the way, was completely lost on a group of teenagers). I led us in a rather martial prayer asking the Lord to protect us from the fury of the sea and the jaws of the great leviathan. Then, my class went down to a fishing pier near the school. I attached the jugs to a length of rope, threw them out and let them float downstream toward us. The potential harpooners were each given a throw. The non-business end of the harpoon was attached by rope to the dock for retrieval purposes, hit or miss "mostly miss." Now, as everyone knows, women were not allowed on whaling ships. Women were a "Jonah" and endangered the ship. So, the females in my class had to do something "manly" before they were given a toss. Their "man impressions and imitations" were often hilarious. Spitting and fake farting noises were common, as was cussing. More than one young lady told me to *"just give me the Goddamn harpoon!!"* Not especially flattering to the guys present. We combined the outing with a short lesson on the whaling industry and an assignment to write a brief paper on the growing transatlantic trade and the mercantile system. The kids were also given a large Styrofoam cup to try their hand at scrimshaw, some of which turned out to be excellent. The kids always expressed their appreciation for this and many of the other recreations. We never walked back to the school without at least one kid thanking me. A bit of advice. Don't let the possibility that a kid or two might misbehave keep you from trying something different. In schools we do way too much of that.

Within the limits created by your own particular teaching situation, try to find ways to inject more of yourself into your presentations. We all have a unique skill set, and frankly, many of the limits we feel are self-imposed. None of the things I've described will improve a standardized test score. A few will address some portions of a state-mandated curriculum, but only indirectly. These few ninety-minute field trips were about school climate and creating the type of positive interactions that turn *a* school into *my* school. In schools, we need to foster a sense of ownership and community. So much of what we consider to be wrong with education can be made better if schools become more engaging and creative places. I wish most teachers would just once follow a student through their day and endure the same amount of tedium and repetition that an average kid is subjected to on a regular basis. Every day does not need to be a dog and pony show. It can't be. But at supper, when most kids are asked, "What did you do in school today?" The occasional smile would be great. These are examples of small things that can be easily attempted with almost no expense. They worked for me, but as I said my circumstances were unique. You probably will have a different set of possibilities to work with. Resolving school climate issues is critical and doable. If you are a teacher reading this, realize how much power you have to shape your classroom, department, or school. You have more agency than you think.

I think I've already put enough bad poetry in this chapter.

XXII

Step One: Get Rid of the Consultants

If schools are to survive and thrive in anything like their present form they must improve, but the ways we choose to go about it currently won't work. In education, we are always looking for what I think of as silver bullets. These are the latest and greatest attempts at improving, restructuring, re-aligning, redefining and of course reforming schools. At a minimum, most will require hiring another administrator. Some may require engaging several consultants to direct this paradigm shattering *novus ordo seclorum*. Oh, and of course, once the consultants depart, yet another administrator must be hired to ensure continued "success." But most dollars spent on these silver bullets is money wasted. Many of these programs have the life expectancy and consequence of a mayfly. They are a series of lounge acts, and nothing more than recycled common sense and 1980's ed. theory *redux*. Meaningful change is more about motivation than methodology, and it is almost always incremental. Attitudes are more difficult to change than institutions, so top-down attempts at reform are usually expensive and futile.

At least in terms of quantity, my career has spanned a really remarkable period of educational research and attempts at innovation. Quality is a separate issue. Almost yearly, it is becoming increasingly obvious that change is desperately needed. By nearly any measure, American schools are underperforming relative to the rest of the world, and even when compared to our own history. Over the years, I have been fortunate to have had the opportunity to instruct a good number of foreign exchange students. By and large, they performed at a higher level than their American classmates. This despite issues with language. I do not know if other countries were only sending us their best and brightest. This is a possibility, but I think it unlikely, as a few were not serious students. Two Italian youngsters who I once had in a college American History class, decided leering at *Playboy* magazines was a better use of their time than taking notes. Neither could they understand my prudish American reaction to Miss October being displayed in all her buxom glory. But on balance, most of these exchange students were very capable and dedicated. Once I had a young lady from Austria who wanted to discuss one of the plays of Goethe. Her questions were much more precise than my answers. Several of my colleagues have had similar experiences as I had with foreign students. In math and science classes, I believe the achievement disparities are even more pronounced.

There are valid reasons for this, but most explanations are really rationalizations which might identify the problems but offer no real solutions. This might help. In most of the industrialized world, the school year is over 200 days long. Some countries, such as Japan, extend this to 230 or 240 days.

In America, most school districts average between 175 and 180 days. W.T.F. are we thinking? This is a very simple-minded and partial solution, but perhaps the first thing we might try is extending the school year. Instead, we continue to look for solutions which are often novel, esoteric, and regrettably, futile. Oh, and by the way, these proposed solutions don't interfere with the state fair or the need for cheap teenage summer labor—coincidence, I'm sure.

Every few years a new initiative is launched, a new theoretician comes into vogue, or a new mandate is imposed. I believe that most of these have been what was once referred to as a "pound of smoke." They seem to have some mass and *gravitas*, but once you get inside them, there is very little there. The only two that I am suggesting might bear a little closer examination are, No Child Left Behind, and the School Choice Movement This is not because they are especially effective, so far they haven't proven to be. But No Child Left Behind offers insight into the thinking of the big decision makers and bureaucrats at the state and federal level, who had somehow determined you could mandate achievement and punish your way to success. In my mind, the school choice initiatives are the more dangerous of the two because they are part of a larger political and social agenda that could ultimately re-segregate all schools and destroy public education.

No Child Left Behind (NCLB) was passed in 2002. The most vivid recollection I have of the passage of the act was a widely circulated picture of President George W. Bush signing the legislation into law while in the background stood Democratic Senator Ted Kennedy, Republican Representative John Boehner and a few other luminaries. Each of them sported a grin as if their collective thought was, "*Damn*, this is easy. Why didn't someone do this before?" This was truly a bipartisan effort, and it was celebrated as an example of what could be accomplished when the political knives were put away. To be honest, the intent of the law was good. Schools were to be held accountable for how well kids learned. It was especially directed towards improving educational outcomes for students living in poverty and students of color. It is also based on the underlying but unstated assumption that underperforming schools simply weren't trying hard enough, or they didn't care enough, or they were inept.

This is a very cursory explanation of how the law was to be implemented. A school's level of success or failure in educating children would be determined using standardized testing, and then more testing, and yet more testing. Each state was to establish a standard of proficiency in reading and math. Schools that weren't making an adequate level of progress towards that standard suffered a series of escalating punishments. If a school underperformed for two consecutive years, it was termed "a school in need of improvement" and it was placed on a watch list. The school would then receive some help in implementing a two-year improvement plan. If the school still underperformed, it was required to offer students from lower income groups free supplemental educational services such as tutoring, and the right to transfer to better performing schools in the same district. In the fourth year, staff and administrators that were deemed to be underperforming could be replaced. By the fifth year, the entire school faced the possibility of being restructured and perhaps being turned into a charter school with a new administration and staff. This was to happen even if the school was making some progress or had a high population of kids with unique challenges, such as limited English language proficiency, or an extremely transient student population. Each year, the learning targets would be adjusted upwards. Improvement should be constant. By 2014, it was expected we would finally reach the "holy land" of universal literacy and numeracy. In other words, *no child* would have been *left behind*. Wow! By legislative fiat, we would have accomplished what no other country in the world had been able to do. What could go wrong? To answer that question even partially would require another book, but the short answer is, **Lots!** In terms of its stated goals, NCLB was a failure. The underlying assumptions of the initiative were both unrealistic and naive. Many schools didn't improve. The sanctions were not enforced uniformly, and the time spent on the endless rounds of testing was a subtraction from instructional time. Few schools are performing better today than they did the day the program was initiated. Many not as well. Every school is different, with a unique clientele. In my opinion, such broad-brush solutions simply will not work. Perhaps had there been rewards for consistent progress, the outcomes would have been more favorable. As structured, the initiative was doomed from the beginning. The promised revolution was another "pound of smoke."

The school choice movement purports to offer a market-based approach to education that I believe certainly will make some schools better. However, I think that most of these newly improved schools will be private or parochial. Parents have an absolute right to decide where their kids will attend school. If they opt for a private or parochial school, that is exclusively a family decision. If parents opt to home school, it is their choice and right. The state of Minnesota provides some support to parents who choose to exercise this homeschool option. In these cases, no one disputes the idea of school choice. Private and parochial schools have a long and successful history. Some are excellent. The first schools in America were private, and today they educate about seven million students, or nearly one in nine children K-12. I went to a parochial school for eight years. The experience was mostly positive, and I don't regret the choice my parents made to send me there.

The real issue is, should public money be used to support these private choices as is now the case in 16 states? Under most choice plans, this money would be given to all students in the form of a voucher. There are also educational savings accounts (ESA), which work essentially as an educational credit card. Other programs are based on tax credits. The student could take this voucher, or any of the other payment schemes, to any school which will accept them, public or private. This does not mean that the school must then accept the student. In a sense, the student has been monetized. This alone is perhaps reason enough to reconsider the rush towards choice.

Under these plans, it is assumed schools will be forced to compete for students, and for all schools it will be a case of improve or perish. This certainly seems plausible. Finally, we will have a free market solution to a nagging social problem. SHAZAM!!, capitalism *uber alles*!! The invisible hand will allocate our human resources in the most efficient way. Perhaps Rex Tillerson said it most plainly when he stated, "Public schools don't understand that the business community is their customer and they are producing a **product** at the end of a high school career ... the question is, if the product is defective or can we use it?" How thoughtful of Mr. Tillerson to provide an epitaph for a tombstone on the grave of liberal arts education. Even if the only goal of education was to create willing cyborgs to better serve corporate America, it would not be that simple.

The possible negative consequences of school choice seem equally plausible. Which students will the schools be competing for? What kids will be left at the back of the queue when schools have filled their classes, or perhaps have added as much "diversity" as they are comfortable with? To many students, the opportunity to choose will be meaningless because choice with no access is not choice. Most students do not live in what we might refer to as a choice rich environment. Educational options are most meaningful to families with the financial ability to explore and exercise those options. Children from less advantaged backgrounds have fewer opportunities to make meaningful decisions. I believe the most likely outcome will not be students choosing schools, rather schools will be choosing students. Even today, some schools require prospective students to take entrance exams. Will more do so? No one knows. Will schools receiving voucher money be forced to offer Special Education services? This is highly unlikely because few private schools offer these services now. Today, many private schools do not require that teachers be certified. Will that become the norm? Would there be diminished oversight of the curriculum and adherence to federal and state mandates? Currently, many families opt for private and charter schools specifically to avoid what they consider to be onerous government regulations. Specifically, those regulations involving diversity and inclusion. What might be the larger social consequences? In all honesty, we already have a two-tiered educational choice system in America. One is mostly white and at least reasonably affluent, the other—everybody else. Vouchers will not address this situation. Nationally, vouchers haven't proven adequate to cover private school tuition. These costs are not coming down. In fact, you could make a pretty good case that with the increased money now available through increased state support, the cost of a private school education will go up significantly. In Minnesota, the average tuition bill for non-public schools, elementary and secondary, is approximately seven thousand dollars a year. The median cost is much higher, and many schools have tuition which is several multiples of that. I have seen no proposed voucher plan that will provide that much support. Vouchers will then serve only to put a nice dent in the tuition bills of parents who really don't need the help and will make no tangible difference for families that really do.

An additional problem creeps in when you look at the effect of vouchers on the schools opted out of. Perhaps at this point I can contribute something I heard a while ago. If a public swimming pool is poorly maintained, the obvious solution is to fix it. If the pool is overcrowded, it would appear to be time to build an additional pool. In either case, the problem cannot be solved by providing certain members of the community with funds to build their own private pools and keep out who they will. This is not a solution. It is anti-democratic and will only exacerbate the problems faced by the public pool. As with our highways and bridges, in many places schools have been neglected for too long. Voucher plans will diminish funding and community buy-in for the public schools. Now public schools will be expected to compete with private schools or corporate schools with diminished funding. At the same time, they will still be required to accept every student who seeks admission, a condition not imposed on the "choice" alternatives. The possibilities that under a voucher system schools will be re-segregated is very real. The ways this might happen are almost limitless. Religion could be used as a basis for admission. So could political affiliation, race, gender, ethnicity or as is most common today, a really exorbitant tuition. An already fractured society might become as a sheet of mica, with clear planes of separation and fault lines, further weakening the whole.

I have come to believe vouchers are inconsistent with the American tradition of a common school. Such schools have been an engine of American prosperity for two hundred years. They have also unified us as a people. Such schemes should not even be considered until some mechanism is put in place which requires private schools to accept all applicants and provide them with services analogous to those demanded of the public system. Replacing funding lost when a student chooses to spend their voucher at a private school is also a possibility. I do not pretend that I have studied the net effect of vouchers on school systems. Certainly, some students have benefitted. But common sense suggests that the bulk of the student population will not.

There is however one consequential innovation that has changed schools in ways which have been unexpected, profound, and in many cases unintended. Its impact can only be expected to grow exponentially in the future. Indisputably, the Apple has landed! The computer has been an educational tsunami and the question now becomes; how to utilize the power of the new technology in a way that will maximize student learning. As a companion question: how can we make this technology compatible with the affective needs of our students?

Computers came upon the educational scene in a rush. In the mid and late seventies, many schools in Minnesota had started computer clubs. The students in these clubs, mostly male, could be connected to a mainframe at the University of Minnesota via a dial-up modem. They then sat around, high-fiving each other as the machines were directed to do something easy and pointless, like calculating pi to the 100th place. Additional time was purchased, and some schools even began to offer classes in computer science. In time, personal computers became common and software was developed for classroom use. The internet was born and computer use grew exponentially.

Sad to admit, but most of this nascent revolution passed me by. I have a very tenuous relationship with all technology. To call me a Luddite is to insult Luddites the world over. Even something as simple as using word processing is difficult for me. Everything I type is done using two fingers. This is an old joke, and not mine, but typing speed is usually expressed as words per minute; my speed is better measured in *minutes per word*. When I was an undergrad, we used these things called typewriters. I survived by buying cases of whiteout, or paying someone to do my typing for me.

The first personal computers that appeared on teachers' desks at my school were used and outdated pieces of technology donated by various corporations and sent to the Minnesota Prison system to be reconditioned for use by school districts. Our faculty was nearly giddy with the acquisition. The machines were under-powered, but free, and *worth every penny!* We were expected to use them for classroom management tasks, like keeping a grade book and attendance. I was cornered, and resistance was futile! After stomping around and cursing for a day or so, I accepted that I had to learn some basic operation skills or retire. I was too young to do the latter and my ceiling was far from finished. I went to a few workshops and actually paid attention. But I never became especially thrilled by, or skilled at, computer use. Every new semester, I selected my student aides based partly on their comfort level with the new silicon deity. These early machines were not reliable. I developed a ritual for dealing with the many glitches. First, after another of the inevitable breakdowns, I closely examined the machine and usually concluded the problem was either demonic possession of the hard drive or a defective SCSI port. I had no idea what a SCSI port was, but it was a techie term and by pronouncing it "skuzzy," I was able to pretty much sum up how I felt about my current machine. After finding no fault with the skuzzy port, I moved on to the problem of demons in the hard drive. First, I slipped on my old graduation robe which I kept for such occasions and began a routine exorcism. First, I glared at the machine and walked around it three times backwards. Then, and in a loud and stern voice I called forth the demons by name. Be gone, Gates! Be gone, IBM! Leave this machine, Jobs! When I had properly intimidated the malevolent spirits, I threw a little salt over my shoulder, banged my chalk erasers together and screamed a couple obscure Latin phrases, then I rebooted; after which I usually called tech support. This happened often enough that the kids chanted the names of the demons with me. Collectively, we gave them a heck of a verbal drubbing! This silly little bit of schtick became less and less useful as computers improved and were replaced by more powerful and reliable machines. (Damn the modernity, I was having fun!) Every classroom soon had at least one computer. The I.M.C. had several, and many of the school departments had classroom sets of Chromebooks. Some schools issued an incoming student a laptop the day they arrived. To use a coaching term, by 2010 or so, computers had pretty much flooded the zone. Soon, textbook salesmen became an endangered species. As a positive, this did save me a good deal of junk mail.

Computers have become to today's classroom what the blackboard was to schools a hundred years ago. Little known fact, when blackboards were first introduced there was something of a debate whether such a *powerful technology* could be entrusted to schoolteachers! A variation of that debate is going on today. Have teachers been given enough training to maximize the potential of this new technology? This should be the case; there are literally hundreds of classes and workshops available that focus on integrating technology into the classroom. Some, I'm sure, are very good. Teachers are often compensated for taking these classes, so in a sense you can choose your desired level of expertise. As far as machines go, no faculty is ever satisfied with the power and capability of the computers they are issued. But in all honesty, most teachers will admit the technology available today probably exceeds their ability to completely and competently use it. (As an aside, by this point I was one of the few teachers in the building who could still use a slide rule. Regrettably, this impressed no one.)

Maybe a more important part of the debate is, should we rely so heavily on technology in education? Maybe we should pause for a while before we risk constructing classrooms that could become almost devoid of interaction between teacher and student. I really believe kids still want to talk to teachers. They want to discuss, they want the occasional lecture, they want to ask questions about *anything* that occurs to them. This is true of all kids, not just your best kids. I freely grant that in my last few years of teaching, my class load consisted of mostly concurrent enrollment students taking my classes for college credit. So by and large they were well-above-average students, but I taught standard classes as well, and the kids in those classes responded to my teaching style in much the same way. If you are a teacher, I would like you to ask yourself this simple question. **If the power goes off, are you still a teacher? If the answer is no, it's time to reassess.** Covid was a dreadful way to learn about the real value of in-person instruction and the power of maintaining personal relationships between teacher and student. It will take years for some kids to recover academically and socially from the isolation. In those two years, students had enough screen time for the next ten. Yet, I know teachers who, even before the pandemic, bragged about having their entire curriculum on the web, including evaluation. Their day consisted of taking attendance, passing out laptops, and monitoring the room. I wanted to ask them, "If that is all you do, why are you necessary?" Oh, that's right, somebody needs to enforce a little order. Then there's hall monitoring, and of course somebody needs to scream at the kids to put away their smartphones and pay attention to their iPads. Somehow, there's a disconnect there. I feel fortunate I never had to deliver an online lesson nor host a Zoom meeting. I have immense respect for teachers who can do it effectively, and I marvel at the technical aplomb they daily demonstrate. There is certainly a place for online instruction, especially at the collegiate level, but I'm glad I never had to attempt it. Very little I did as a teacher would have worked in a Zoom meeting. I'm basically a storyteller with a pretty elaborate set of props. Perhaps it is no more than a function of me getting older, but I have very deep reservations about the ways computers are reshaping education. Or it may be that I am uncomfortable that older education models which stressed the centrality of the teacher have been replaced with a kind of computer-centric classroom. This was probably inevitable. The last few years I taught, the words "teaching" and "technology" were becoming synonyms. They are not, and never will be.

There is one form of technology with which I tried to reach at least a partial accommodation in the last few years before I retired; that being cellphones. Cell phones suck!! I believe every secondary teacher in America hates these damn things with a passion, myself included. But I also hate death, war, famine, conquest and the Yankees. All of these I can also do nothing about. Smartphones are like the black flies you occasionally have to endure if you want to spend any time in the Boundary Waters. A real pain in the ass, but an unavoidable part of the ecosystem. My policy with regard to the infernal things was this. In class, when I am lecturing, your phone can be on the top left corner of your desk, *if you are recording*. During group work, they may be out *for reference*. Of course, you will want to use them for many *other things* … but resist the urge. If we are on a field trip, the occasional check is OK. The only call you may always accept when in class is one from your mother. No one will ever love you as she does, so you should always answer. There were no real penalties for breaking these rules, except a stern finger shaking and an absolute refusal to consider giving an offending student an extension on any assignment. This I saw as a logical consequence. If you have time to screw around checking your status on Facebook, having papers done in a timely fashion should be a piece of cake.

When I was younger, I tried to put the squelch to cell phone use all together. One of my better students was an extremely social young lady, who I had warned repeatedly about her phone use. She was also a great kid with an obvious sense of humor. After class, I asked her if she had an old flip phone or something equally antiquated that I could smash. She indicated she had several, Surprise, surprise! I asked her to bring one the next day. During class, she pretended to take a call from her "bestie." I yelled for a bit, worked up all the *faux* anger I could, and grabbed the phone. I placed it on a desk and began smashing it with a stone ax from one of my primitive tools displays. I crushed the phone, broke the desk, and scared the room into absolute silence. Finally, one kid mumbled under his breath, "You can't do that." I agreed and said, "Of course I can't, it was fake! Jeanine and I set this up yesterday. But do you want to bet your phone that McLean won't lose it completely someday. Remember, I'm the guy who walks around the halls singing, dresses like Aristotle, goes whaling on the Rum River, and believes that he's a timelord from a planet called Gallifrey. Most of the people in this building think that I'm at least two sandwiches short of a picnic. Maybe next time it won't be faked!" We had a good laugh, and the phones stayed in their pockets—for about two weeks. A very small and short-term victory.

In my career, I never really came up with a policy that was effective against a resourceful kid and their smartphone. Surely, I am among the last teachers in America to realize the average kid can text while their phone is in their pocket. Neither do I have a solution for what I view as the overuse and abuse of technology in the classroom. In all honesty, I am not sure if it actually *is* a problem. I do have opinions, but perhaps it may be as simple as getting back to the question I suggested earlier. Every teacher should ask themselves—If the power goes out, am I still a teacher.? If the answer is no, it's time to reassess your use of technology.

In this narrative I make no claims that I was the best teacher in my building, my department, or even in the carpool I occasionally used. However, in time I came to know my students as well as any teacher could. I think that's partly true because in 43 years in the classroom, I never once put a screen between myself and a kid. I asked them to use computers for research and word processing, but no lesson I ever taught them originated as part of a canned program or the support material that came with a textbook purchase. *None* of my greatest failures in the classroom were attributable to my pathetic computer skills. My greatest failures were all attributable to the occasions when I didn't respond in a meaningful way to what a student was telling me: the times I did not see the confusion behind the smile, the despair behind the silence, or the real issue behind the anger.

I wrote the next chapter a few years ago. At the time, and as you will see, I had a wonderful opinion of myself as a teacher. I thought I was funny and clever. I was popular. Kids liked me. But as with David all those years ago, many things I should have noticed were ignored, and questions I should have asked weren't even considered. In so many cases I wish that I had been better, or perhaps more observant. In my career, I don't know how many more kids like Stacy passed through my classroom on their way to becoming less than they could have been. This was the day I stopped considering myself to be a good teacher; and really started becoming one.

*You **must** try our new program.*
It's new, it's grand, it's great
It will render what you're doing now,
much worse than the second rate!

It comes with tons of software,
and it's easy to install.
The kids will go bananas,
when they come back in the fall.

We've redesigned the classroom,
with this brand new paradigm.
Your kids will leap two years ahead
in only one year's time!

*The **only** problem you might have,*
now they're learning so much more.
Is we're finding it real difficult
*To get kids **out** the door.*

And if any problems do arise,
*you can hire **me** for a year.*
In fact you better do it now,
while my calendar is clear.

I'll help you with the upgrades,
Tell your teachers what to know.
And make sure your staff is ready
When we roll out 2.0

XXIII

Ashes and Defeat

It was the type of day that might only occur on the earliest edges of autumn. The summer had long since grown tired. July and August were a succession of days memorable only for caustic sunshine and oppressive humidity; but summer's quiver was nearly empty now, and it was a scant two weeks until the equinox. Tomorrow or tomorrow or tomorrow might still be unpleasantly warm, but on some day after that I would first wear a jacket to school. Then, I might be thankful for the warmth, but not on this day. In all of its aspects, this day was perfect. It was early September, and the morning sky was beautifully cerulean. I had just survived all the bullshit fall teacher workshops, and a new school year was finally beginning. The world was totally correct and satisfying beyond description.

With classes again in session, the focus came back into my world, and for nine months I would be complete. I was a teacher again and Lord how I had missed school! The sights of it, the sounds of it, the smell and the purpose of it; especially the purpose of it. Regrettably, in most areas of my life, the passing years have gradually inclined me towards cynicism. But I will never become cynical about school, kids, and teaching. To me, the classroom will always be a place of faith and optimism. More than ever, I was still a charismatic and a true believer in the common school. God willing, I always will be.

That year would be my twentieth in the classroom, and as with most of the good teachers I have ever known, teaching had gradually become both livelihood and life to me. I had long since ceased to enjoy the summer recess. Extended breaks now made me listless and surly. This fixation with my work may cost me dearly someday, but not then, and not yet. That day was a twentieth new beginning and another bite of the apple. Each bus load of students was another infusion of excitement into the building. School was again in session and for now, and for nine long months, that would be enough.

The sound of a school in September becomes starkly different. During my summer classes, the emptiness of the halls had made every noise an echo and an interruption. Now, the building was loud and vibrant. There was a constant hum. Quick giggles merged and mingled with banging lockers. Everywhere there were overly loud conversations and shouts of recognition. The cumulative effect was a kind of white noise, something that I have come to recognize as the elevator muzak and pulse of a good high school.

The activity level in the building increased exponentially as summer stasis yielded to frenetic fall. Freshmen moved to class in a kind of pinball panic. The boys jostled, and they bumped; these collisions often led to feigned indignation and mock combat. It was all done to impress freshman girls, who had just discovered sophomore guys, and now viewed such behavior as "like, immature." By November, these same freshmen will usually have lost most of their middle-school feistiness, but until then, the poor little neophytes looked rather silly and out of place. In time, they would come to realize ennui was now the true epitome of high-school coolness. The seniors understood. They were already a study in practiced indifference. They bitched about being back, but there was no real acid in their gripes, for they spit their invective through smiling lips and then winked at me. Old relationships were reaffirmed, and old animosities were temporarily forgotten. I knew that soon the cliques would re-aggregate, but until then, goths chatted amiably with preps, burn-outs discussed football with jocks, and all the males stared openly at the too-high skirts and too-low halter tops. The air was laden with pheromones, cheap cologne, the smell of breakfast in the cafeteria, and carpet cleaner. School was back in session, and almost everyone in the building was partially giddy with the sensory overload. For a day, or perhaps as long as a week, even the grumpy old bastards who were well into their retirement slide remembered why they had become teachers in the first place. The bell rang, and new pens were applied to clean notebooks. In synchrony, 2,000 minds resolved to do better this year. Maybe the bulk of these resolutions would not survive period one, but in any case, school was in session and for a few golden moments, novelty would trump apathy and most things seemed possible.

My first period was a Political Science class. After the briefest of introductions, we were soon discussing the deep ruminations of Aristotle and his political ethics. The kids ate it up. In second period American History, our topic was the Constitutional Convention. During that class, a student with a perpetually malicious smirk asked me if I believed that Ben Franklin had slept around. An impertinent question to be sure, but a beautiful segue into the foibles of Ben and other "great" men from the founding generation. The discussion which followed was interesting, engaging, and funny as hell.

I was now totally in my element: philosophy, history, and stand-up comedy. New students, old material, raucous laughter, loud enough that every kid on the floor heard it and wished that my name was on their class schedule. That first morning passed in a heartbeat, and as I walked across the street to get a sandwich for lunch, I was positive that if teaching talent and personal satisfaction could be converted to cash, I would be the richest, as well as the happiest man in the whole of American public education. I was smug in the certainty I was a great teacher, maybe the best in the building. Heck, maybe the best in the state. Hubris perhaps, but what I did was important, I did it well, and I truly believed that I was making a difference,

I saw her somewhere between the deli counter and the checkout. Though I guessed her to be only in her mid-thirties, she possessed not a single feature one might associate with youth or vitality. She wore no make-up, and from appearances she probably regarded her short-cropped hair as more nuisance than adornment. Had time and perhaps circumstance been more kind, she might still have been striking. Or maybe, she had simply heard one too many empty flattering lies and no longer saw any advantage in the effort it took to be attractive to men. I imagined that she was a shift worker, or perhaps a waitress. It was obvious that she worked with her hands, or on her feet, and that payday probably didn't happen often enough. She looked so incredibly tired. Fatigue enfolded her even more tightly than her well-worn jeans. She was a walking weariness which eight hours of sleep would not fix, nor even much improve. I could pass by her a thousand times and never see or imagine more than that. Perhaps, if she came here often enough, we might eventually exchange nods of recognition or one phrase pleasantries, all essentially meaningless, unaffecting and unaffected.

I was slightly nonplussed when my casual glance and nanosecond analysis was met with a guarded smile of recognition. "Hi, McLean, I thought it was you."

Eventually, every career teacher will come face to face with a very human fragment of a poorly remembered year in the classroom. It was obvious she had once been a student of mine, and for two awkward seconds I tried to retrieve a name, or perhaps a small personal factoid that I might relay to her, and by relaying it convince her I had not forgotten her entirely. From somewhere within that two-second eternity, a name began to emerge, "Stacy?" Immediately, her face and posture told me my guess had been correct. The severe woman who had initially regarded me with a self-protective indifference and an unspoken question perceptibly softened. Her tattooed hands emerged from the pockets of a dirty red windbreaker, and she moved easily towards me for a hug. In that minute she was 18 again, it was graduation night, and she still had dreams of becoming a dancer. More memories, I recalled a girl who had been an earnest student. She had also been a gymnast of the highest order. She was once cute and perky, popular, and well regarded by her teachers. She worked hard and listened intently. She laughed at the appropriate times. I vaguely recalled that she had trouble with tests, but her daily work was always neatly and conscientiously done. Her penmanship was beautiful. I remembered her graduation picture. Though a city kid, she had chosen to be photographed clad in blue jeans and seated on a split rail fence. A bright yellow rope served as a belt. In the photo, she also wore a red flannel shirt and a straw cowboy hat with a blue neckerchief. There were hay bales in the foreground. The entire motif was faux-country, and common enough to be a cliché. I remembered that she had given me an invitation to her graduation open house, and unlike many I received, it was not offered as a simple and perfunctory courtesy. She had really wanted me to come. She had made me promise I would come. To this day I can't remember why I was unable to attend, but after 15 years she still willingly offered me a hug, and with her tobacco-scented embrace she now multiplied whatever guilt I had long since forgotten for not having been there to congratulate and wish her well.

I asked her how things were, and really expected no more response than a superficial banality, but her halting reply came from a place that was infinitely more deep and complex. Within a random and choppy narrative, she tried to compress the last 15 years for me. Every word was carefully guarded and considered, but the pain in her eyes begged me to inject my darkest imaginings into the long pauses between each sentence. It seems that when she left high school, she had tried college for a year. There had been some success, but "College just wasn't like high school, McLean. They found out pretty quickly I couldn't read. Bet you didn't know that; none of my teachers knew that."

Realizing that she had already said more than she intended, she paused, and when she started again her monotone voice barely animated her newly flat affect. But to me, every word was now the stroke of a hammer. With a simple admission she had made herself vulnerable, and word by word she was now rebuilding and reinforcing the arrogant crust necessary to stem the bleeding of a million small wounds newly reopened. Thank God she didn't cry then, for a single tear might have melted the façade entirely; and me with it. But 15 years ago, and disarmed by the certainty of failure, she had decided to quit school. In retrospect, the decision was a bad one, and her remorse was evident.

The times weren't any too prosperous back then, work was scarce, and she soon began drifting through a series of temporary jobs and equally transient relationships. As a result of one of these casual liaisons she was now a mother, and had been for five years. The father was long gone, and her voice betrayed no sorrow at his absence. Her boy was in kindergarten then, and she really didn't have much time to visit with me anymore, because he would be getting off the bus soon, and she wanted to meet him at the stop. It was his first day of school, too. In an almost offhand way, she told me she had been sober for almost a year now, and the bar scene was behind her. She hoped things might be getting better for her soon. She knew a guy that might hire her to help him install hardwood flooring, and if she did a good job, he might take her on permanently. It would be a union job, and there would be health insurance, maybe even dental, and she really hoped I would still be teaching when her kid got to high school, "Cuz, you were the best, McLean, I always enjoyed your class."

In the silence which followed, an overpowering sense of failure and inadequacy began to well up within me, choking off my every attempt at acknowledgment. I'm sure at that moment, as my gaze fell to the dirty floor tiles, I must have looked every inch a humble and self-effacing public servant. I think I even appeared to be blushing. What I really felt was a raw and unmitigated shame. In one quick thrust, the reality of this woman's life had deflated my pumped-up pretensions of teaching excellence, of making a difference. No more rationalizations, no more delusions, only a question. What had I really done for Stacy? What had any of her teachers done? The evidence of my own eyes shouted that a beautiful and happy girl had somehow become a sad and marginalized woman. In my entire career, no criticism ever purposefully leveled at me had cut so quickly and brutally as the sincere and guileless compliment just offered to me by a very tired former student. "Cuz you were the best, McLean,

I always enjoyed your class." To me, those words now carried the sting of a well-deserved slap or a heartfelt curse.

I had the most powerful impulse to hold her, to kiss her on the forehead and apologize to her. I wanted to shout at her, and I wanted to cry for her. In that instant, I wore the mantle of collective guilt for every man who had failed to protect her from all the predators and predations that had devoured her ambition and innocence, then moved on to younger and still naïve fields, and in the awful light of that moment, I had to confront the possibility that I had been no better than any of them. I was her father, and I was her husband, and I was her brother. Most painful of all, I had been her favorite teacher, and perhaps, if I had truly been "the best," on this most perfect of days, I would be hugging a dancer and sharing in her success.

As she said goodbye to me, she promised to stop by school sometime for a longer visit. She then took her meager collection of items to the register, and somewhere between the checkout and her car the perky 18-year-old died and a flint-faced woman in her mid-thirties drove silently home to a small, rent-subsidized apartment, a five-year-old child, and perhaps a few hours of sweet oblivion.

I have not seen Stacy since that one chance meeting, and her son's name has never appeared on any of my class rosters. In all these years, she has yet to walk into my classroom, but she often comes to visit me. Usually, she appears like a storm cloud to mar my smuggest of days, my sunny and perfect days. Those rare occasions when my lectures are interesting, engaging, and funny as hell. The type of days that I still live for; when if personal satisfaction and teaching talent could be converted to cash, I'd be the happiest, as well as the richest man in the whole of American public education. Often on these days, I still walk across the street to buy a sandwich to take back to my room for a quiet lunch. There, surrounded by a dozen vacuous awards and at least as many stained Styrofoam coffee cups, I will think about questions still unanswered, and my sandwich will probably taste mildly of ashes and defeat.

The spring after that chance encounter with a former student in a grocery store, I enrolled in a reading certification program at Saint Cloud State University. I never intended to again become a full-time reading teacher, but I also resolved that I would not again miss kids who were successful non-readers. I was given some invaluable instruction in reading across the curriculum and identifying kids with undiagnosed learning issues. It was a fantastic program that helped me often during the balance of my career. I would recommend at least a couple of developmental reading classes as part of every secondary teacher's preparation for licensure. A writing class would also be a must. In high school, we graduate so many kids who end up taking remedial reading or math classes when they go on to college or technical training. The students will pay for these classes, and the credits will not count towards their graduation. There are things that could be done to reduce those numbers.

For a period of time, we linked high-school graduation to passing competency tests. I never supported that kind of high stakes testing, but the data generated painted a grim picture. I think the program was abandoned when the tests started to tell us so much more than we were comfortable knowing. I never would advocate that a school implement a "return to the basics" curriculum that is again coming into vogue in certain states and districts. But literacy must underpin the entire educational system. Having a high-school degree has never been a guarantee a person could read and write. Sadly, that is more true today than it ever has been. Somewhere in each of the four years of high school, there has to be a carve out for students who need continued support in developing functional literacy and numeracy. In Minnesota, we have mandated that students take a large number of courses. In many respects, our schools are becoming a mile wide and an inch deep in most subject areas. But literacy is crucial and the foundation of all other classes. Reading instruction must be ongoing. Goal one: We should be able to promise every student who enters our school that they will leave as a literate citizen. That must become a realistic expectation. I think it is possible.

I've waited at a convenience store checkout while a young cashier struggled to give me the proper change.

I've listened to grandparents as they stumbled while trying to read a children's book to an impatient toddler.

I've filled out check blanks for customers to complete a purchase. But they did sign their name ... with difficulty.

I've seen a young man stare intently at the front of a bus. Then he turned to ask me, "Where is this bus going?"

I've wondered what our future holds if we don't fix this. Is this really all the better we can do?

XXIV

Seniors

In high school, each grade level is unique. The freshman I have often thought of as being like a big litter of puppies. They are cute, but the noise they generate can drive you nuts. Many lack social grace or simple awareness. If I have a class full of freshmen, I know that at least once during the semester I will need to give a deodorant lecture. Amazing thing about freshman boys, they can't stop touching or grabbing each other. With girls, you will have the occasional primal grooming ritual as they fiddle with each other's hair. The quest for split ends can occupy an entire hour. Couple these behaviors with raging hormones and you sometimes find yourself presiding over a baboon colony with acne. In our building, we teach civics at the freshman level. This assignment usually goes to the low person on the seniority totem pole. Not a class avidly sought after.

Sophomores and juniors have usually figured a few things out. Most are rule followers; most of the time, and they are kind of on the near edge of adulthood. The more conscientious ones are already looking at colleges, building a resume, and are worried about their grades and class ranking. They are *all* exploiting the freedom that comes with a new driver's license. Some have jobs and relationships, most can't wait to graduate.

The seniors are different. Many of them have already made some pretty important decisions about their future, and this year will be about implementation. It will also be about friends and letting go. At my high school, every year in early September we have a ceremony called Senior Sunrise. In the morning before classes, the seniors gather on the football field. They usually aggregate in small groups. Sometimes these groups share a blanket spread on the dew-covered grass. As per usual, the blankets are provided by the females in the group. The guys haven't yet figured out the relationship between wet grass and soggy pants. The school provides doughnuts and hot drinks. It's kind of the unofficial ceremonial beginning of the senior year. The senior leadership and a couple of faculty members are often asked to address the group. I had done so in the past, and my comments were usually brief and as funny as I could make them. That year I decided on a different tone. I really liked this class. There were almost 450 of them, and there weren't any more than forty that I would have been uncomfortable writing a letter of recommendation or reference for. This hasn't always been true, many times in the past I had told students I couldn't give them a strong recommendation. Now, as I was aging, I realized I had said that too often. In the last few years, I always tried to find something positive to write and usually I did. If I couldn't describe the student with superlatives, I could always come up with some 'positive generalities.' By doing this, I was returning a favor once done for me by one of my favorite teachers years ago. I would urge most of my teaching colleagues to do the same. Find the good. It's always there in some measure.

September 17, 2017

I understand that this morning is for classmates and friends, and that a preachy old man can do little to improve the occasion. However, if you would indulge me for a minute or two, I would like to share with you a few things which I did not learn until it was too late for me to do anything about them. Looking back, there were at least ten things that I didn't do in my senior year that I wish the heck I had.

One, in my senior year I never made a friend outside of my own little clique. Because of this, it took me years to accept and appreciate people who were different from me.

Two, I never once stopped a bully from making life difficult for a kid who had committed the unpardonable sin of being different. I easily could have done so. But because I was a coward, my school was a terrible place for a large part of the student body, and less than it might have been for everyone else, myself included.

Three, I was a pretty good student, but never once did I offer to help anyone who was struggling. Because of this, I missed my first opportunities to teach.

Four, I never stopped a friend from telling a racist, sexist, or homophobic joke. I am ashamed to say that I told a few myself. Because of this, I helped to perpetuate racism, sexism, and homophobia in my school.

Five, I never went to a concert or play. My group just didn't do that, I never went to an event such as this one. Because of that, I never realized or appreciated the talents and creativity of many of my classmates.

Six, I never said thank you to staff who really went out of their way for me. I never expressed my thanks for the example some of my teachers set for me. Because of this, as the year went on, fewer and fewer people were willing to go out of their way for me, or cut me a little slack when I most needed it.

Seven, I never really challenged myself academically. Because of this, I was unprepared for college and nearly dropped out after the first semester. For me, that would have changed everything.

Eight, outside of sports, I never joined a group or organization. Because of this, I missed a dozen opportunities to explore different things. I never developed leadership skills, and for years I was awkward in many social situations.

Nine, I never volunteered for a community service project. There is really a joy to be had in giving, and I didn't discover that until much later in life.

Ten, I never went to my own graduation, and because of these reasons I have been back for only one reunion. The one word which best describes my senior year is, forgettable. Today, I do not have a single close friend remaining from a class of over 700.

Whatever you do this year, make it a point to step outside yourself. You have spent the last twelve years becoming the person who you are. Now, try to spend this year becoming the person you hope to be for the rest of your life. Do something kind, do something memorable, and try something difficult. I truly hope on graduation night we will meet here again, and you can honestly say you saved the best for last. Good Luck!

It was a speech that I should have given to many of my senior classes over the years. The longer I taught, the more I came to appreciate them. So close to adulthood, yet so much more to process before they left childhood behind. So often, the character of the senior class set the tone for the entire building and school year. In the best classes, you see a group of kids who have grown closer together, and who really saw the best interest of the school as their common purpose. They individuate, but are proud of their collective identity. Sometimes they come back to visit, and those have been some of my best moments. I try to guess at the year they graduated. Invariably, if I think it was ten years ago, it was 20. This is usually good for a laugh and a comment on my advancing age and receding memory and hairline. Most are proud of what they are doing or have done. They are adults physically and mentally. Most of the time they thanked me before leaving, and with a handshake or a hug they made me wonder why in the hell anyone would ever want to do anything else but teach.

I thought I would be jubilant the night I graduated.
To finally wear a mortar board, Oh god! how long I'd waited.

To hear some pomp and circumstance, endure a boring speech,
and put my fingers in my ears, when the mic begins to screech.

At last I'll walk across the stage, I can hear my parents yell.
I'm handed a diploma, then the tears begin to well.

It's time to flip my tassel, our caps soon fill the air,
The principal said not to; but the senior class don't care!

Tonight's for celebrating! At least we're going to try.
But our happiness is tempered by the need to say goodbye.

To friendships lasting thirteen years. To the staff that really cared.
To the kids who filled my classes. To the memories we shared.

Some things so dearly wanted, you really didn't want at all,
and I'd put up with the hassles, if I could come back in the fall.

XXV

Teachers in Freezers

Over the course of their high-school careers, many students are developing a worldview that diverges from their parents. This is in the order of things. At times during my career, a few of my parent-teacher conferences were mildly confrontational because I was telling kids things their parents didn't necessarily want them to hear. One parent suggested that I was a communist, and another actually accused me of being a Democrat!! Today it is so much worse and the few taunts thrown at me were mild by comparison to the invective sometimes hurled at current teachers. This also includes professors at some major universities. In the cruelest of ironies, some schools are now in the business of perpetuating falsehoods, and some school boards and collegiate administrations have determined that their true mission in this world is to shield their students from having to think or being made the least bit uncomfortable.

Until a few years ago, I did a little adjunct work in the state college system. At the time, I was only dealing with the leading edge of today's frontal assault on truth and common sense. Besides, in my case, I really believed there was little controversy to be generated in lecturing about the ratification debates of the Constitution, or the election of 1800. In this I was wrong. One of my students objected to what he considered my "revisionist" interpretations of history and complained to the department chair. I was informed of the complaint and questioned a bit, but nothing further came of it. Not a big deal. This has changed.

At every level, it is so much worse now. We have moved beyond the place where certain groups were merely trying to ban opinions. Now, they seek to rewrite well-documented facts, and censure teachers who refuse to be cowed by their bellicose ranting. Currently, I am on the outside looking in. As a retiree, I will never have to suffer the consequences of my opinions. Today, teachers who speak up against believers in the latest *conspiracy of the illuminati* might be silenced by gubernatorial decree, or perhaps even lose their job for refusing to lie to their students. If I could offer a bit of encouragement from the sidelines. The *truth* doesn't care if fools or people of bad intent choose not to believe it. Your role as a teacher hasn't really changed, and if we as teachers have done our jobs correctly, many of our students will start to see and relate differently to the larger world in both a physical and intellectual sense. They have to. As has been said many times, "Change isn't optional." Kahlil Gibran wrote a beautiful piece titled, *"On Children"* that every parent of a high school or college student should read and think about. I especially love these poignant and powerful lines, *"You may give them your love but not your thoughts, For they have their own thoughts. You may house their bodies but not their souls, For truly their souls do dwell in the house of tomorrow, which you cannot visit, not even in your dreams.*" That will remain true despite the best efforts of people who wish to freeze America in some fondly remembered past decade. I believe that the kids will still manage to be better than we were. In my career I have seen so many examples. This one especially stands out.

In January 2010, Haiti was leveled by a powerful earthquake. The world rushed to respond, and there was an urgent need for money to fund the non-governmental organizations trying to offer relief. I had two concurrent enrollment classes that were almost entirely made up of seniors. One student had a personal connection with Haiti. Each class decided we should take up a collection and donate it to Feed My Starving Children, for use in Haiti. I thought it to be a good idea and a great charity, so I asked that they bring in what they could the next day. We collected about $60, and while I thought our donations to be pretty impressive, one of my senior boys thought that compared to the actual need, our donation was kind of pathetic. A young lady suggested we organize a fundraiser. The floor was opened to ideas. A few things were suggested, but all were rejected. Most involved selling something, and every spring sport or organization in the building was already fundraising and there were limits to what people would buy. I had long before discovered this was a generous community, but to ask people for another contribution to buy another product that they really didn't need was perhaps too much. Instead, it was suggested we have a contest, maybe something between classes or involving the faculty. It could be done in a day with minimal planning. That suggestion became the genesis of something that we later christened "Teachers in the Freezer."

The original suggestion involved me sitting on a block of ice in a pair of gym shorts during the halftime of a basketball game. The kids would pledge so much money for each minute that I lasted. The opposing fans would also be free to donate. This was something that I hadn't thought through completely before I agreed to it. Regrettably, my teaching career has been liberally sprinkled with equally poorly considered plans. After about a day, during which I had time to fully consider the possibilities for long-term bodily damage and a really embarrassing trip to the doctor's office, I nixed the idea. Thankfully, I did so before we had really started to advertise it. As a Plan B, I thought we should get ten teachers and put them in the school freezer in shorts and tees. It was ten below in there and uncomfortable enough to get your attention. We would then ask the crowd to bail them out. With each hundred dollars donated, the crowd could spring one of the incarcerated staff. I promised to be the last one out but would only leave when we had raised $1000. The head football coach who was to be there with us got on the school news telecast the next day and suggested that, "Old man McLean should probably be the first one sprung because the cold will make his rheumatism flare up, and he will be cranky the rest of the semester." He thought that a real man such as himself would be a more logical candidate for the honor of risking severe frostbite. The war of words was on! The next day, on the school news, I suggested that he was right. He had much more practice than I at doing stupid things, but he was a wimp who wore a parka to coach football games when it dipped below forty degrees, and he wouldn't make it past the jump ball that started the game. Then I took a roll of duct tape, wrapped it around my arm and jerked it off while screaming, "Beat this for tough, freezer boy!" Admittedly, his next salvo was the best of the week. He was also a health teacher, and he responded by suggesting that with me as the last one out, the contest couldn't go on too long because I would need to pee within half an hour. His explanation about old guys and prostate problems was a bit over the top, but so funny. This went on for four days. The school buy-in was tremendous. There was a great crowd at the basketball game and the kids and parents came ready to donate. The opposing crowd also stepped up for us. We had a thousand dollars in no time. The coach and I decided to milk it for as long as we could and didn't leave. By the middle of the second half, we had almost $2400. The donations had slowed to a trickle by then, so we walked out together holding a sign that simply read 'Thank You.' The ovation from the students was as much for themselves as it was for the two frozen fools holding the sign, and the eight other teachers who also had spent their evening shivering in a school freezer raising money to help feed kids they didn't know. That same night, we did a "sleep out" in the school parking lot to buy clothing for the homeless. Donations were accepted. I think we got about $350. That sleep out was entirely initiated by my seniors. This is a terrible admission, but it got down to ten degrees that night. I crapped out at about 3:00 A.M. and curled up next to a heater in one of the school entryways. None of the kids followed suit, and I felt like the biggest wimp on the planet. My craven performance was all over the building the next day. The ribbing I took was deserved. Throughout the fund raiser and the night in the parking lot, those kids made me so proud and hopeful. I learned that, as with much of life, there are a million things that can be a source of inspiration. My students were never the least of these. Get past the preconceptions and stereotypes, and most kids are amazing. Many times during my career, I found that all that was required for me to do was point them in the right direction, and then get the hell out of their way.

Different classes helped me on a few other projects over the next couple of years. At a parent-teacher conference the fall previous, the father of one of my sophomore students told me he had access to several large rolls of paper. It was the end of a production run, but there was still a lot of it. Mostly black or white, but some red and blue were also included. These offered endless possibilities! My classes covered the walls and hallways in our entire department and did a timeline of the black experience in America. We unrolled the black paper on the floor, had kids lay down on it and traced them. We cut out the silhouettes, stapled them on the walls, and had over 100 kids each write a short biography of a historically significant African-American. These were attached to the black figures on the walls. This gave us a rather impressive visual timeline. To add an auditory element, we set up five tape recorders that played different black musical genres as a person progressed through the exhibit. A viewer could move from Spirituals and Gospel Music, to Jazz, to Blues, to Rock and finally Hip Hop and Rap. I do not present this as an inclusive musical list, but it added a lot to the exhibit. Across the top of the wall, we had Dr. Martin Luther King, Jr.'s entire *I have a Dream Speech*. This was done with red paper and ripped letter by letter from six-inch squares. The ragged look of the letters seemed perfect over the black figures, all of them were depicted wearing paper chains, and linked to one another.

Subsequent classes helped me to do something similar to honor the history of Native Americans, and a history of immigration. Later, we did the Civil Rights movement. In all of this, I was dependent upon the help and tolerance given me by my colleagues in the Social Studies department and the building admin. These exhibits stayed up for a couple of weeks at a time, and the vast majority of our student body was respectful of the theme and the work required to build the display. I usually took it down after a few of the figures started to show evidence of "freshman cleverness." Putting up some type of display became an expectation for each incoming class. We did the history of flight, the Second World War, the Cold War and Twentieth Century inventors and inventions. There were others but memory fades. The last one I'll discuss was perhaps the single most difficult thing I ever attempted in all my years of teaching. As always, the kids and my colleagues would be absolutely integral to what I hoped would become a kind of a capstone to my career.

*We're done with all you liberals who refuse to tell **our** truth!*
*We're done with all the crap you spread to **wokify** our youth!*
*We're done with history teachers, and their preaching **C.R.T.**!*
*We're done with "educators" who refuse to think like **me**!*

We're done with English teachers, and the novels our kids read!
*We're done with making students think. **We'll tell them what they need!***
We're done with Science teachers, and this talk of the climate crisis!
*We're done with lies you people spread, you're just as bad as **ISIS**!*

We're done with all professors, and the liberal pap they smear!
*We're done with free inquiry, it's the **thinking** that we fear!*
*We're done with all the **grooming** that you people try to do!*
*We're done with all you teaching that the **gays** are people too!*

*We're done with textbooks telling us that **slavery was all bad**!*
We're done with hearing anything that makes our students sad!
*We're done with all you **socialists**, who think their lunch is free!*
*We're done with tolerating all this **damned diversity!***

*We're done with sitting idly by as you **commies** wreck our schools!*
*We're done with all the times you tried to make us look like **fools!***
*We're done with **stupid pronouns**: such talk we just can't stand!*
*We're done with mere requesting. From now on we **demand***

XVII

Douglass Day

Schools are daily confronted with all the same problems being manifested in most other parts of society. This has always been true, but it has never been more apparent. Accepting diversity, both racial and cultural, has never been easy or comfortable. As different groups have become more assertive in expressing their rights, the schools have become more politicized. My school was not a place you would describe as racially charged. Our minority enrollment was small, our immigrant population small but growing. There are schools where the racial tension is palpable, but that was never the case with us. We did have the occasional ugly incident. Some fights seemed to have no apparent cause other than the color of the participants. Vile sexual things were occasionally scratched into the doors of bathroom stalls. The very occasional N word fell out a few mouths, but lately, it was the homophobic stuff that tended to dominate the restroom art and literature scene. It seemed that calling someone "gay" was still relatively consequence free. Anti-Semitism had always been here, but it never was the dominant pathogen in a very ugly collection of local viruses. While our district was becoming more diverse, we were years away from having an enrollment that mirrored the state demographic characteristics.

Many of my kids were aware of the problems that most of America had begun to recognize and address but few saw racism as part of their daily reality. 2009, was many years after the Rodney King beating and a few years before the murder of George Floyd. We hardly seemed to be the type of school that needed a massive intervention or consciousness raising session. After all, the election of Obama was supposed to usher in a new post-racial America, wasn't it?

Several years ago, I would have been comfortable with at least part of that belief. It was a trip to Washington, D.C. that changed my understanding of the central role race can play in our society. I was going to lunch and had heard a few good things about a Mongolian grill near Chinatown. Armed with a vague set of directions, I began what I thought would be a walk of about a mile. As I said, at times I tend to be oblivious to my surroundings. After walking for about half an hour, it occurred to me that I should have reached my destination. I also noticed for the first time I was nearly the only white man on the street. Despite my generally liberal worldview, I grew increasingly uncomfortable, and was disappointed in myself because of it. Finally, I stopped a gentleman walking past me and asked if he could direct me to the restaurant. He looked at me as if I had two heads, pointed in a different direction, and kept walking. As he got a little bit farther away from me, I heard him mutter, "Dumb ass!" I will remember my discomfort with the situation and the gentlemen's response for the rest of my life. For those few minutes, I was the minority member being spoken down to. I was no longer part of the dominant culture. Strange comparison to make, but I felt threatened and naked. Some things were clarified for me in a way now far removed from my casual and academic understanding of the issues of race and privilege. I thought this to be an important insight.

For years afterward, I considered how I might help all the students in my high school arrive at that same understanding. For one day at least, I wanted them to think about what every day might be like for the few students of color that we had in the building. How a trans kid might see our school, or how much casual misogyny, or bigotry, and racism we were willing to tolerate. As the sand was moving through my professional hourglass, I hoped that now it might be possible to try. Maybe I had become aware and organized enough to attempt a lesson on this scale.

I thought that perhaps the best way I could do this was for the entire building to spend time in every class discussing the issues surrounding race, or listening to the history that framed these issues. I wanted these discussions to focus on a person who was relatable, well-known, and almost leonine. I did not want someone who was a sympathetic figure. No part of this day was to be about pity; in the long run, this only clouds understanding. I wanted someone who projected personal power and agency. I thought Frederick Douglass to be a good choice—the perfect choice! For one day I hoped that we could become Frederick Douglass High School.

The first thing I had to do was run the project by my students to gauge their interest and determine if they thought it was worthwhile to pursue. I knew my classes didn't represent the entire school, but I thought I had a good cross-section and enough rapport with them to get an honest answer and a thoughtful discussion. Their enthusiasm encouraged me. Buoyed by the kids' positive reaction, I put the proposal before the district administration and set up a meeting with the school board.

Before then, I met with each of the departments in the high school individually. Each voiced at least tentative support. I got on the agenda for our next faculty meeting and answered every question I could, as well as outlining possible difficulties. Initially, there was concern that the entire student body could essentially miss most of a day of formal instruction. I agreed, but tried to outline what I thought were the possible benefits and assured my colleagues that attendance at any of the proposed events and lectures would not be mandatory. Teachers could decide if they wished their classes to participate. It was at this point in the discussion that several teachers began to carry the argument for me. There was a passion there. There is a saying among car salesmen that "once you've made the sale, stop selling." I shut up. The motion carried with almost 70% support. On my way out the door, one of the more taciturn members of our faculty asked if I thought I could do it. I said no, but that, "I'm pretty sure that *we* can do it!"

At the subsequent board meeting, getting approval was remarkably easy. The body language of several of the board members told me they were not completely comfortable with the idea, however, with the support of the superintendent and the high-school staff there were no formal objections. I had to clarify *twice* that I was not asking for any funds. I really think the board believed it probably wouldn't happen. Two years prior, I went before the same group with a proposal to reenact the charge of the First Minnesota Regiment at the Battle of Gettysburg. On the second day of battle, the men from Minnesota likely saved the Union by holding the federal center against an overwhelming force of Confederates. The cost was gruesome. The regiment suffered 84% killed or wounded. This is the highest casualty rate suffered by any American regiment in any American war. (At the time, it was Minnesota's sesquicentennial, so I felt it called for a celebration of all things Minnesota.) That plan ultimately crashed and burned when I tried to raise enough funds to get over 1000 kids into something that could pass for a blue or butternut uniform and give them some facsimile of a firearm. Selling a few kepis didn't get me even a quarter of the way there. That failure followed me around like a bad credit rating for quite a while.

Changing the name of the high school initially seemed more doable. Doing a few simple estimates, I thought if we could raise $2500, we could make it work. We were going to need to purchase a lot of stuff. I decided to sell buttons that read *Douglass for a Day*. If I could hang at least one button on every student, teacher, administrator, lunch lady, custodian, and visitor who walked into the building for a month or two, we might get there. My students began selling, and enough money came in that we could begin. I asked a few of the staff to help me with the initial planning, and again was surprised so many were willing to take on additional work for a project that at this point was little more than a concept: and a sketchy one at best. At our group's first meeting, it was decided that, if possible, we should expand the scope of the day to include presentations on Native American culture and treaty rights. At the next meeting, we decided to include presentations on LGBTQ issues and to invite our small Southeast Asian community to contribute. Thankfully, at this point, the woman who directed our diversity and inclusion program got involved in every aspect of the planning and implementation. I think ultimately, she had more to do with the success of the day than I.

Step one was to secure the use of the facilities. Fortunately, the high school had five areas suitable for large group instruction. It was required that each be provided the sound and video capability to make the presentations. Thankfully, one of the people in our group was willing to take this on. This was great because my expertise with microphones and video equipment was almost comparable to my mad computer skills. It would have looked terrible if on the day we needed the equipment to work, I had to dawn a graduation robe, clap a few erasers, and chant obscure Latin phrases to exorcize the demons from the projectors and sound systems.

We needed historians. I had done some work in the history department at Saint Cloud State University and three of their professors were willing to come down for the day to make presentations on Frederick Douglass and the general topic of racism in Minnesota past and present. There would also be presentations on the treaty process, and how Indigenous land claims have been ignored. We were able to include the issues surrounding the Dakota War of 1862. We could pay our visiting profs very little, but they were willing to do this for no more than gas money and a slice of pizza for lunch. Their generosity and scholarship become the cornerstone of the entire day.

We thought we needed to change the signage in the building, and if I could redo one aspect of that day, it would be even attempting to do so. If we were going to put an FD over every school logo in the building, we would need 266 of them in five different sizes. There were four monuments outside the building that required a full 4x8 sheet of plywood to cover them. The school marquee facing the road required something 50 by 30 feet to cover it completely on both sides. For this, we used a painter's drop cloth with a huge FD painted on both sides. Getting it up was a bitch, but doable. For the script across the roofline of the building, we needed a banner 70 feet by three feet. There was not a day that went by from February until mid-April that I did not have at least one moment of "What the hell were you thinking with these damn signs!!"

To do any of this, I needed the assistance of our industrial tech classes. The instructors and students were willing to make metal stencils with the letters FD cut in the sizes required. They used routers to write in script, *Frederick Douglass High School* across six 4' x 8' plywood sheets These were to be painted and then mounted on the outside of the building. My students, armed with dozens of cans of spray paint, set about using the stencils to make almost 300 signs in the appropriate sizes to change the logos on the inside of the building. In the middle of this process, a school secretary noticed I had made a mistake on the work order for the larger signs being made in the industrial tech area. I had spelled Douglass with only one S. I have no real excuse for this. I was tired, and I confess I am not detail-oriented; at times I can be blind to events swirling around me. But this level of "dumbassery" was completely novel. I had reached an entirely new and undiscovered level of incompetence. Three of the plywood sheets had already been manufactured with the incorrect spelling. I got to the instructor to stop the process before any more damage could be done and apologized profusely. He agreed with my assessment that I was indeed a dumb ass, and then simply said, "We'll fix it." It was at that point I began to believe the whole day was actually going to happen. An industrial tech teacher and a secretary had saved the school and myself from a huge potential embarrassment. For the first time I was beginning to realize that no matter what broke, the people helping me had my back, the kids had my back, the administration was supportive, and all I needed to do was to let them in. Later that night, that short phrase, "We'll fix it," became a moment of reflection for me. I thought back over a career that had by then stretched almost 40 years. I remembered how once an occasionally morose 20-something McLean had spent time in the Boundary Waters sitting on a big-ass rock staring at the night sky and looking for a direction in life. That dumb, confused kid would have been amazed if he knew then how much his future self would come to depend upon other people to help him accomplish anything of note or consequence. I had once believed that as my career evolved, I would become more independent, self-assured, and confident. A knight errant with a history degree and a whistle. Instead, I was now a better teacher than I had ever been because, over time and by degrees, I had changed. I now accepted my dependence on others, and at least occasionally was willing to substitute their judgment for my own. In a sense, this was both humbling and liberating.

As preparations proceed, almost every department in the building contributed something to the effort. Two art class students drew and painted a 12' x 8' mural of Frederick Douglass, then built a frame for it. Their handsome portrait was affixed to the front of the building. They nailed exactly the proud, defiant look on Mr. Douglass' countenance I was hoping for. There were additional 4' x 8' drawings of Crazy Horse and Caesar Chavez, also wonderfully rendered. The P.E. department agreed to hold classes outside for the day and would get the gym decorated. Math gave up a team teaching space. With about a month to go, the program was beginning to fill in. The middle school also became involved. One of their social studies teachers had his classes create a "Hall of Heroes." Using the same format I used with the civil rights display, they cut out dozens upon dozens of figures and put biographies on the individual figures. They accompanied their biographical display with a well-thought-out and rendered art exhibit focused on black history. The teacher brought over several groups of middle-school students throughout the day of the actual event. We arranged for an African drumming company to give two presentations to the whole school and one to the middle school. They also explained the significance of the drum in African culture. A Native American dance company was going to give two performances and explain the significance of the dance and costumes. An LGBTQ rights advocacy group from Saint Cloud State was scheduled to give presentations throughout the day. At a general assembly at the end of the day, our own jazz band would perform. Every two hours, our visiting profs offered another lecture on the topics outlined. I asked the governor to stop by and do a cameo, but it didn't work with his schedule. One of my students also penned a brief letter to President Obama. No joy on that one either.

We began the day with a short address by the superintendent in which he declared the purpose of the activities and made the official proclamation that for one day we were Frederick Douglass High School. Then the language arts department agreed to collectively read portions of *What to the Slave is the Fourth of July*? The department chair would read Martin Niemoeller's poem *"First They Came..."* Throughout the day, our counseling department and other staff would lead panel discussions focusing on various topics related to the overall theme of racism and gender bias. The night before, the National Honor Society agreed to help me change the signage and get the banners spread over the front of the building. The mural went up in three separate pieces and really dominated the main entrance to the building. A couple of my senior boys volunteered to hang out in the parking lot all night to guard the Douglass picture. They thought it was a good idea because, "There are some real rednecks around McLean." I told them no, but when I came out in the morning they were there and asleep in their cars—"Thanks guys." For good measure, we changed the directional signs on the roads around the high school. The last of my decorating crew left at midnight. I stayed in the building that night on a couch in the coaches' office, caught a little sleep, and hoped.

The day dawned beautifully. I didn't ask them to, but well before school, the teachers who had helped throughout the planning, showed up on their own; four brought coffee! I have seldom been as touched and grateful. For at least the hundredth time in my career, I looked at the people who I worked with and thought, "I am so proud that I share a profession with you." I have often thought that as a society, our collective prosperity and happiness really depends upon so many people who we will never take the time to thank. If you are a parent reading this, your kids' teacher is one of these people; appreciate them, please!

Considering the moving parts that had to mesh, Frederick Douglass day went off well. The superintendent's speech was short but well-written and received. The language arts department did a wonderful job with the reading; the second the Niemoeller verse was completed, the Native American group began their performance. They did a fantastic job, the crowd almost hypnotized by the rhythm. The explanations of the symbolism of the dance and costumes were insightful and informative. The same may be said about the African drumming company. A couple of the younger members of that group were students of mine at the time, and they just beamed throughout the performances. Each group welcomed questions at the end of their performance; the fact there were more questions than time allowed for answers spoke volumes about how the presentations were received by the kids. As the day progressed, events were scheduled in such a way students always had at least two possible presentations per hour to choose from, and by the end of the day it was possible for a student to fill their entire day with lectures, discussions, or performances offering insights into issues likely to dominate and change the world they were shortly to inherit. Admittedly, there were kids who opted out of participating in most of the day. There were students who used the day as an opportunity to skip. But I was thrilled at the number of kids who participated enthusiastically, and how often the performers were thanked for making it happen. At the end of the day, I was exhausted. Probably more from stress than physical activity. The next day, the National Honor Society would help me clean up the school and remove the signage; but that was tomorrow. On Frederick Douglass Day, my last act was to sit by the river and think about all that had worked well, what might have been done better, and the number of people I was going to need to thank for making whatever level of success we achieved possible.

It took about a day before the first email arrived, suggesting I could have found someone else to rename the high school after. Not directly said, but it was implied that one of the dead white guys we have been studying for years would have been a better choice. After all, Ben Franklin or George Washington hadn't received nearly the exposure and props they were due. I almost responded to that person, suggesting that perhaps next time I tried this I would consider their thoughtful suggestion, and wondered if I could borrow their statue of Nathan Bedford Forrest or Jefferson Davis as a centerpiece. I didn't, but I was tempted. A couple of the letters referenced the LGBTQ group and were aggressively stupid. They were also vulgar, and one was threatening. Oddly, I think I had communicated with this person several times that year. His ability to massacre the language was notably singular, and the random use of "f......g queers" was a dead giveaway. Besides, how many sterling minds such as his could one school district produce? The explanation of Native American treaty rights got a couple of pretty strongly worded reactions, primarily dealing with walleye spearing on Mille Lacs Lake. One of these messages quickly digressed into a rant against the odds of winning at a Native American casino. Student reactions were more in line with the day's intent. I was asked by several students why they had never been taught about the Dakota War of 1862. The kids wondered why the war and the mass hanging which followed got no mention in their textbook. I told them that sometimes the things omitted from history books teach the most powerful lessons about our history.

Everything considered, there was actually less blowback than I expected. I think that, as has happened many times during my career, I got lucky. My timing was good. I believe a few years ago, people were more willing and able to see the good in what I was attempting to do—to share differences and express diversity in our society in a positive light—than they are today. Or perhaps I was lucky that bigots then felt less empowered than they do today. Certainly, with Obama's election we had not suddenly created a social climate accepting of diversity, but it did foster discussion. Douglass Day happened before the election of Trump and the legitimization of white male grievance politics. Now, elements of a community can scream some poorly informed bullshit about CRT and all attempts at understanding and supporting diversity and equity end. As do many attempts at teaching a true and inclusive history of the United States.

I'm glad I was allowed to do this. As with much of teaching, I have no idea what was accomplished. You can't measure attitudes changed or insights gained. In the sonnet, *On His Blindness*, Milton wrote one of my favorite verses. *"When I consider how my light is spent, Ere half my days in this dark world and wide."* Often over the years as I was driving home that short line occurred to me. Usually, it was on a day that hadn't gone so well, and I would find myself wondering at the roads I had not taken in life. This was still true even though my career was nearly at an end. I believe all of us involved in Douglass Day—planning, preparing, performing or partaking—walked away considering that at least for that day, it was light well spent. As a friend of mine once said, "Every once in a while, the universe decides to smack you with a Styrofoam two-by-four just to get your attention." I really am thankful for that grumpy pedestrian in D.C. who suggested that I was a dumb ass because I got lost on the way to a Mongolian grill, and for a little while at least, I was able to feel what it was like to be the other.

I believe that at least once in their career, every teacher should try to do something big. Something that will engage the entire school in a common purpose. For me, that was Frederick Douglass day. There are a million other possibilities; pick one, then go with it! Many of your colleagues will help you. Your students will help you. Most parents will be thrilled to see their kids excited about working towards a common goal.

You will also be opening yourself up to criticism. There is no possible topic that won't offend someone on the staff or in the community. Do it anyway, take a chance. Remember that you are in this business for the kids; and of course the extravagant salary! Should you decide to try, I wish you all the luck in the world.

XXVII

Nihil Aeternum Est

When my students asked me when I was going to retire, my standard response was "Never." I often joked that I would probably just keel over in my classroom someday. So, if I didn't report to class one morning, call 911 and then check for my body in the assorted piles of junk I had accumulated over the years. Hopefully you guys will find my carcass before putrefaction sets in. A poor joke, but the year after Douglass Day, I did begin to think about retirement. I think I had always been a high energy teacher, and I knew I was slowing down. There was less spontaneity in my teaching, I was less willing to drag a class down to the river at the drop of a hat. One of my best friends in teaching had retired and reported that it wasn't awful. Perhaps most telling, I was spending more time dwelling on my failures than celebrating my successes. In a way, I began to feel very much as I did when I was contemplating resigning from Eagle River almost forty years ago. Back then, I was sure I wasn't doing anything significant, that I wasn't moving the needle. I thought that maybe I needed to leave teaching. It wasn't exactly like that now. I was 100% convinced I had been right when I decided that teaching would become my career. I knew that what I did was significant. I had come to see it as perhaps the best thing I was capable of doing. As I said previously, I am a person with limits, and certainly not a brilliant man. The thing I most excel at is being ordinary, no more than a Delphic knife. But I could teach. The few skills that I do have often worked in concert to make me an effective instructor. There were small corners of the world I thought that I might still be able to improve. But now, I felt things were moving too fast, and I was walking too slow. Cashiers at convenience stores started to call me, "honey." The top of my head was more skin than hair, and my hearing sucked.

The kids still seemed to enjoy my classes, and their interest level and behavior were all that I could ever wish for. I had always assumed that at some point the kids would tell me when it was time to go, and that wasn't happening—yet. In fact, they started to get a kick out of my total ineptitude with modernity and eagerly volunteered to help me muddle through any tech-related activity, like using a smart board, a projector, my own cell phone, or on-line class registration. Once, one young lady announced that my class was just like a trip to her grandfather's house. "All he ever wants to do is swear at his remote control, ask me really silly questions about his computer, and talk about the old days." At the time, that sounded like a good description of a history teacher. I did not however immediately take to my new nickname: Gramps. But in time I was amazed how little it came to bother me.

As I aged, I was worried that perhaps the district would one day need to decide between letting go of a younger and better teacher or keeping me on staff. They would have no choice, really. At this point, I had a job for as long as I wanted one. Unless I did something really egregiously stupid, tenure rules required that seniority be given primacy when making decisions about staffing. I have come to think of this as a mistake. It was once required by the state that teachers retire at age 65, and as I passed that milestone, I saw some wisdom in the policy. Experience has its advantages, but being old has its drawbacks. If a district is to grow and thrive, it is important that it renew itself with new blood and fresh ideas.

At this point in my career, I had also started to think about legacy issues. For now, I still thought of myself as a competent teacher, but would I have the grace to leave before I become a bad caricature of myself? There were things happening which shouted at me that I was slipping. Sometimes I would be lecturing and couldn't find the word I needed. Occasionally now, a name or a date eluded me. Toward the end of that year, I had one of the most embarrassing moments I had ever had in front of a class. I bent over to pick something up off the floor and passed gas. Not just a little, and not quietly. I will give the kids all the credit in the world. They really tried not to laugh. Most tried to ignore it and it wasn't until I offered an over-the-top apology, complete with an outlandish explanation for my flatulence that the laughter began. But as I drove home that night, I couldn't help thinking, "What the hell comes next, incontinence? Someday soon, will the kids start laughing at me instead of with me? Any chance that I might become a doddering old fool who dribbled stuff on himself and occasionally left his zipper open?" A classroom isn't like the U.S. senate, silly gaffs, mumbling incoherently, and memory lapses really do matter. This is perhaps the thing which frightened me the most. Someday would I walk into a department meeting and everyone would just kind of go silent? Maybe I would feel some animosity. Throats would clear, and then someone would begin a novel strand of conversation, eagerly engaged in by everyone at the table. That scenario terrified me. Sometimes the hardest and most necessary conversations to have are those you have with yourself, and a mirror can be a very cruel thing.

I remembered a man I used to teach with. I thought he was probably a good instructor once, but each year there was a little less joy in his demeanor. A little less laughter came from his classroom, and student work piled up in random spots on his desk. More often than not, his glasses were crooked on his face, and he seldom shaved. When he did, he did half a job.

If the stories he told were to be believed, he was once a high energy teacher. Not so anymore. It seemed that every year he took less pride in his physical appearance, and the kids spent more of his class being out of control. Sometimes he screamed almost incoherently, demanding that a student "Get out of my room!" Once I saw him take a break when he reached the top of the stairs. He just stood there staring down the hall in the direction of his classroom. He had an absolutely vacant expression. I asked him what was wrong and got no answer. Then he started to shuffle down the hall. I am positive that he never heard the question. When he finally retired, many of his colleagues remembered only the confused old man. They had forgotten the quality instructor. Did *he* know he was losing a step? Did he continue to work because retirement wasn't financially possible? I started to think it would be so darned easy to stay too long at the fair. I resolved to leave when I was sure I was still competent and wanted.

Later that year, before summer break, I met with the district's personnel director and told him I was willing to cut back to a three-quarters teaching load in the upcoming year. Our enrollment was shrinking and there were rumors of staff cuts. I had taught Political Science and History classes in our concurrent enrollment program for the past several years and wanted to continue doing so. Essentially, I would be dropping three general American History classes. I thought he would jump at the opportunity to lose a quarter of my salary. He didn't; he suggested that my resigning would be a better alternative as far as the district was concerned. This kind of surprised and disappointed me. First, on a personal level, I didn't want to see myself as so easily dispensable. Second, because I have an advanced degree in American History and additional graduate work in Political Science, I was able to teach college-level classes in both areas. There was no one else in the department who could. I had about 90 kids registered for my college classes, and these kids would need to be accommodated. Some of them had petitioned to be allowed into my class, and they had no good options as far as other courses went. I had promised these kids I would be there for them. Also, retiring is something that you need to think seriously about for a while before you actually do it; and I hadn't yet. So, I resolved to teach a full load again the following year. It didn't disappoint me that by the end of that school year I was notified that cutting back to three-fourths would be doable if I was still interested. I was given no reason as to why the change in plan, but it was welcomed. I could now get a little more sleep. There would be less preparation and correcting. More time to think and plan a retirement.

As I recall the next three years were blessedly uneventful, and the beginning of what I came to think of as "harvest time." It wasn't that I was getting lazy in my old age, but I had taught the same things so often that there was little additional planning involved. There were always new things which I included in my syllabi, but mostly I knew what I was going to do in class. I had accumulated excellent resources over the years, and I knew when and how to use them. I knew what would work, and I knew when the kids would laugh. I was playing a role I had been rehearsing for most of my adult life. Oddly, for a while now I had begun to really look forward to parent-teacher conferences. Over the years, as I had grown older and grayer my relationships with my kids' parents changed. In some cases, I became almost a confidante; a time or two I was a shoulder to cry on. I came to understand that most children will never know how deeply they are loved and the extent of their parent's concern.

I had never been more at ease in the classroom. A million things that at one time may have gotten under my skin were irrelevant now. In graduate school, I once had a professor who described the perfect teacher as being like water, always adaptable and capable of assuming the shape of any vessel into which they are poured. An incredible thing to think about, but after 40 or so years in the classroom, I think it described me.

The year following, I was further reduced to half-time, and some of the kids who were originally scheduled for my concurrent enrollment classes were put into Advanced Placement courses instead. In March of the next year, I was told there would be no concurrent enrollment classes in the upcoming year, and my services would no longer be needed. Seems that offering AP classes was cheaper and no special coursework was required to be an instructor. I knew it was coming, but the finality of the situation still surprised me. My first thought was, "but my room isn't finished yet!" It wasn't, I still had to get a student to draw the final tile in the ceiling. It was to be me walking out of my room with a fishing rod over my shoulder. After I thought about it for a while, I decided that it really wasn't important anymore. That also surprised me. What I had done in the room was ending. That was the important thing. My last act that year was to gradually start cleaning out over thirty years of books and memories. I eventually filled a dumpster with one and was kind of overwhelmed by the intensity of the other. I was amazed by what I had accumulated. File cabinets full of things I once thought to be important—into the garbage can. Student projects, some very well done; into the dumpster. Pictures of former students—in a box to keep. Reference books were donated to the school library—why? They would be more at home in an antique store. That year, on one of the last days for teachers, they held a get-together in the library for staff who weren't returning. A cake, coffee, and best wishes sort of thing. I was asked to come and respectfully declined. I didn't want to be called upon to mumble a few words and blubber. The folks in my department held a small fishing outing for me. I appreciated that a lot. They also had the good grace to let me catch the most fish. I had always thought the best way to make my exit would be to simply not show up for August's Who Buddy icebreaker at the opening workshop some year. The people in my department could explain I had called it quits, and life would go on.

I wish that teachers were like architects. Every building they plan and help to construct is a monument to their efforts, and will probably last for years, perhaps outlasting the builders. Teachers will be largely forgotten, perhaps called to mind at reunions. Or maybe they will someday be attached to a different set of memories and become an indistinct part of a larger childhood collage. I thought I would be remembered about as long as I had a former student in the building. I thought that five years from now, somebody would have turned my room back into storage space and the occasional kid who wandered in would probably say something pithy like, "What the hell was all this about?" Maybe someone in the department will overhear and say, "The guy that used to teach here was a bit eccentric." I hope they will follow that comment with something like, "He was a really solid teacher though."

It took three days to finally get rid of my stuff. I took as many of the books with me as I thought my wife would let me store. A bunch of others the department took and set up a small library in the social studies office. I appreciated that, even if I held no real expectation that they would be used. The rest were tossed or given away. The kids heard I wasn't going to be back, and a few filtered in to say goodbye and wish me luck. A few more stopped in to tell me they were sorry they had never gotten to take a class from me. I probably made some lame joke about how lucky they were, but I thanked them. When I was done, I looked at the empty sagging shelves, the ceiling tiles, the desk and everything else that was no longer mine. That was maybe the hardest thing for me to grasp. There was no longer any such thing as *my* room, no more just plain *McLean's* room, and in a moment of clarity I realized that there never really had been such a thing. Every kid who walked through the door had a better claim on this space than I ever had. They were just kind of letting me store my junk here for a while, darn good of them. Now there was emptiness and echoes. It's amazing how different a room sounds when everything is off the walls. For the first time ever, I heard the ticking of my clock. I felt cold standing there. There were places where things had been hanging only three days before. A copy of the Constitution, a picture of Jefferson, a few plaques, and diplomas that I was proud of. The space they had occupied, now a lighter color than the rest of the walls. I wondered how long it took to darken up the paint on a wall that way. Silly question really. I took one more walk around the room. I stared at the drawings and tried to put a face with each signature. It disappointed me that so many former students were just a cipher now. I found the drawings and signatures of two young ladies who had died together in a car crash about twenty years before. I had watched one of those girls grow up. Her father was also a teacher and had been a friend of mine. We had coached together. We went fishing together. I remember that I was so upset at the funeral that I had put on shoes from two different pairs, one brown one black. In my career, it was not the only funeral I attended for a student or former student. I lost count of how many. I know that all were sad. The last thing I always said to my senior classes before they graduated was this, "I have been to more funerals for students and former students than I want to remember. Don't you dare do something stupid and make me attend yours. I'm too damned old!!" They laughed; I wasn't trying to be funny.

I pulled my broken-down desk chair to the middle of the room, sat down, and imagined the room as it had looked over thirty years ago when the department chair told me I could have it for a classroom. There was no real flood of nostalgia, but I thought of a million things which I might have done better. Oddly, I thought about Eagle River. Makes sense I guess; to contemplate the beginning when you've come to the end. I didn't linger as long as I thought I might have.

On the way out, I wondered if there was some way I could take my classroom door with me. A while ago two students had painted on it a very good picture of the Starship Enterprise going into warp. The legend above the picture read, "To Boldly Go Where No Man Has Gone Before, Social Studies At Warp Ten. Captain Jean Luc McLean …Engage." (For the record I know that warp ten is impossible, and if you really could attain that speed you would be everywhere all at the same time. But thinking back on it, this did kind of describe how I did things.) *Damn*, I *loved* that picture. I left Yoda up on the wall. I didn't have the heart to rip him down. I then went around the building to say goodbye to a few friends. Most were so much younger than I. One was a former student of mine. The teachers who had started at the same time as me were all gone now. A few at a time, they had retired to planned communities in Somewhere, Arizona. A couple of the youngsters had already arranged for me to do some subbing for them the next year. I was looking forward to it. It was ironic, but just a few days previous the district had passed a huge referendum, and the summer I left they were beginning to plan a massive remake of the high school. It would be a year or so yet, but I understood my old room was one of the first scheduled for demolition. They really didn't need the room anymore, no one would ever teach in that space again. Almost without thinking, I began whistling *My Grandfather's Clock.*, kind of analogous I guess. *Nihil aeternum est*: nothing lasts forever. I wish I had gone back and taken pictures of everything before that happened. It's too late now, obviously. Thankfully, one of the ladies I taught with did take a few. She sent me some a while back. A nice trip down memory lane. On my way out of the main door, I really had to fight the urge to scream, "The last dinosaur has left the building!"

That summer may have been the most difficult in my life. It was one of the few times I was not teaching summer school, nor was I taking a class. Depression occasionally returned. I fished and volunteered. My wife and I began to catch up on some of the travel that we'd promised ourselves when we were poverty stricken young parents. I took a job at a hardware store. Just kind of an on-call thing. I learned how to run a cash register, and to bite my tongue when the occasional customer decided that today was a really magnificent day to be an asshole. I found that I enjoyed working in a place where the most urgent problem I had to deal with was trying to help a customer get rid of crabgrass in their yard or spiders in their crawl spaces. I discovered that I had a real talent for sharpening lawnmower blades and making keys. People usually thanked me for the help. It was a good gig.

I did get a little subbing the next fall and early winter. I even got an occasional opportunity to give a lecture that was interesting, engaging, and funny as hell. I became an A.P. English teacher for a couple of weeks. I loved it. Covid ended all that, as well as a few things that I had started doing as volunteer work. In a way, it was a mercy that I retired when I did. As I said, nothing I ever did in a classroom would translate well into a Zoom meeting. It was fortunate, I wouldn't be required to put my full-blown computer ineptitude on display for a whole new group of students. When covid passed I thought about applying for another teaching job, but it just seemed too late for me to get back on the horse, so the narrative ends here.

Now when I think about my years in teaching, my memory usually puts a warm patina around most of it, and the people I will never forget will always outnumber the people I really want to forget. I think that to be a good way to look at any career. I really have no idea how many thousands of kids I have been privileged to teach. I tried to approximate the number once, but it was only a poor guess. I have also worked beside hundreds of caring and competent teachers and administrators, and each gave me a gift. I know that over the years they have all taught me, and they have all helped to define me. Today, I can honestly say that I came to like and appreciate almost every kid who ever walked through my classroom door, and I grew to respect most of the men and women who had the courage to teach. I do not use the word lightly. It takes courage to teach. My students and my colleagues in education changed me profoundly, and always for the better.

In my last couple of years teaching, I was easily the most experienced member of the faculty, and the youngsters would occasionally ask if kids were "better" back in the day. In all honesty I told them that kids were really little changed from when I started back in the 1970s. Today, they are technologically savvy, but incredibly naive about the power of social media. They will not respect you simply because you are an adult, but they still need school, and they need to be surrounded by as many caring teachers as possible. That is perhaps more true today than it even has been, and that may be the biggest difference. Today, teachers are more urgently needed than at any point in our history. In an anomic world, teachers and schools must offer stability. People criticize schools because they have failed to change and adapt. This is partly true. But the interaction between a teacher and their class is timeless. *In loco parentis*. May this never change. I believe that one simple Latin phrase once encapsulated the promise, hope, and future of America's schools. But recently, we seem to have lost something: faith in each other and our public institutions. In education, I believe that faith and trust were once the glue that bound parents, teachers, students, and the community to a common purpose. America was the first country to try and educate every student to the highest level possible. We came to assume that education was a birthright and a promise made to all children regardless of social status or zip code. That promise burns less brightly today. As I said earlier, we once had an intergenerational covenant, an unspoken obligation to the future. Is this still true? Have our personal agendas supplanted any notion we once had of community? I don't know. I am now in my seventh decade and am not sanguine about the trajectory of America's schools. But I think that a solution lies somewhere in those simple Latin words. It does take a village to raise and nurture the next generation. All of us need to be role models, mentors, and teachers. Until we recover that sense of community obligation, schools will not improve.

I taught for forty-three years, but it was only in the last few of these I learned what my students really wanted from me; what they had always wanted from me. It was never to give them any kind of deep historical understanding, or a complete explanation of the Constitution and Bill of Rights. In a semester or two, that simply wasn't going to happen. They needed me to listen to them. In all the really significant conversations I ever had with kids, the topic of history or political philosophy seldom came up. What they wanted from me, whether they said so or not, was maybe to offer them a few tips on growing up, and they wanted honesty. Not a collection of gold stars or participation awards. They wanted to know that with me, both praise and criticism were sincere, and came from a place of caring and concern. That's all, and maybe a s'more after a particularly stirring historically significant group activity. I have the rest of my life to work on becoming anything like Atticus. I'm not there yet, probably never will be, but I hope that in 43 years of trying, I may have moved the needle a little.

If you are a teacher, I know that throughout this narrative I have offered you very little that you can take back to your classroom and run with it. That is because I sincerely believe that there are no prescriptions for teaching efficacy. You are probably already a competent caring person. Start from there, let that become your center. Then, think, reflect, study and work your tail off. Finally: find the joy. It seems a very simple thing, but it may be the most important advice I can leave you with. There are a million ways to be a great teacher and every one of them starts with truly enjoying the students placed in your keeping. Internalize this: *In loco parentis*. That is a truly amazing thing to reflect upon. McLean

I had hoped to finish this book with a few super clever and meaningful verses. But try as I might this is all I could come up with.

Forty-three years is too long a time to synthesize into a rhyme.
Too many joys, Too many tears, Too many kids, Too many years.
So much water has flowed on by, I'd be a fool to even try … To summarize.
Finis!